LIBRARY OF NEW TESTAMENT STUDIES

689

formerly the Journal for the Study of the New Testament Supplement series

Editor
Chris Keith

Editorial board
Dale C. Allison, Lynn H. Cohick, Kylie Crabbe, R. Alan Culpepper, Craig A. Evans, Jennifer Eyl, Robert Fowler, Juan Hernández Jr., John S. Kloppenborg, Michael Labahn, Matthew V. Novenson, Love L. Sechrest, Robert Wall, Catrin H. Williams, Brittany E. Wilson

The Countercultural Victory of 1 John in Greco-Roman Context

Conquering the World

Ahreum Kim

LONDON • NEW YORK • OXFORD • NEW DELHI • SYDNEY

T&T CLARK
Bloomsbury Publishing Plc
50 Bedford Square, London, WC1B 3DP, UK
1385 Broadway, New York, NY 10018, USA
29 Earlsfort Terrace, Dublin 2, Ireland

BLOOMSBURY, T&T CLARK and the T&T Clark logo are trademarks of
Bloomsbury Publishing Plc

First published in Great Britain 2023
Paperback edition published in 2025

Copyright © Ahreum Kim, 2023

Ahreum Kim has asserted her right under the Copyright, Designs and Patents Act, 1988, to be identified as Author of this work.

For legal purposes the Acknowledgments on p. ix constitute an extension of this copyright page.

All rights reserved. No part of this publication may be reproduced or transmitted in any form or by any means, electronic or mechanical, including photocopying, recording, or any information storage or retrieval system, without prior permission in writing from the publishers.

Bloomsbury Publishing Plc does not have any control over, or responsibility for, any third-party websites referred to or in this book. All internet addresses given in this book were correct at the time of going to press. The author and publisher regret any inconvenience caused if addresses have changed or sites have ceased to exist, but can accept no responsibility for any such changes.

A catalogue record for this book is available from the British Library.

Library of Congress Cataloging-in-Publication Data
Names: Kim, Ahreum, author.
Title: The countercultural victory of 1 John in Greco-Roman context : conquering the world / Ahreum Kim.
Description: London ; New York : T&T Clark, 2023. | Series: Library of New Testament studies, 2513–8790 ; 689 | Includes bibliographical references and index. | Summary: "This book demonstrates that a consistent countercultural narrative permeates the First Epistle of John, and identifies the Johannine community as conquering the polytheism of the Greco-Roman world with their pistis (belief/faith) in Jesus as the true Son of God"– Provided by publisher.
Identifiers: LCCN 2023008258 (print) | LCCN 2023008259 (ebook) | ISBN 9780567712073 (hardback) | ISBN 9780567712110 (paperback) | ISBN 9780567712080 (pdf) | ISBN 9780567712103 (epub)
Subjects: LCSH: Bible. Epistle of John, 1st–Criticism, interpretation, etc. | Christianity and other religions–Greek. | Christianity and other religions–Roman.
Classification: LCC BS2805.52 .K56 2023 (print) | LCC BS2805.52 (ebook) | DDC 227/.9406–dc23/eng/20230406
LC record available at https://lccn.loc.gov/2023008258
LC ebook record available at https://lccn.loc.gov/2023008259

ISBN: HB: 978-0-5677-1207-3
PB: 978-0-5677-1211-0
ePDF: 978-0-5677-1208-0
ePUB: 978-0-5677-1210-3

Series: Library of New Testament Studies, volume 689

ISSN 2513–8790

Typeset by Newgen KnowledgeWorks Pvt. Ltd., Chennai, India

To find out more about our authors and books visit www.bloomsbury.com and sign up for our newsletters.

Contents

List of Figures	vii
List of Tables	viii
Acknowledgments	ix
List of Abbreviations	x

1 Introduction — 1

2 Victory in the Greco-Roman World — 7
  2.1 Victory in Competition — 8
    The *Agōnes* — 8
    An Iconic Nike — 11
    Johannine Competition? — 15
  2.2 Victory in War — 16
    Nike with Artemis, Ares, and Athena — 16
    Nike in Battle — 20
    Nike in Power — 23
    The Johannine Battle — 25

3 The Conquered — 27
  3.1 The Evil One — 27
    The Young Men Conquer the Evil One — 28
    The Evil One and the Murderer — 32
    The Evil One Threatens *Pistis* — 37
  3.2 The Antichrists and False Prophets — 40
    Conquering the Docetists? — 45
  3.3 The World — 48
    The Desires of the World — 48
    Contention with the World — 52
    Conquering the World in John's Gospel — 54
    The Ruler of This World — 55

4 A Countercultural Letter — 61
  4.1 Against the Culture of Fear — 61
    Positive Jewish Fear? — 62

		Fearing the Gods in the Greco-Roman World	65
		The Greco-Roman Response to Fear	68
		The Johannine Response to Fear	72
	4.2	Avoiding the Idols	74
		A Confusing Ending?	74
		The Greco-Roman "Idol"	77
		Jewish Idolatry	81
		Warning against the Idols in 1 John	84
5	Conquering the World with *Pistis*		89
	5.1	*Pistis* and Greco-Roman Victory	89
		Pistis of the Romans	89
		Pistis to the Roman Empire	94
		Pistis/Fides, Nike/Victoria, and the Emperor	100
		Pistis to the *Divi Filius*	104
	5.2	A Countercultural Battle over *Pistis*	106
		Emphasizing *Pistis* in 1 John	107
		Pistis in the Son of God	112
		Testifying to Johannine *Pistis*	118
		Victorious *Pistis* and Eternal Life	123
6	Conclusion and Final Reflections		131
Bibliography			135
Index of References			145

Figures

1. Panathenaic Prize Amphora with lid. Attributed to the Painter of the Wedding Procession (Greek [Attic]), signed by Nikodemos. 363–2 BCE. J. Paul Getty Museum no. 93.AE.55. 10
2. "Le Jupiter Olympien vu dans son trone et dans l'interieur de son temple." Etching and watercolor version of Phidias's celebrated statue at Olympia. Frontispiece of Antoine-Chrysostome Quatremere de Quincy's book, *Le Jupiter Olympien, Ou, L'art De La Sculpture Antique Considere Sous Un Nouveau Point De Vue: Ouvrage Qui Comprend Un Essai Sur Le Gout De La Sculpture Polychorme, L'analyse Explicative De La Toreutique, Et L'histoire De La Statuaire En or Et Ivoire Chez Les Grecs Et Les Romains: Avec La Restitution Des Principaux Monuments De Cet Art Et La Demonstration Pratique Ou Le Renouvellement De Ses Procedes Mecaniques* (Paris: Firmin Didot, 1814). 12
3. Part of Mosaic no. 8: Les divinites de la semaine (Mars). Mosaiques romaines d'Orbe-Bosceaz. Archeologie cantonale de l'Etat de Vaud, picture Fibbi-Aeppli, Grandson. 18
4. Varvakeion Athena, plaster cast. Cambridge, Museum of Classical Archaeology inv. no. 145. (Original: Athens, National Museum inv. no. 129.) CC BY-NC-ND 4.0. 20
5. "Roman Forum: Arch of Titus." (c.81 CE) depicting Titus crowned by Nike (top right) for his military victory. Photograph by Gary Lee Todd. 101
6. A bronze dupondius of Marcus Aurelius showing Pistis/Fides with Nike in her right hand (170–1 CE), Rome. (RIC III Marcus Aurelius 999) ANS 1944.100.49173. Courtesy of the American Numismatic Society. 103
7. A gold quinarius aureus of Tiberius (22–3 CE), Lugdunum, imprinted with 'TIDIVIF' (Tiberius *divi filius*) and with Nike sitting on a globe and holding a victory wreath. (RIC I [2nd edn.] Tiberius 8) ANS 1956.184.18. Courtesy of the American Numismatic Society. 105

Tables

1. You Have Conquered the Evil One (1 Jn 2:12-14) — 29
2. The Devil and the Evil One (1 Jn 3:8, 11-12) — 33
3. Conquering the World (John 16:33; 1 Jn 5:4-5) — 54
4. The Testimony (1 Jn 5:9-10) — 122

Acknowledgments

This manuscript is a revised version of my doctoral research at the University of Cambridge. In completing this work, I am ever grateful to Professor George van Kooten for his invaluable knowledge, guidance, and support as supervisor. From my initial months as an MPhil student, and through the challenging times of the pandemic, he never hesitated to give his time, energy, and encouragement. I am also thankful to Drs Justin Meggitt, James Carleton Paget, and Gerhard van den Heever for their helpful comments regarding my research.

My sincere thanks to Chris Keith, Sarah Blake, and the T&T Clark/Bloomsbury members who helped make this publication possible. Much appreciation is also extended to the people and institutions who have contributed to the images in this manuscript, including the J. Paul Getty Museum, Pro-Urba, the Museum of Classical Archaeology at Cambridge, the American Numismatic Society, Gary Lee Todd, and Antoine-Chrysostome Quatremère de Quincy.

The support and prayers from friends abroad (especially Rachael Uddo, Della Kim, Moonjung Kim, Jina Nam, Sharon Kim, Hannah Chong, Swift Memorial UMC, Torch Trinity Graduate University, and SNU Church) and from Cambridge colleagues and friends were vital to the completion of this work—thank you! Finally, I am immensely grateful for the encouragement and prayers of my family and my financial supporters. I am truly humbled and obliged, as I would, in a very real sense, be unable to endeavor in this work without them.

Abbreviations

AB	Anchor Bible
ACS	American Classical Studies
BECNT	Baker Exegetical Commentary on the New Testament
Bib	*Biblica*
CBQ	Catholic Biblical Quarterly
CEV	Contemporary English Version
ClQ	*Classical Quarterly*
CurBR	*Currents in Biblical Research*
EC	Epworth Commentary
ESV	English Standard Version
ExpTim	*Expository Times*
HALOT	*The Hebrew and Aramaic Lexicon of the Old Testament.* Ludwig Koehler, Walter Baumgartner, and Johann J. Stamm. Translated and edited under the supervision of Mervyn E. J. Richardson. 4 vols. Leiden: Brill, 1994–9
HTR	*Harvard Theological Review*
ISV	International Standard Version
JBL	*Journal of Biblical Literature*
JSNT	*Journal for the Study of the New Testament*
JSNTSup	Journal for the Study of the New Testament, Supplement Series
JTS	*Journal of Theological Studies*
LCL	Loeb Classical Library
LSJ	Liddell-Scott-Jones Greek–English Lexicon
NAC	New American Commentary
NASB	*New American Standard Bible*
Neot	*Neotestamentica*
NICNT	New International Commentary on the New Testament
NICOT	New International Commentary on the Old Testament
NIV	New International Version
NKJV	New King James Version
NLT	New Living Translation
NovT	*Novum Testamentum*
NRSV	New Revised Standard Version
OCD	*Oxford Classical Dictionary*
OED	*Oxford English Dictionary*
PNTC	Pillar New Testament Commentary
SP	Sacra Pagina

TDNT	*Theological Dictionary of the New Testament.* Edited by Gerhard Kittel and Gerhard Friedrich. Translated by Geoffrey W. Bromiley. 10 vols. Grand Rapids: Eerdmans, 1964–76
TNTC	Tyndale New Testament Commentaries
VT	*Vetus Testamentum*
WBC	Word Biblical Commentary

1

Introduction

The First Letter of John, though brief in content, has prompted volumes of exegetical and theological scholarship addressing the contention that permeates the rhetoric of the Letter. The sense of conflict is apparent not only in the Johannine author naming several opponents who must be "conquered," including the evil one (2:13, 14; 3:12; 5:18, 19), antichrists (2:18, 22; 4:3), false prophets (4:1), and the world itself (5:4, 5), but also in the way he concludes with the warning: "Little children, keep yourselves from idols" (5:21).[1] Many twentieth-century scholars, including Rudolf Bultmann and Rudolf Schnackenburg, interpreted the central issue in 1 John to be a concern over proper theology;[2] they presumed that the Johannine author is writing out of a concern for budding heresies that have created a sectarian divide among the members of the Johannine community. Indeed, a schism has apparently already taken place as the antichrists "went out" from the community (2:18). While there has been significant debate over what specific heresies these opponents might represent, the general consensus has been that the conflict in 1 John is primarily an intra-Johannine one contending over different understandings of Jesus.

The reference to the antichrists who "went out" offers little doubt that there has been some intra-Johannine conflict; it is questionable, however, whether the author of 1 John repeatedly asserts that the young men of the community have "conquered the evil one" (2:13, 14), or even more prominently, that the Johannine believer "conquers the world" (5:4-5) out of a desire to address heresy. The writer's many references to "the world"[3] and the evil one, antichrist, and false prophets being associated with "the world" (4:1-5; 5:19) suggest that the contention referenced in the Letter is more than an internal issue limited to theological disputes between current and former Johannine members.

---

[1] All English translations of biblical writings are taken from the New Revised Standard Version (NRSV) with minor adjustments where appropriate. Classical abbreviations are taken from the Oxford Classical Dictionary (Simon Hornblower, Antony Spawforth, and Esther Eidinow, eds., *The Oxford Classical Dictionary*, 4th edn [Oxford: Oxford University Press, 2012]).
[2] See, for example, Rudolf Bultmann, *The Johannine Epistles*, tr. R. Philip O'Hara with Lane C. McGaughy and Robert Funk (Philadelphia: Fortress Press, 1973); Rudolf Schnackenburg, *The Johannine Epistles*, trs Reginald and Ilse Fuller (Tunbridge Wells: Burns & Oates, 1992); cf. I. Howard Marshall, *The Epistles of John* (NICNT; Grand Rapids: Eerdmans, 1978), 14–22; Stephen Smalley, *1, 2, 3 John* (WBC; Waco, TX: Word Books, 1984), xxiv–v.
[3] Cf. 1 Jn 2:2, 15 (3x), 16 (2x), 17; 3:1, 13, 17; 4:1, 3, 4, 5 (3x), 9, 14, 17; 5:4 (2x), 5, 19, cf. 2 Jn 7.

The tendency toward this sectarian view of 1 John seems to be influenced by the presumption of a schism in the Fourth Gospel. Because of literary similarities, the First Letter has often been interpreted based on the premise that it presupposes the Gospel. While I do not dispute this, scholarship on the First Letter appears to have been skewed by assumptions from John's Gospel. J. Louis Martyn has been influential in much of twentieth-century Johannine scholarship[4] as one of the first to draw attention to the specific historical and social contexts of the Johannine community. He worked primarily on the Gospel of John, cautioning against any "timeless and placeless" reading of the text,[5] and his monograph, *History and Theology in the Fourth Gospel*, framed future Johannine scholarship with its emphasis on the expulsion of Jewish Christians from the synagogue.[6] Martyn worked closely with fellow Union Theological Seminary scholar Raymond Brown,[7] who further engrained a sectarian view not only in relation to the Jews and Jewish Christians in John's Gospel but also in the Johannine Letters by grouping the antichrists, false prophets, and liars together as "hostile secessionists" who left the Johannine community.[8] In his extensive scholarship on both the Gospel and the Letters, Brown postulated complex theories about the Johannine community and how it developed, for which he was criticized and which led to his later simplifying his ideas.[9] Yet, the sectarian approach established by Martyn and Brown prevailed, and subsequent scholarship has read the contention in 1 John as an intra-Johannine issue over opposing theological views of Jesus, even suggesting that the antichrists who "went out" from the community were those who decided to go back to the synagogue.[10]

This study reconsiders the contention of the First Letter, following increasing twenty-first-century scholarship that examines New Testament texts in light of their broader cultural context.[11] In Pauline literature, the religious and political influence of the Roman Empire has been addressed by scholars, such as Richard Horsley[12] and N. T. Wright,[13] with respondents, such as John Barclay, insisting that the imperial cult

---

[4] See examples of Martyn's influence in John Ashton, *Understanding the Fourth Gospel* (Oxford: Oxford University Press, 2007), 6, and Paul Anderson, "Beyond the Shade of the Oak Tree: Recent Growth in Johannine Studies," *ExpTim* 119, no. 8 (2008): 367–8.

[5] J. Louis Martyn, "The Salvation-History Perspective in the Fourth Gospel" (PhD Diss, Yale University, 1957), 87.

[6] J. Louis Martyn, *History and Theology in the Fourth Gospel*, 3rd edn (Louisville, KY: Westminster John Knox Press, 2003), 46–66.

[7] Serene Jones, "Union Mourns Professor Lou Martyn," *Union News*, June 10, 2015, https://utsnyc.edu/union-mourns-professor-lou-martyn.

[8] Raymond Brown, *The Epistles of John* (AB; London: Geoffrey Chapman, 1982), 127.

[9] Anderson, "Beyond the Shade of the Oak Tree," 366.

[10] Paul Anderson, "The Community that Raymond Brown Left Behind: Reflections on the Johannine Dialectical Situation," *Faculty Publications—College of Christian Studies* (2013): 275; Paul Anderson, "Antichristic Crises: Proselytization Back into Jewish Religious Certainty—The Threat of Schismatic Abandonment," in *Text and Community: Essays in Commemoration of Bruce M. Metzger, Vol. 1*, ed. J. Harold Ellens (Sheffield: Sheffield Phoenix Press, 2007), 217–40.

[11] See, for example, Stanley E. Porter and Andrew W. Pitts, eds., *Christian Origins and Greco-Roman Culture* (Leiden: Brill, 2013); David E. Aune and Frederick E. Brenk, eds., *Greco-Roman Culture and the New Testament* (Leiden: Brill, 2012); Teresa Morgan, *Roman Faith and Christian Faith* (Oxford: Oxford University Press, 2015).

[12] See Richard A. Horsley, ed., *Paul and Empire: Religion and Power in Roman Imperial Society* (Harrisburg, PA: Trinity Press International, 1997).

[13] See N. T. Wright, "Paul's Gospel and Caesar's Empire," in *Paul and Politics: Ekklesia, Israel, Imperium, Interpretation: Essays in Honor of Krister Stendahl*, ed. Richard A. Horsley, 160–83 (Harrisburg,

is not so prominent to the social, political, and religious context of the early Christian churches as the imperial cult was no single entity but a large range of practices by various kinds of people across the empire[14] and therefore not making so forceful an impression on the cities' inhabitants as Wright suggests.[15] While I agree that Wright takes things a step too far, Barclay is rightly criticized by Christoph Heilig as "too pessimistic" regarding the value of background.[16] The imperial cult being an integral part of the cultural context across the empire, including the late first and early second centuries when 1 John was likely written, is precisely the point. The religious and political culture of the Greco-Roman world was as prevalent and integral as the internet is in most cities on the planet today. Any letter at any time can hardly be divorced from the cultural context within which it is written, and this study attempts to draw attention to the context to further illuminate what the writer of the First Letter might have intended and how the audience would have received its message, and it reexamines the contention expressed through the conquering language in 1 John within the context of the Greco-Roman world.[17]

When referring to the "culture" of the Greco-Roman world, I mean "the distinctive ideas, customs, social behavior, products, or way of life of a particular nation, society, people, or period."[18] Every writer comes from a culture, and thus, every text—possibly every *word*—can have cultural connotations. As an example, the word "trump" was an everyday part of my vernacular until 2015 when the word acquired an indelible cultural attachment to a specific person, which would provoke an image and even strong emotions whenever this word was used. For twenty-first-century readers to truly understand the language and message of 1 John, the letter should be read within its cultural context. Thus, the approach to this study is both exegetical and contextual, with a philological analysis of the First Letter of John and an attempt to understand possible cultural implications by drawing on classical sources, extant material culture, and secondary scholarly literature. Determining cultural connotations is admittedly limited by the material available and by the perspectives and biases of the sources themselves. Despite these limitations, however, the attempt to analyze the language of

---

PA: Trinity Press International, 2000). Wright detects "echoes of Caesar" in Paul (N. T. Wright, *Paul: Fresh Perspectives* [London: SPCK, 2005], 61–2, 70–1), drawing on the method of Richard Hays (Richard Hays, *Echoes of Scripture in the Letters of Paul* [New Haven, CT: Yale University Press, 1989]).

[14] John M. Barclay, *Pauline Churches and Diaspora Jews* (Tübingen: Mohr Siebeck, 2011), 345.

[15] Barclay, *Pauline Churches*, 368.

[16] Christoph Heilig, *Hidden Criticism?: The Methodology and Plausibility of the Search for a Counter-Imperial Subtext in Paul* (Tübingen: Mohr Siebeck, 2015), 158.

[17] The term "Greco-Roman" is admittedly problematic in that there are elements that are unique to the Greeks and to the Romans. However, the term is applicable to the culture of the early-centuries CE, which adopted a Hellenistic culture but existed under Roman rule. In that sense, it is both Greek and Roman, and the term Greco-Roman includes these attributes. There is also a convergence in the religion of the time in the deities, which had Greek and Roman equivalents, and in the worship of the emperor, which was an expected part of the culture under the Roman Empire. Just as an overarching culture might be attributed to the United States or the UK, which are made up of distinct cultures, the term "Greco-Roman" is applied to refer to the general religious and political culture of the time.

[18] Oxford English Dictionary, "Culture," 2nd edn (Oxford: Oxford University Press, 2004).

1 John within its cultural context helps construct a better picture of what the Johannine writer is indeed trying to convey and how the audience may have responded.

When Christianity was still in its nascent stages, the audience for the First Letter of John would have been a small minority in the largely polytheistic culture of the Greco-Roman world. While there may have been some insular form of "Johannine culture," many would have had to work and interact with those who did not subscribe to the same *pistis* (belief/faith)[19] that had formed the Johannine community. For those who did not come from a Jewish background and were raised in an environment that regarded polytheistic worship and worship of the Roman emperor as the norm, the shift to the Johannine *pistis* may have been particularly challenging.

When examining the conquering language of 1 John, I was particularly intrigued by the distinct, substantive use of *pistis* (belief/faith) and *nikē* (victory) in the final chapter: "For everyone who is born of God conquers the world. And this is the victory that has conquered the world, our faith" (5:4). It prompted me to question: What does it mean to "conquer the world," and how can this victory be "our *pistis*"? Moreover, because the conquered evil one, antichrists, and false prophets are all affiliated with "the world" (4:1-5; 5:19), I began to question previous scholarship, which presumed that the conflict of the letter was primarily an intra-Johannine, theological debate.

Through this study, I will demonstrate that the contention in 1 John extends beyond the Johannine community and that the writer is presenting a consistent *countercultural* narrative:[20] He is identifying the Johannine community as separate and *counter to* the predominant customs and norms of the broader Greco-Roman culture. Thus, he uses conquering language to reflect the battle of the Johannine *pistis against* the *pistis* of the Greco-Roman world and proclaims the *nikē* of *pistis* for those who believe in Jesus as the true Son of God. First, we will look at the *nikē* of 1 John in light of the associations of *nikē* in the Greco-Roman culture in order to have a better framework for the type of victory that the Johannine author is trying to convey. The most obvious cultural *nikē* is the goddess Nike, the personification of victory, who appears frequently in the contexts of competition and war. Athletic and artistic competitions known as the *agōnes* were popularized from the early fifth century BCE but continued to flourish under the Roman Empire. If the *nikē* in 1 John is referring to a competition-based victory, then the writer would be like many other New Testament authors who use the popular metaphor. We will then look at the cultural association of *nikē* in the context of war, and the military victories that were attributed to the victory goddess. It becomes clear that the combative language of the Johannine letter seems to align more closely with this type of victory.

---

[19] In 1 Jn 5:4, *pistis* is usually translated as "faith" in English (e.g., NIV, ESV, NLT, NKJV, NASB, CEV, NRSV), but could generally be translated as "belief," "faithfulness," "trust," or a combination of these. The challenges of defining *pistis* will be addressed in Section 5.2, but I will broadly connote "belief" when referring to *pistis*.

[20] April DeConick offers a helpful example of a countercultural movement when she identifies the Gnostics as "countercultural" because they challenged religious convention in their orientation toward a transcendent God (April DeConick, *The Gnostic Age: How a Countercultural Spirituality Revolutionized Religion from Antiquity to Today* [New York: Columbia University Press, 2016], 4–5). The countercultural character of the Gnostics and the Johannine community may explain why some have aligned the two.

Having identified the more militaristic undertones in 1 John, we will examine the nuances of the conflict with each of the opponents of the letter: the evil one, the antichrists, the false prophets, and the world. The study will identify what their monikers signify, whether these opponents are spiritual or literal, and how they are (or are not) being conquered by the Johannine believers. Because all of the opponents are related to "the world," and the world itself is conquered by the Johannine believers in the victory proclamation (5:4), identifying "the world" is an integral part of this analysis. The discussion will include a helpful point of comparison in the conquering language of the Gospel of John. Jesus uses conquering language that is similar to that of 1 John when he tells his disciples that he has conquered the world (Jn 16:33, cf. 1 Jn 5:4). The allusions to violence in both Johannine battles suggest that the conflict with "the world" is not simply spiritual. This analysis will show that the conquering of the world in both John's Gospel and 1 John involves conquering the literal Greco-Roman world as well.

Although the Johannine author proclaims that his readers are victorious conquerors (5:4-5), his language indicates that he has some concerns about the culture. The next chapter will look at two examples that reveal his countercultural narrative: the allusion to fear (4:18) and the warning at the close of the letter to "keep yourselves from idols" (5:21). Both references indicate that the writer is aware of the Greco-Roman culture and how it may affect his audience. This chapter will demonstrate that the reference to fear in direct opposition to love (4:18) is not referring to the positive Jewish conception of fear that includes a reverence for God. Instead, it suggests the more negative fear of the divine, which is discussed in the writings of historians and philosophers in the Greco-Roman culture. Another indication of his countercultural narrative is the warning in the final verse to "keep yourselves from idols" (5:21). Because his underlying concern is the *pistis* of the Johannine community, the author gives a warning to be vigilant against any influences that might threaten their *pistis*. His final word is a countercultural message to avoid the idolatry of the polytheistic Greco-Roman world.

Finally, we will focus on the victory of *pistis* both in the Greco-Roman culture and in the letter of 1 John. In the culture, Roman soldiers achieve victory by encouraging their opposition to submit in a *pistis* to the Romans, and there are deliberate attempts by emperors to foster loyalty from their subjects by aligning themselves with the goddesses of Pistis/Fides and Nike/Victoria.[21] Through this study, we see that the writer of 1 John intentionally counters the culture of *pistis* to the emperor, who was often known as the *divi filius* (the son of god), with a repeated emphasis on Jesus as the *true* Son of God. The analysis will show that the writer is concerned about the influences of the Greco-Roman world, and that he is proclaiming a countercultural victory because he considers the prevailing culture to be a threat. Thus, the author emphasizes the true *pistis* that is proven through the testimony from people and from God, and he conveys the gravity of this battle against the culture by emphasizing the result of their *pistis*: eternal life.

---

[21] For the sake of consistency, I will mostly refer to the gods and goddesses by their Greek names but will also include the Roman names when appropriate.

2

Victory in the Greco-Roman World

For the modern-day audience reading the letter of 1 John in English, the proclamation of victory in the final chapter would probably be received quite differently in comparison to its original audience. Firstly, readers today would not notice the distinct substantive of the noun "victory," *nikē* (νίκη), which only appears once in the letter (and indeed in all of the New Testament)[1] (5:4):

> For everyone who is born of God conquers the world. And this is the victory that has conquered the world, our faith.
>
> ὅτι πᾶν τὸ γεγεννημένον ἐκ τοῦ θεοῦ νικᾷ τὸν κόσμον· καὶ αὕτη ἐστὶν ἡ νίκη ἡ νικήσασα τὸν κόσμον, ἡ πίστις ἡμῶν.

The declaration of *nikē* in the final chapter builds upon the verbal forms throughout the letter, but the nuances in English are lost because the verbal forms tend to look and sound quite different from the noun. A person does not "victor" over someone; they "conquer," "overcome," or perhaps "defeat." For the original Johannine audience, however, the word *nikē* would have stood out, not only because of its distinct usage in the letter, but also because there was a strong association of the word *nikē* with the victory goddess in the surrounding culture.

Nike (Roman: Victoria) is the personification of victory, which was reinforced in literature and material culture from about the sixth century BCE to well into the fourth century CE. The goddess often appears in the context of athletic and artistic competition, indicating whom she favors by crowning wreaths on the victors. She also appears to be a significant figure in war, as both military and political leaders attribute their victories

---

[1] The noun νῖκος (conquest), a later form for νίκη, appears four times in the New Testament, three of which reference LXX passages: Mt. 12:20 (cf. Isa. 42:3); 1 Cor. 15:54-5 (cf. Isa. 25:8; Hos. 13:14), 57. However, the word νῖκος does not appear in the LXX passages themselves. The passage in Mt. 12:20 may be a conflation of the Isaiah passage (42:3-4) to indicate that justice is being put forth "successfully" rather than "to victory." In 1 Corinthians (15:54-5), the emphasis on victory is likely to emphasize the triumph over death as a result of the resurrection. Cf. Robert Kraft, "*Eis nikos* = Permanently/Successfully: 1 Cor 15.54, Matt 12.20," in *Septuagintal Lexicography*, ed. Robert Kraft (Missoula, MT: Scholars Press, 1975): 153–6; Richard B. Hays, *First Corinthians* (Louisville, KY: John Knox Press, 1997), 276–7. See also LSJ s.v. "νικάω" and "νῖκος." The word νῖκος is often translated "victory" in English (cf. NIV, NRSV, ESV, NKJV, NASB). Thus, even though the words are indeed related, the distinctiveness of the νίκη in 1 John (5:4), and its cultural association to the goddess of the same name, would be lost to those reading the NT in English.

to her regardless of their resources and strength. This chapter will consider the *nikē* of 1 John in the context of the cultural associations of the goddess Nike in order to identify more closely with the original Johannine community. This background can illuminate the nuances of the *nikē* that is proclaimed by the Johannine author including how he intends this victory to be achieved.

2.1 Victory in Competition

The *Agōnes*

When referring to *nikē* in the Greco-Roman world, one likely context was the athletic and artistic competitions or festivals known as the *agōnes* (ἀγῶνες).[2] In its earliest forms, before the eighth century BCE, the events were smaller and centered around a shrine or sanctuary, but by the sixth and fifth centuries, the competitions became popularized Panhellenic events.[3] Some of the Panhellenic *agōnes*, like the Pythian Games, included music and art,[4] but many, like the Olympic Games, were more oriented toward athletic competition. Each *agōn*, whether local or Panhellenic, was dedicated to a deity, but the Panhellenic festivals were especially momentous as they brought together people from multiple cities. Seeking *nikē* in the *agōnes* may have become increasingly popular because the competitions were a way to assert dominance and attain victory without the extreme losses of seeking victory in battle.[5]

Although the *agōnes* had started with the Greeks, the Romans became just as passionate about the competitions.[6] The emperor Domitian established a regular *agōn* in Rome itself, the Capitoline Games, which was included in the list of Sacred Games that celebrated a deity, and was considered to be second only to the Olympics.[7] Herod the Great had also fostered the popularity of athletic competition in Judea with his

---

[2] The *agōnes* referred to athletic and artistic competitions, but the term *agōn* (ἀγών) and its derivates could also denote the general struggle for survival and success, rivalry in philosophical and legal debates, opposition in war, and medical disputes. For example, Hesiod, *Works and Days* 11–26, Polybius 9.32.4; Thucydides 2.89. Cf. LSJ s.v. "ἀγών."
[3] Cf. Thomas Francis Scanlon, *Eros and Greek Athletics* (Oxford: Oxford University Press, 2002), 25; Stephen Instone and Antony Spawforth, "*agōnes*" in *OCD*.
[4] Pliny (the Elder), *Naturalis historia* 35.58; Plutarch, *Moralia* 674D–5B.
[5] Cf. Donald G. Kyle, *Sport and Spectacle in the Ancient World* (Chichester, West Sussex: John Wiley and Sons, 2015), 6. Ironically, intense, violent fighting could be seen in the *agōnes*, notably in the *pancration* (παγκράτιον) event in which every form of power possible was allowed to defeat the other contestant. Like the ultimate fighting championships of the modern day, *pancration* contestants battled with a combination of wrestling, boxing, and street fighting until one of the contestants could no longer continue or would formally indicate defeat. Cf. Xenophanes, *Fragments* 2.5; Pindar, *Nemean Odes* 5.52; Herodotus 9.105; David C. Young, *A Brief History* (Malden, MA; Oxford: Blackwell, 2004), 43. Another irony is that the Romans found a way to assert dominance in war without the need for bloodshed in the *pistis* to the Romans (see Section 5.1).
[6] The Greeks tried to affirm their ethnic superiority by limiting participation to Greeks, but the festivals became a popular and active part of the Roman world as well. Cf. Kyle, *Sport and Spectacle*, 7.
[7] Cf. Suetonius, *Domitian* 4.4; *IG* XIV, 747 (an inscription about a first-century CE athlete winning at the Capitoline Games); cf. Stephen G. Miller, ed., *Arete: Greek Sports from Ancient Sources* (Berkeley: University of California Press, 2004), 166, 171.

building a hippodrome stadium in Caesarea Maritima in the first century BCE.[8] Victory in the athletic context could therefore be seen among Greeks, Romans, and Jews.

When the *agōnes* victories were represented in literature and material culture, the depictions frequently included the goddess Nike with the winners. She can be seen, for example, in victory odes (ἐπινίκια)[9] from the fifth century BCE, when the *agōnes* were gaining in popularity. These commissioned poems celebrated the winners by glorifying the events of the victory. The poems could then be set to music and performed at the victory party.[10] The odes were a way for the champions to receive a more lasting glory through the Greek poets, "for the word lives longer than deeds."[11]

The lyric poet Pindar includes Nike in his descriptions of the winners of the *agōnes*. In a poem about the Nemean Games, one of the most prestigious Panhellenic festivals, Nike appears to embrace the winner:

Inherited Destiny decides the outcome of all deeds. Euthymenes, twice from Aegina did you fall into Nike's arms and enjoy elaborate hymns.[12]

Πότμος δὲ κρίνει συγγενὴς ἔργων πέρι πάντων. τὺ δ' Αἰγίναθε δίς, Εὐθύμενες, Νίκας ἐν ἀγκώνεσσι πίτνων ποικίλων ἔψαυσας ὕμνων.[13]

Pindar poetically describes how the athlete Euthymenes was victorious in two different games and fell into the arms of the goddess. Similarly, in a victory ode about the Isthmian Games, Pindar depicts a winner falling on the knees of Nike.[14] The inclusion of the goddess reflects much of the culture of the Greco-Roman world, in which religion is interwoven into every activity; in the context of athletics, the competitors may have the physical ability to win, but they cannot be victorious without the favor of the gods, and of Nike in particular.[15]

Bacchylides, a contemporary of Pindar, describes Nike at the start of a victory ode about a winner from the Pythian Games:

Nike, giver of sweetness, to you the father (son of Uranus) on his high bench (has granted glorious honor), so that in gold-rich Olympus you stand beside Zeus and judge the outcome of prowess for immortals and mortals: be gracious, daughter of thick-tressed, right-judging Styx; it is thanks to you that Metapontion, the god-honored city, is now filled with the celebrations and festivities of strong-limbed

---

[8] Josephus, *Ant.* 15.341. Herod also constructed most of the public buildings at Nicopolis, the city founded to commemorate Augustus's victory at Actium (Josephus, *War* 1.425; *Ant.* 16.137); see Joseph Patrich, "Herod's Hippodrome-Stadium at Caesarea and the Games Conducted Therein," in *What Athens Has to Do with Jerusalem: Essays on Classical, Jewish, and Early Christian Art and Archaeology in Honor of Gideon Foerster*, ed. Leonard V. Rutgers (Leuven: Peeters, 2002), 29–68.
[9] Cf. LSJ s.v. "ἐπινίκιος."
[10] Young, *A Brief History*, 67.
[11] Pindar, *Nemean Odes* 4.6 (Race, LCL); cf. Young, *A Brief History*, 74.
[12] All English translations of classical literature are taken from the (digital) Loeb Classical Library with minor adjustments where appropriate.
[13] Pindar, *Nemean Odes* 5.42 (Race, LCL).
[14] Pindar, *Isthmian Odes* 2.26.
[15] Cf. Pindar, *Isthmian Odes* 5.8-11.

Figure 1 Panathenaic Prize Amphora with lid. Attributed to the Painter of the Wedding Procession (Greek [Attic]), signed by Nikodemos. 363–2 BCE. J. Paul Getty Museum no. 93.AE.55.

youths, and they sing the praises of the Pythian victor, the marvelous son of Phaiscus.

Νίκα γλυκύδωρε· κλυτὰν γὰρσοὶ πατὴρ τιμὰν ἔδωκεν ὑψίζυγος Οὐρανίδαςἐν πολυχρύσωι τ' Ὀλύμπωι Ζηνὶ παρισταμένα κρίνεις τέλος ἀθανάτοισίν τε καὶ θνατοῖς ἀρετᾶς· ἔλλαθι, βαθυπλοκάμου κούρα Στυγὸς ὀρθοδίκου· σέθεν δ' ἕκατι καὶ νῦν Μεταπόντιον εὐγυίων κατέχουσι νέων κῶμοί τε καὶ εὐφροσύναι θεότιμον ἄστυ· ὑμνεῦσι δὲ Πυθιόνικον παῖδα θαητὸν Φαΐσκου.[16]

Before any other proclamation in the poem, Nike is honored *first*. She is not simply present when the athletes compete;[17] she can play the role of judge, determining which person will be victorious. Yet, she is more than an umpire or referee; Nike decides the victory, and it is because of *her* that even a city, like the city of Metapontion above, will receive honor.[18]

Extant material culture supports the descriptions of Nike in the victory odes. Just as the poems allude to her role in athletic victory, the visual depictions of winners in the *agōnes*

---

[16] Bacchylides 11.1 (Campbell, LCL).
[17] Cf. Bacchylides 3.5.
[18] Cf. also Bacchylides 12.5.

include Nike's presence as well. A fifth-century BCE Athenian *stamnos* (liquid container), for example, depicts victorious athletes offering sacrifices in honor of the gods, and a winged Nike hovering above them.[19] Similarly, on a Rhegium silver coin from the fifth century BCE, Nike is seen flying over Anaxilas, the tyrant of the city, and crowning him with a wreath after he wins a race at the Olympics.[20] In a terracotta *amphora* (jug) from *c.* 363 BCE, Nike crowns a winner of a boxing match (Figure 1).[21] Nike seems to have been the primary icon of victory associated with the games, and this fostered the popularity of the goddess among the Romans as well, who built their own temple to Nike/Victoria in 294 BCE.[22] According to Livy, people would throng to the temple at Palatine Hill bearing gifts for the goddess, and they would attend a banquet and games held in honor of the gods.[23] In the following year, the Romans wore laurel wreaths for the first time at the games and presented each victor with a palm branch, another symbol of victory.[24] The crowns and palm branches that victors received at the *agōnes* were made of perishable leaves,[25] but they became a prize that even an emperor would covet.[26]

An Iconic Nike

The association of Nike with the *agōnes* was likely solidified through one of her most iconic images in material culture: the Statue of Zeus at Olympia (Figure 2), which showed Zeus seated on a throne with Nike uplifted in his right hand. The massive chryselephantine sculpture was a substantial representation of victory for several centuries in the city that hosted the Olympic Games, and was so impressive that it was later considered one of the Seven Wonders of the Ancient World.[27] Pausanias describes the Nike, who was prominently displayed not only in Zeus's right hand but also in four more images of her around his throne:

> The god sits on a throne, and he is made of gold and ivory. On his head lies a crown which is a copy of olive shoots. In his right hand he carries a Nike, which, like the statue, is of ivory and gold; she wears a ribbon and—on her head—a crown ... The throne is adorned with gold and with jewels, to say nothing of ebony and ivory. Upon it are painted figures and wrought images. There are four Nikes, represented as dancing women, one at each foot of the throne, and two others at the base of each foot.

---

[19] British Museum no. 1839,0214.68; cf. descriptions of festival sacrifices in Pausanias 5.13.8–5.14.2.
[20] Richard Rawles, "Early epinician: Ibycus and Simonides," in *Reading the Victory Ode*, eds. Peter Agócs, Chris Carey, and Richard Rawles (Cambridge: Cambridge University Press, 2012), 22.
[21] J. Paul Getty Museum 93.AE.55.
[22] Livy 10.33.9; cf. Stefan Weinstock, "Victor and Invictus," *HTR* 50, no. 1 (1957): 215–18; Michael McCormick, *Eternal Victory: Triumphal Rulership in Late Antiquity, Byzantium, and the Early Medieval West*, Past and Present Publications (Cambridge: Cambridge University Press, 1986), 12.
[23] Livy 29.14.13.
[24] Livy 10.47.3.
[25] Cf. Lucian, *Anacharsis, or Athletics*, 9.
[26] Nero in 67 CE supposedly "won" at least 1,808 crowns of victory at multiple *agōnes*, cf. Suetonius, *Nero* 22–5; Miller, *Arete*, 165.
[27] Cf. Martin Price, "The Statue of Zeus at Olympia," in *The Seven Wonders of the Ancient World*, ed. Peter A. Clayton and Martin J. Price (New York: Dorset, 1989), 59–77.

Figure 2 "Le Jupiter Olympien vu dans son trone et dans l'interieur de son temple." Etching and watercolor version of Phidias's celebrated statue at Olympia. Frontispiece of Antoine-Chrysostome Quatremere de Quincy's book, *Le Jupiter Olympien, Ou, L'art De La Sculpture Antique Considere Sous Un Nouveau Point De Vue: Ouvrage Qui Comprend Un Essai Sur Le Gout De La Sculpture Polychorme, L'analyse Explicative De La Toreutique, Et L'histoire De La Statuaire En or Et Ivoire Chez Les Grecs Et Les Romains: Avec La Restitution Des Principaux Monuments De Cet Art Et La Demonstration Pratique Ou Le Renouvellement De Ses Procedes Mecaniques* (Paris: Firmin Didot, 1814).

Καθέζεται μὲν δὴ ὁ θεὸς ἐν θρόνῳ χρυσοῦ πεποιημένος καὶ ἐλέφαντος· στέφανος δὲ ἐπίκειταί οἱ τῇ κεφαλῇ μεμιμημένος ἐλαίας κλῶνας. ἐν μὲν δὴ τῇ δεξιᾷ φέρει Νίκην ἐξ ἐλέφαντος καὶ ταύτην καὶ χρυσοῦ, ταινίαν τε ἔχουσαν καὶ ἐπὶ τῇ κεφαλῇ στέφανον … ὁ δὲ θρόνος ποικίλος μὲν χρυσῷ καὶ λίθοις, ποικίλος δὲ καὶ ἐβένῳ τε καὶ ἐλέφαντί ἐστι· καὶ ζῷά τε ἐπ᾽ αὐτοῦ γραφῇ μεμιμημένα καὶ ἀγάλματά ἐστιν εἰργασμένα. Νῖκαι μὲν δὴ τέσσαρες χορευουσῶν παρεχόμεναι σχῆμα κατὰ ἕκαστον τοῦ θρόνου τὸν πόδα, δύο δέ εἰσιν ἄλλαι πρὸς ἑκάστου πέζῃ ποδός.[28]

Seeing five Nike images on this statue alone would suggest the significance with which the Olympians regarded her, and the gold and ivory Nike in Zeus's right hand seems to offer a focal point for viewers to see the uplifted personification of victory. Notably, both

---

[28] Pausanias 5.11.1-2 (Jones and Ormerod, LCL).

Nike and Zeus also wear crowns on their heads to symbolize their victory, and this may have contributed to the icon of crowns being attached to both Nike and to the *agōnes*.[29]

The statue of Nike and Zeus in Olympia became an iconic image because of the popularity of the competitions in the city, which were originally held in honor of Zeus. During the Golden Olympic decade of the 470s BCE, a new temple was built in Olympia in honor of the deity,[30] and in *c.* 435 BCE, the Eleans, the custodians of the Olympic Games,[31] hired Phidias to design and install a cult statue within the temple because he was one of the most well-known Greek sculptors of the time. He had completed the impressive Athena Parthenos statue, which also highlighted the goddess Nike in Athens a few years before (see more on this statue in the next section), and the Eleans seemingly wanted him to do an even greater work in Olympia.[32] Phidias seems to have satisfied his clients as he almost doubled his previous efforts, constructing a nearly twenty-meter (sixty-five foot) display that was placed inside the immense new temple, which was about $70 \times 30 \times 21$ meters ($230 \times 98 \times 69$ feet).[33] The sight was so grandiose that Strabo centuries later noted that the statue gave "the impression that if Zeus arose and stood erect he would unroof the temple."[34]

The sheer expense and effort spent on the statue leave no question as to why it might be considered one of the Seven Wonders of the Ancient World, but it was also an apparently beautiful and inspiring sight. In a discourse before the immense Olympic statue in 97 CE, Dio Chrysostom proclaimed, "Of all the statues which are upon the earth [it is] the most beautiful and the most dear to the gods," and he thought that whoever "stood before this image, would forget all the terrors and hardships that fall to our human lot."[35] According to Epictetus, some believed that it was "a misfortune to die without seeing [it]," and Quintilian commented, "The beauty of [the statue] is said to have added something to the traditional religious concept of the god."[36]

Based on the writers mentioned above, there was a high regard for the Nike and Zeus at Olympia, and many people probably did see the statue as the Olympics was considered to be the most prestigious of the Panhellenic Games, and competitors and spectators from both inside and outside of the city would have had access to it. However, it seems doubtful that it would have been as inspiring and beautiful if the goddess Nike had not been included. In the male-dominated society, desirable abstract values such as victory were personified as beautiful female figures.[37] Thus, Nike was a

---

[29] See more on Nike with crowns in Sections 2.2 and 5.1.
[30] Ulrich Sinn, *Olympia: Cult, Sport, and Ancient Festival*, tr. Thomas Thornton (Princeton, NJ: M. Wiener, 2000), 56.
[31] Cf. Thomas James Dunbabin, Robert J. Hopper, and Antony Spawforth, "Elis" in *OCD*.
[32] Cf. Rashna Taraporewalla, "Size Matters: The Statue of Zeus at Olympia and Competitive Emulation," in *Statue of Zeus at Olympia: New Approaches*, ed. Janette McWilliam et al. (Newcastle upon Tyne: Cambridge Scholars Publishing, 2011), 42.
[33] Young, *A Brief History*, 60.
[34] Strabo, *Geography* 8.3.30 (Jones, LCL).
[35] Dio Chrysostom, *Discourses* 12.25, 51–2 (Cohoon, LCL).
[36] Epictetus *Discourses* 1.6.24 (Oldfather, LCL); Quintilian 12.10.9 (Russell, LCL).
[37] Emma Stafford suggests that, in the male-dominated society, extremes such as the Fates were represented in female form as "the other," and desirable abstract values such as victory were represented as the desirable female. Cf. Emma Stafford, "Masculine Values, Feminine Forms: On the Gender of Personified Abstractions," in *Thinking Men: Masculinity and Its Self-representation in the Classical Tradition*, ed. Lin Foxhall and John Salmon (London: Routledge, 1998), 53.

source of inspiration toward the ideal, and the muscular, staid Zeus was representative of the power needed to reach it.

One can imagine the message this statue might convey: The god is literally holding victory in his hand. Nike is like the seal of assurance that Zeus holds power and victory over his opponents, and all who honor him will likewise have favor with him, and with Nike, to be victorious in their endeavors. Though the main figure of the statue is Zeus, Nike seems to be a major focus as she is the winged goddess who serves as a source of inspiration, conveying the image of victory and success that one can achieve. She is certainly a major reason, if not the primary reason, why the statue is revered so highly as beautiful, and causing people to forget their hardships, just as Quintilian and Dio Chrysostom suggested above.

The Nike images within the temple would be enough to convey the significance that was attributed to the goddess, but additional figures of her outside the temple further demonstrate her prominence. Pausanias comments that a golden Nike crowned the west pediment peak of the temple,[38] and a marble statue of the goddess was excavated at Olympia from 1875 to 1876 along with parts of the base and an inscription. Known today as the Nike of Paionios, the statue dates from around 425 to 420 BCE, and it originally stood near the temple of Zeus on a triangular six-meter-high pillar.[39] The accompanying inscription says, "The Messanians and the Naupaktians dedicated this statue to Zeus Olympios from the spoils of the wars. Paionios of Mende made it, who also won the competition to make the akroteria of the temple."[40] The specific note that the sculptor Paionios won a competition seems appropriate in a city known for its competitions, and there is poetic logic in a victor sculpting the victory goddess.

From the multiple Nikes placed in noteworthy places, one can see why someone would think of the goddess first when discussing *nikē* in the city of Olympia in fifth century BCE. Nike would have been a visible representation of victory, not only for the everyday residents of the city but also for visiting competitors and spectators from all over the Greco-Roman world. Her image ingrained the sense of the importance of victory to the culture. However, the prominence of Nike was not limited to one location or time period. The Statue of Zeus with Nike lasted for over 800 years,[41] and it was probably as iconic and well known as the Eiffel Tower in Paris or the Statue of Liberty in New York, both of which have stood for less than 150 years.

As with many iconic statues both in antiquity and the modern day, copies were made, and Pausanias notes a bronze image of Zeus holding a figure of Nike as one of the most noteworthy sights in the port city of Piraeus.[42] Another copy was found during a nineteenth-century excavation of a villa of the emperor Domitian from the first century CE in Rome, which is on display at the State Heritage Museum in St

---

[38] Pausanias 5.10.4.
[39] Cf. Pausanias 5.26.1.
[40] "Nike of Paionios," University of Cambridge Museum of Classical Archaeology Databases, accessed May 24, 2021, https://museum.classics.cam.ac.uk/collections/casts/nike-paionios.
[41] In 475 CE, it was carried off to Constantinople by Emperor Theodosius I, where it was destroyed by a fire. Cf. Tom Stevenson, "The Fate of the Statue of Zeus at Olympia," in *Statue of Zeus at Olympia*, 167.
[42] Pausanias 1.1.3.

Petersburg, Russia.⁴³ It is not surprising that the emperor would have made a copy, as he seems to have been fond of the *agōnes* (as mentioned above). Even this smaller version of the original is still an impressive sight at almost three-and-a-half meters (11.4 feet) tall. It likely represents the power of Zeus and the triumph of Nike that the emperor wanted to display and foster in his home.

The many references to Nike in material culture and literature seem to indicate that she had a close association with athletic, competitive victory for several centuries. Indeed, her connection was so solidified that she is still associated with athletic victory and success today.⁴⁴

Johannine Competition?

Because of the prevalence and popularity of the *agōnes,* it is understandable as to why the author of 1 John might want to allude to a competitive *nikē*. Several New Testament letters make references to the competitions, as they were a palpable metaphor for the readers of the time. The most obvious, perhaps, is the metaphor of running and boxing in 1 Cor. (9:24-6):

> Do you not know that in a race all the runners run, but only one receives the prize? Run in such a way that you may win it. Every athlete exercises self-control in all things; they do it to receive a perishable crown, but we an imperishable one. So I do not run aimlessly, nor do I box as though beating the air.
>
> Οὐκ οἴδατε ὅτι οἱ ἐν σταδίῳ τρέχοντες πάντες μὲν τρέχουσιν, εἷς δὲ λαμβάνει τὸ βραβεῖον; οὕτως τρέχετε ἵνα καταλάβητε. πᾶς δὲ ὁ ἀγωνιζόμενος πάντα ἐγκρατεύεται, ἐκεῖνοι μὲν οὖν ἵνα φθαρτὸν στέφανον λάβωσιν, ἡμεῖς δὲ ἄφθαρτον. ἐγὼ τοίνυν οὕτως τρέχω ὡς οὐκ ἀδήλως, οὕτως πυκτεύω ὡς οὐκ ἀέρα δέρων.

Corinth was the city that hosted the Isthmian Games, and so the Corinthians would have found the references to the *agōnes* to be familiar and compelling.⁴⁵ They would have recognized the language of *agōnizomai* (ἀγωνίζομαι) alluding to the struggle of the *agōnes,* and the individual competitors training for months, exerting tremendous effort for a victory that was represented by a perishable crown made of leaves (στέφανος, 1 Cor. 9:25).⁴⁶ The metaphor emphasized the point about winning a prize as a result of

---

⁴³ "Statue of Jupiter," The State Heritage Museum, accessed May 25, 2021, https://bit.ly/3fiH79x.
⁴⁴ Nike has appeared on almost every Summer Olympics medal since 1896 ("Olympic Medals," Olympics, accessed June 16, 2021, https://olympics.com/en/olympic-games/olympic-medals). Nike is also in the name of a company known for athletic footwear, and it has produced sneakers that reference the goddess specifically ("Women's Air Force 1 Shadow: Goddess of Victory," Nike, accessed June 16, 2021, https://www.nike.com/my/launch/t/womens-air-force-1-goddess-of-victory; Ellie Abraham, "Nike Trainers Mocked over Incorrect Use of Greek Lettering," *The Independent,* June 9, 2021, https://www.independent.co.uk/life-style/fashion/nike-trainers-greek-letter-mythology-b1862636.html).
⁴⁵ Hays, *First Corinthians,* 155.
⁴⁶ Cf. Lucian, *Anacharsis, or Athletics,* 9; Hays, *First Corinthians,* 156; F. W. Grosheide, *Commentary on the First Epistle to the Corinthians* (NICNT; Grand Rapids: Eerdmans, 1972), 214–15; Leon

discipline and self-control (similarly in 2 Tim. 2:5).[47] References to running races and fighting appear in many other epistles as well (e.g., Gal. 2:2, 5:7; Phil. 2:16, 3:12-14; 2 Tim. 4:7; Heb. 12:1), indicating the popularity and relevance of the *agōnes* at the time.

The author of 1 John may have considered using an *agōnes* metaphor as well to declare his victory in the final chapter of the letter. However, the language he uses does not seem to relate with athletic and artistic competition. There is no reference to *agōnizomai* (ἀγωνίζομαι),[48] and there is no mention of running (τρέχω),[49] a prize (βραβεῖον),[50] or a crown (στέφανος).[51] Instead, the language in the Johannine letter suggests a different sort of victory. Although the noun *nikē* appears only once in 1 John (5:4), the verbal cognate occurs several times.[52] In each case, there is a distinct opponent: the evil one (2:13, 14); false prophets and antichrists (4:4; cf. 4:1-3); and the world (5:4-5). (These opponents will be examined further in Sections 3.1–3.3.) The Johannine audience does not seem to be in competition with these opponents, racing against the false prophets or boxing the antichrists. Instead, the conquering language with these opponents, and especially with the evil one in 1 John,[53] suggests a combative fight that is more akin to the context of victory in military battle. We will now examine the concept of *nikē* in war, which was also represented through the victory goddess in the Greco-Roman world.

2.2 Victory in War

Nike with Artemis, Ares, and Athena

In addition to her association with the *agōnes*, the Nike, who personified victory in the Greco-Roman culture, also appeared frequently in the context of war. This is perhaps unsurprising as one of the earliest known references to the goddess is in reference to a battle; in Hesiod's *Theogony*, the goddess is described as the daughter of Pallas and Styx, and she is honored alongside her sisters Zelus, Cratos, and Bia (Rivalry, Supremacy, and Force, respectively) for siding with Zeus in the battle against the Titans.[54] As the god of thunder and lightning, Zeus has significant power on his own, but the depiction

---

Morris, *The First Epistle of Paul to the Corinthians: An Introduction and Commentary* (TNTC; London: Tyndale Press, 1969), 139.

[47] Jerome H. Neyrey, *Paul, in Other Words: A Cultural Reading of His Letters* (Louisville, KY: Westminster/John Knox Press, 1990), 144.

[48] The word ἀγωνίζομαι occurs at Lk. 13:24; Jn 18:36; 1 Cor. 9:25; Col. 1:29; 4:12; 1 Tim. 4:10; 6:12; 2 Tim. 4:7.

[49] Cf. Gal. 2:2; Phil. 2:16; Heb. 12:1.

[50] The noun for "prize," βραβεῖον, occurs only at 1 Cor. 9:24 and Phil. 3:14 in the NT.

[51] The word στέφανος appears twenty-five times in the NT and can be translated "wreath" or "crown"; cf. LSJ s.v. "στέφανος." See, for example, 1 Cor. 9:25; 2 Tim. 4:8; Jas 1:12; cf. 2 Tim. 2:5; Rev. 2:10. There is also the more ominous crown of thorns in Mt. 27:29; Mk 15:17; Jn 19:2, 5.

[52] The verb νικάω (conquer) appears only in the First Letter of John among the Johannine letters at 2:13, 14; 4:4; 5:4 (2x); 5:5 cf. the sole occurrence in John's Gospel at 16:33 (see more on John 16:33 in Section 3.3).

[53] See references to the evil one at 1 Jn 2:13, 14; 3:12; 5:18, 19; cf. references to evil at 1 Jn 3:12; 2 Jn 11; 3 Jn 11.

[54] Hesiod, *Theogony* 383–403.

of Nike taking his side seems to imply an assured victory.[55] In the context of war, surely everyone would want victory to be on their side, and this may explain why Nike was also affiliated with the cult of other deities related to violence and warfare, most notably Artemis, Ares, and Athena.

One of the oldest extant sculptures of Nike shows her connection with Artemis, the goddess of the hunt. The sculpture, believed to date as early as 570 BCE, was found on the island of Delos, in front of the Temple of Artemis.[56] The inscription on the base of the sculpture attributes the work to "Archermos," who appears to have been one of the first to depict the winged Nike.[57] The statue being found outside the Temple of Artemis shows that Nike was likely connected with the huntress goddess, who was known as a death-bringing deity.[58] If the audience of 1 John was in Ephesus, as is traditionally thought,[59] then this connection may be especially relevant as the citizens of Ephesus in the first centuries CE believed that the key to understanding their city lay in the cult of the huntress goddess.[60] There are also inscriptions thanking Nike in Ephesus dating to the second and third centuries.[61] This offers support for the connection between the two goddesses and further shows Nike's significance to the culture in multiple cities.

The victory goddess appears to have had a closer affiliation with Ares, the god of war. One Homeric hymn even calls Nike the daughter of Ares.[62] Their connection is understandable given that soldiers would want to achieve a victory in war, and both Greeks and Romans honored Nike alongside Ares and associated them together in their expeditions.[63] In the British Museum, a richly decorated scabbard called the "Sword of Tiberius" (c. 14–16 CE) shows the ceding of military victory, with Tiberius presenting a statuette of Nike to Augustus, who is himself sitting in the pose of Zeus, and accompanied by Nike and Ares.[64]

The association of Nike and Ares can also be seen today in the Villa of Orbe-Boscéaz in Switzerland,[65] in which a series of second-century CE mosaics portray the days of the week (Figure 3). The mosaic for "Tuesday" displays a strong, muscular Ares sitting with spear, helmet, and shield, flanked on either side by the victory goddess Nike and Phobos, the god of fear. The imagery is appropriate because the Latin name

---

[55] The early association of the two deities may also explain why Zeus and Nike were depicted together in the Statue of Zeus at Olympia; they were already seen as a team.
[56] "Nike of Delos," University of Cambridge Museum of Classical Archaeology Databases, accessed May 27, 2021, https://museum.classics.cam.ac.uk/collections/casts/nike-delos.
[57] Cf. Aristophanes, *Birds* 573.
[58] Cf. Homer, *Odyssey* 11.171–3.
[59] Smalley, *1, 2, 3 John*, xxxii; cf. Robert W. Yarbrough, *1–3 John* (BECNT; Grand Rapids: Baker Academic, 2009), 17–19.
[60] Mary Beard, John North, and S. R. F. Price, *Religions of Rome, Vol. 1* (Cambridge: Cambridge University Press, 1998), 360. The book of Acts also refers to the fierce passion of the Ephesians to the goddess Artemis (Acts 19:24-41).
[61] IE IV 1069.2; 1077.2; cf. Guy MacLean Rogers, *The Mysteries of Artemis of Ephesos Cult, Polis, and Change in the Graeco-Roman World* (New Haven, CT: Yale University Press, 2012), 306, 435 n. 26.
[62] Homer, *Homeric Hymns* 8.4.
[63] Cf. Plutarch, *Sulla* 19.5; *Moralia* 873B; Athenaeus, *The Learned Banqueters* 6.243e.
[64] British Museum no. 1866,0806.1.
[65] Cf. Sophie Bujard, "La Mosaïque aux Divinités d'Orbe-Bosceaz (Suisse): une lecture a choix multiples," in *La Mosaïque Gréco-romaine, 9*, Collection De L'École Française de Rome, 352, ed. Hélène Morlier (Rome: École Française de Rome, 2005), 227–34.

Figure 3 Part of Mosaic no. 8: Les divinites de la semaine (Mars). Mosaiques romaines d'Orbe-Bosceaz. Archeologie cantonale de l'Etat de Vaud, picture Fibbi-Aeppli, Grandson.

for Tuesday, *dies Martis* (literally "day of Mars") is in honor of the war god Mars, the Roman equivalent of Ares. However, it is also a triumphant message to place Nike alongside Ares (and Phobos) in the mosaic. The image seems to portray a victorious Tuesday, one that inspires and conveys a sense of success over others (enemies).

One of the most impressive displays of Nike in antiquity, especially before the Statue of Zeus was erected in Olympia, was the Nike housed in the Parthenon in Athens. The Athena Parthenos, a now-lost gold and ivory sculpture, showed Nike's association with Athena, the goddess of wisdom and warfare. The immense statue is described by Pausanias:

> The statue of Athena is upright, with a tunic reaching to the feet, and on her breast the head of Medusa is worked in ivory. She holds a statue of Nike about four cubits high, and in the other hand a spear; at her feet lies a shield and near the spear is a serpent.
>
> τὸ δὲ ἄγαλμα τῆς Ἀθηνᾶς ὀρθόν ἐστιν ἐν χιτῶνι ποδήρει καί οἱ κατὰ τὸ στέρνον ἡ κεφαλὴ Μεδούσης ἐλέφαντός ἐστιν ἐμπεποιημένη· καὶ Νίκην τε ὅσον τεσσάρων πηχῶν, ἐν δὲ τῇ ἑτέρᾳ χειρὶ δόρυ ἔχει, καί οἱ πρὸς τοῖς ποσὶν ἀσπίς τε κεῖται καὶ πλησίον τοῦ δόρατος δράκων ἐστίν.[66]

---

[66] Pausanias 1.24.7 (Jones, LCL).

The statue of Athena was probably about 12.7 meters tall (41.6 feet) with a 1.8-meter (6 foot) Nike in her hand.[67] As the patron goddess of the city of Athens, Athena was valued and honored for her protection, but the Athenians' need to show that Nike was also on their side reveals her value. The towering figures undoubtedly left a lasting impression, and it is yet another visual display of the good fortune and success that the culture placed with Nike. The Athenians honored Athena as a goddess who knew warfare, having fought in many battles including the one in which she sided with Zeus and Nike.[68] She was the patron saint and warrior who would protect Athens and keep peace in the city.[69]

Like Olympia, Athens seems to have had several representations of Nike over the years. A second-century CE marble head of Nike was found in a 1970 excavation on the slope of the Areopagus, just south of the Athens Agora.[70] It may have been a copy of the Nike of Paionios (discussed in the previous section) or a copy of the Nike from the Athena Parthenos. The inclusion of the victory goddess in the prodigious statue at Athens conveys a different message to the viewers of the statue in comparison to the statue at Olympia. The Nike in Athens is a victory of war, which may offer greater confidence and reassurance to the Athenians and serve as a threat or warning to those who may try to attack the city. The message is that Nike is on the side of Athens, and so opponents should beware.

The Athena Parthenos did not survive antiquity, but remnants of the iconic image remain as it was copied to reflect power and victory in war for many years after. A silver coin from King Lysimachus (r. 305–281 BCE) of Thrace in Northern Greece, for example, which commemorates his conquests in Asia Minor, shows Athena Parthenos with Nike crowning a wreath on the inscription of his name.[71] Much later, coins from Domitian also show Athena (Roman: Minerva) holding Nike,[72] and a one-meter version from the third century CE called the Varvakeion Athena Parthenos (Figure 4)[73] indicates the popularity with which this association of goddesses continued for centuries. The iconic image seems to have represented good fortune and success,[74] but may also have functioned as an icon of protection against enemies, as the original Athena Parthenos did.

---

[67] Taraporewalla, "Size Matters," 41; Judy Barringer, "The Legacy of the Phidian Zeus at Olympia," in *Statue of Zeus at Olympia*, 63.
[68] Hesiod, *Theogony* 383–403. The depiction of this battle, including Zeus, Athena, and Nike fighting alongside one another, can be seen on the East frieze of the second-century BCE gigantomachy frieze from the Great Altar, which was excavated at Pergamum in the nineteenth century, and now resides at the Pergamon Museum in Berlin; cf. Pausanias 1.25.2; Evamaria Schmidt, *The Great Altar of Pergamon*, tr. Lana Jaeck (London: Owen, 1965), 5–6, 29.
[69] Cf. Erika Simon, *The Gods of the Greeks*, tr. Jakob Zeyl, ed. Alan Shapiro (Madison: University of Wisconsin Press, 2021), 199–232.
[70] Agora Museum, Athens. Inv. No. S 2354.
[71] British Museum no. 1919, 0820.1.
[72] For example, *RIC II²*, Part 1 Domitian 61.
[73] "Varvakeion Athena Parthenos," University of Cambridge Museum of Classical Archaeology Databases, accessed May 27, 2021, https://museum.classics.cam.ac.uk/collections/casts/varvakeion-athena-parthenos.
[74] Images of Nike appear to represent such fortune and success today. For example, the "Spirit of Ecstasy" ornament on the luxury Rolls Royce car bears a strong resemblance to the goddess.

Figure 4 Varvakeion Athena, plaster cast. Cambridge, Museum of Classical Archaeology inv. no. 145. (Original: Athens, National Museum inv. no. 129.) CC BY-NC-ND 4.0.

Nike in Battle

While Nike appeared alongside other deities such as Zeus, Artemis, Ares, and Athena, she also appears in material culture and literature as an icon of her own in the context of military battle. As with the *agōnes,* Nike became so associated with military victory that her image is still used in the modern day to represent victory in war.[75] One of the most well-known extant representations of Nike in war is the Nike of Samothrace, sometimes referred to as the Winged Victory of Samothrace, which is displayed in the Louvre Museum in Paris. The marble statue, which was discovered in the nineteenth century on the Greek island of Samothrace, dates to around 250 to 150 BCE and sits atop a base in the shape of the front of a ship, standing on a low pedestal, totaling 5.6 meters

---

[75] More recent statues of Nike can be seen all over the world today to represent victory, including those in the United States, Canada, Mexico, England, Germany, India, and China. In San Francisco, she is part of the Dewey Monument, which celebrates an 1898 victory in the Spanish-American War. In downtown Mexico City, an immense Nike covered in 24 karat gold overlooks bustling traffic as a part of the Monumento a la Independencia, which was built in 1910 to commemorate the centennial of the beginning of Mexico's War of Independence.

(18.4 feet) high.⁷⁶ There were numerous naval battles during the Hellenistic period in the fight for control of the Aegean Sea, and thus battle fleets were a vital military resource. The monumental Nike was one of the offerings made at the sanctuary for the Great Gods of Samothrace,⁷⁷ to invoke protection against the threat of shipwreck or battle.

Nike is not portrayed as a violent goddess herself, fighting alongside soldiers. She is more akin to a figure of fate than to the many other deities who are brutal figures of war.⁷⁸ Nike is often portrayed in Greco-Roman literature as a silent portent, a sign in the midst of battle that either inspires soldiers to courage and assurance of victory, or ironically, drives them to gripping fear and assumed defeat. In *Parallel Lives,* Plutarch gives several accounts in which the victory goddess plays a defining portent in the context of war. In Plutarch's account of the life of Brutus, Nike is a portent that signals victory, but it is a victory for his enemies. In the Battle of Philippi in 42 BCE, Brutus and Cassius are about to fight Octavius and Antony. They all make their respective ceremonial purification rituals before battle, but Cassius is said to have signs of his downfall during his rites that relate specifically with the goddess Nike:

> However, it was thought that Cassius had a baleful sign during the lustration; for the lictor brought him his wreath turned upside down. And it is said that before this, also, in a procession at some festival, a golden Nike belonging to Cassius, which was being borne along, fell to the ground, its bearer having slipped. And besides, many carrion birds hovered over the camp daily, and swarms of bees were seen clustering at a certain place inside the camp; this place the soothsayers shut off from the rest of the camp, in order to avert by their rites the superstitious fears which were gradually carrying even Cassius himself away from his Epicurean doctrines, and which had altogether subjugated his soldiers.

> οὐ μὴν ἀλλὰ σημεῖον ἐν τῷ καθαρμῷ μοχθηρὸν ἔδοξε Κασσίῳ γενέσθαι. τὸν γὰρ στέφανον αὐτῷ κατεστραμμένον ὁ ῥαβδοῦχος προσήνεγκε. λέγεται δὲ καὶ πρότερον ἐν θέᾳ τινὶ καὶ πομπῇ χρυσῆν Κασσίου Νίκην διαφερομένην πεσεῖν, ὀλισθόντος τοῦ φέροντος. ἔτι δ' ὄρνεά τε σαρκοφάγα πολλὰ καθ' ἡμέραν ἐπεφαίνετο τῷ στρατοπέδῳ, καὶ μελισσῶν ὤφθησαν ἑσμοὶ συνιστάμενοι περὶ τόπον τινὰ τοῦ χάρακος ἐντός, ὃν ἐξέκλεισαν οἱ μάντεις ἀφοσιούμενοι τὴν δεισιδαιμονίαν ἀτρέμα καὶ τὸν Κάσσιον αὐτὸν ὑποφέρουσαν ἐκ τῶν Ἐπικούρου λόγων, τοὺς δὲ στρατιώτας παντάπασι δεδουλωμένην.⁷⁹

Interestingly, Cassius has tried to adopt Epicurean doctrines that negate the idea of the afterlife, presumably in response to the superstitious fear permeating the culture (see more in Section 4.1), and to likely assuage his own personal fears in battle. Yet, he

---

⁷⁶ Cf. Andrew F. Stewart, *Art in the Hellenistic World: An Introduction* (Cambridge: Cambridge University Press, 2014), 83–4.
⁷⁷ Cf. Hugh Bowden, *Mystery Cults in the Ancient World* (London: Thames & Hudson, 2010), 49–67.
⁷⁸ For example, Zeus with his thunderbolt, Poseidon with his trident, and Ares with his spear were all feared for their violent power.
⁷⁹ Plutarch, *Brutus* 39.3-6 (Perrin, LCL).

has his own golden statue of Nike brought into war to help foster success, and when it falls to the ground, it is seen as a sign that Cassius will not acquire victory. Cassius and the soldiers are overtaken by the fear that they will lose because of the negative portent, which indicates that Nike is not on their side. Note that the wreath or crown (στέφανος), which was usually connected to victory, was also turned upside down, indicating another negative sign of their impending defeat.

In the Battle of Pharsalus in 48 BCE, the goddess Nike appears to give a more active sign than the one in Philippi, in which the bearer dropped a statue. Both Plutarch and Roman historian Cassius Dio mention the portents of victory surrounding the battle because of the unlikely win of Julius Caesar against Pompey the Great. Caesar was in the much weaker position with fewer soldiers and limited provisions, but in the temple of Nike at Tralles (now modern-day Turkey), a palm tree is said to have shot up at the base of Caesar's statue.[80] The palm tree appearing in Nike's temple is seen as a portent that Caesar will win the battle, and indeed he does. In Cassius Dio's account, the goddess is even recorded as having turned toward the image of Caesar, indicating his impending victory. The sign from Nike serves as the explanation as to how Caesar could have succeeded, when by all physical appearances, he would presumably have lost. Nike becomes the indicator of who will win the war.

In a similar account of Nike indicating the victor, Cassius Dio reports on the Battle of Teutoburg Forest in 9 CE, when Germanic tribes decimated the Roman legions under Augustus:

> For a catastrophe so great and sudden as this, it seemed to him, could have been due to nothing else than the wrath of some divinity; moreover, by reason of the portents which occurred both before the defeat and afterwards, he was strongly inclined to suspect some superhuman agency. For the temple of Ares in the field of the same name was struck by lightning ... and a statue of Nike that was in the province of Germany and faced the enemy's territory turned about to face Italy.
>
> τό τε γὰρ πάθος οὐκ ἄνευ δαιμονίου τινὸς ὀργῆς καὶ μέγα οὕτω καὶ ἀθρόον ἐδόκει οἱ γεγονέναι· καὶ προσέτι καὶ ὑπὸ τῶν τεράτων τῶν πρό τε τῆς ἥττης καὶ μετὰ ταῦτα συμβάντων δεινὴν ὑποψίαν ἐς τὸ θεῖον ἔσχεν. ὅ τε γὰρ τοῦ Ἄρεως ναὸς ὁ ἐν τῷ πεδίῳ αὐτοῦ ὢν ἐκεραυνώθη ... καὶ Νίκης τι ἄγαλμα ἔν τε τῇ Γερμανίᾳ ὂν καὶ πρὸς τὴν πολεμίαν βλέπον πρὸς τὴν Ἰταλίαν μετεστράφη.[81]

Up until that point, Augustus had been a very successful emperor, annexing many regions and enlarging the Roman Empire. Yet, his failure to secure the region of Germania left him fearful that his enemies would come all the way to the city of Rome. The victory of his enemies, Augustus reasoned, was certainly related to the deities of Ares and Nike. Her statue had turned around to come against Italy, and this portent was an indication that there were supernatural forces at work.

Oftentimes, the portents from the goddess Nike are more influential than the strength or skill of the soldiers themselves. Indeed, the morale of the presumed

---

[80] Plutarch, *Caesar* 47.1; Cassius Dio, *Roman History* 41.61.4.
[81] Cassius Dio, *Roman History* 56.24.3-5 (Cary and Foster, LCL).

winners can completely shift to assumed losers simply based on a sign from her, as seen in Plutarch's biography of Sulla.

> And it is said that about the time when Sulla was moving his armament from Italy, Mithridates, who was staying at Pergamum, was visited with many other portents from Heaven, and that a Nike with a crown in her hand, which the Pergamenians were lowering towards him by machinery of some sort, was broken to pieces just as she was about to touch his head, and the crown went tumbling from her hand to the ground in the midst of the theatre, and was shattered, whereat the people shuddered, and Mithridates was greatly dejected, although at that time his affairs were prospering beyond his hopes.
>
> Λέγεται δὲ ὑπὸ τὰς ἡμέρας ἐκείνας ἐν αἷς ὁ Σύλλας ἀπὸ τῆς Ἰταλίας ἐκίνει τὸν στόλον, ἄλλα τε πολλὰ Μιθριδάτῃ διατρίβοντι περὶ τὸ Πέργαμον ἐπισκῆψαι δαιμόνια, καὶ Νίκην στεφανηφόρον καθιεμένην ὑπὸ τῶν Περγαμηνῶν ἐπ' αὐτὸν ἔκ τινων ὀργάνων ἄνωθεν ὅσον οὔπω τῆς κεφαλῆς ψαύουσαν συντριβῆναι, καὶ τὸν στέφανον ἐκπεσόντα κατὰ τοῦ θεάτρου φέρεσθαι χαμᾶζε διαθρυπτόμενον, ὥστε φρίκην μὲν τῷ δήμῳ, ἀθυμίαν δὲ πολλὴν Μιθριδάτῃ παρασχεῖν, καίπερ αὐτῷ τότε τῶν πραγμάτων ἐλπίδος πέρα προχωρούντων.[82]

Plutarch is describing Nike's role as Sulla planned an attack against Mithridates VI of Pontus during the First Mithridatic War in the early first century BCE. Before Sulla became dictator of the Roman Republic, he was a consul who was assigned to quell insurgents like Mithridates. Although Mithridates had a strong army, the support of many locals, and substantial riches to sustain his cause, his soldiers shuddered and lost all hope because of the portent from Nike. Mithridates was completely despondent, and he lost the war to Sulla. They all believed that the Romans retained their power because Nike indicated that they would win.

Though Sulla was a strong military leader, he did not ascribe his successes simply to his abilities. When he later won the Battle of Chaeronea in 86 BCE against Archelaus, Mithridates's general, Sulla, "inscribed upon his trophies the names of Mars, Victory and Venus [Ares, Nike, and Aphrodite], in the belief that his success in the war was due no less to good fortune than to military skill and strength."[83] Like many others of the time, Sulla associated victory in battle with favor from the supernatural gods, and of Nike especially.

Nike in Power

Nike functioned as a quiet, ominous portent in Greco-Roman wars, but she was not a deity who was altogether devoid of power. She did not cast down lightning bolts like Zeus or shoot arrows like Artemis. Yet, the Greeks and Romans believed that Nike still had the power to affect their lives, and they therefore made sure to honor her

---

[82] Plutarch, *Sulla* 11.1 (Perrin, LCL).
[83] Plutarch, *Sulla* 19.5 (Perrin, LCL).

lest they lose her favor. They honored her because they knew that she had the power to assign great victories or hand them over to death. An inscription on an altar of Zeus Eleutherios[84] shows the honor attributed to Nike and the distinction between her power and the work of Ares, the god of war:

> When Greeks by Nike's power and work of Ares' hand
> Drove forth the Medes, this common altar here they raised
> Of Zeus, the god of Freedom, for Free Greece.
>
> τόνδε ποθ᾽ Ἕλληνες Νίκης κράτει, ἔργῳ Ἄρηος,
> Πέρσας ἐξελάσαντες, ἐλευθέρᾳ Ἑλλάδι κοινὸν ἱδρύσαντο
> Διὸς βωμὸν Ἐλευθερίου.[85]

Plutarch was critical of this account regarding the Greco-Persian wars (fifth century BCE) from the historian Herodotus, and he doubted the timing and motives for this inscription. However, the message within the inscription still indicates that the Greeks attributed military victory to the gods Nike and Ares. It is by her power and his hand that they were able to conquer their enemies. She was responsible for the Greek victory and thus deserved recognition.

Cassius Dio offers his perspective of history including the role that Nike played as a source of power to Roman leaders. In one description of Augustus Caesar, Cassius Dio writes about a statue of Nike that was taken from Tarentum, which Augustus placed in the Curia Iulia, the Senate House in the city of Rome:

> After finishing this celebration Caesar dedicated the temple of Minerva, called also the Chalcidicum, and the Curia Iulia, which had been built in honor of his father. In the latter he set up the statue of Nike which is still in existence, thus signifying probably that it was from her that he had received the empire.
>
> Ἐπεὶ δὲ ταῦτα διετέλεσε, τό τε Ἀθήναιον τὸ Χαλκιδικὸν ὠνομασμένον καὶ τὸ βουλευτήριον τὸ Ἰουλίειον, τὸ ἐπὶ τῇ τοῦ πατρὸς αὐτοῦ τιμῇ γενόμενον, καθιέρωσεν. ἐνέστησε δὲ ἐς αὐτὸ τὸ ἄγαλμα τὸ τῆς Νίκης τὸ καὶ νῦν ὄν, δηλῶν, ὡς ἔοικεν, ὅτι παρ᾽ αὐτῆς τὴν ἀρχὴν ἐκτήσατο.[86]

Having been built in his father's honor, the Curia was a very significant place for Augustus,[87] and according to Cassius Dio, the Roman leader placed a statue of Nike there because he attributed the goddess with his having won control of the Roman Empire. Augustus saw her power as the reason for why he won the battles; despite putting much of his own effort and skill into these wars, he regarded his victory as having come from her and through her. It was Nike who granted the empire, and so

---

[84] The altar of Zeus Eleutherios was at the center of the Festival of Freedom, a celebration held every four years to honor the Greek triumph over the Persians in fifth century BCE.
[85] Plutarch, *Moralia* 873B (Pearson, LCL); cf. Herodotus, *The Persian Wars* 8.77.
[86] Cassius Dio, *Roman History* 51.22.1-2 (Cary and Foster, LCL).
[87] Cf. the inscription called the *Fasti Maffeiani* that reports Augustus dedicating an altar of Victory in the Senate House (Dessau, *ILS* 8744).

Augustus felt the need to have a statue setup in her honor in his most valued place. Cassius Dio mentions that the Nike statue was still existing in his time, demonstrating that well into the second century CE, the visual reminder of this important victory in Greco-Roman history remained for all to see.

Some Greco-Roman leaders took advantage of the power associated with Nike. Gaius Caesar, also known as Caligula, reigned as emperor from 37 to 41 CE, but as Cassius Dio reports, Caligula was seemingly more manipulative than his predecessor. Caligula exploited the people's fear of Nike's power to attain unrestrained personal power for himself.

> Indeed, even before this he had been demanding that he be regarded as more than a human being, and was wont to claim that he had intercourse with the Moon, that Nike put a crown upon him, and to pretend that he was Zeus, and he made this a pretext for seducing numerous women, particularly his sisters
>
> ἠξίου μὲν γὰρ καὶ πρότερον ὑπὲρ ἄνθρωπον νομίζεσθαι, καὶ τῇ Σελήνῃ συγγίγνεσθαι καὶ ὑπὸ τῆς Νίκης στεφανοῦσθαι ἔλεγε, Ζεύς τε εἶναι ἐπλάττετο, καὶ κατὰ τοῦτο καὶ γυναιξὶν ἄλλαις τε πολλαῖς καὶ ταῖς ἀδελφαῖς μάλιστα συνεῖναι προεφασίσατο[88]

The image of Nike bestowing a crown appears again as a symbol of victory and success from the goddess. By insisting that he had the favor of the gods and that Nike especially had bestowed power on him, Caligula tried to garner approval from the people and further their inclination to see him as a demi-god or god himself (see more on divine rulers in Section 5.1), even though he was a wicked and corrupt leader.

If Nike had the power to win wars and assign seemingly unexpected leaders to rule, then the people of the Greco-Roman world surely had to submit to her whims. It is no wonder that she was simultaneously pursued and feared by soldiers engaged in battle and political leaders who sought to rule. Those who were able to curry her favor could expect great military victory and immense political power, while those without Nike on their side suffered powerlessness and even the consequence of death in battle.

The Johannine Battle

Nike as the representation of victory in the Greco-Roman world was clearly well-established in the context of war; she was so well-regarded that both military leaders and emperors attributed their victories to her. In the pursuit of *nikē* in 1 John, the writer seems to allude to a similar context of victory in war in which the readers are engaged in a type of Johannine battle. The readers are portrayed as conquerors facing several opponents, including "the evil one" (2:13, 14; 3:12; 5:18, 19), antichrists (2:18, 22; 4:3), false prophets (4:1), and even the world itself (5:4-5). The militaristic

---

[88] Cassius Dio, *Roman History* 59.26.5 (Cary and Foster, LCL).

undertone is particularly evident in the first appearance of the verbal cognate νικάω (conquer, 2:13b):[89]

> I am writing to you, young men, because you have conquered the evil one.
>
> γράφω ὑμῖν νεανίσκοι, ὅτι νενικήκατε τὸν πονηρόν

It is specifically the young men (νεανίσκοι), who have conquered "the evil one" (ὁ πονηρός), and the designation suggests some sort of combat as the "young men" would be those of military age.[90] More of this battle will be explored in the next section.

One challenge to understanding the nature of the battle is that the *nikē* of 1 John is identified with *pistis* (5:4):

> For everyone who is born of God conquers the world. And this is the **victory** that has conquered the world, our **faith**.
>
> ὅτι πᾶν τὸ γεγεννημένον ἐκ τοῦ θεοῦ νικᾷ τὸν κόσμον· καὶ αὕτη ἐστὶν ἡ **νίκη** ἡ νικήσασα τὸν κόσμον, ἡ **πίστις** ἡμῶν.

One might presume that a fight related with *pistis* might involve a mental or spiritual battle over what the combatants believe. Indeed, references to the word "spirit" (πνεῦμα)[91] in the letter do support that there is a spiritual element to the Johannine conflict. However, there are also several references to murder[92] and death,[93] which may suggest that there is a more literal cost involved.

The severity of these references indicates the extreme nature of the battle that is being fought in 1 John. Although the writer offers assurances that the members of the Johannine community are ultimately triumphant over their opponents (2:13-14; 5:4-5), he also gives several warnings throughout his letter (e.g., 2:15-18; 4:1; 5:21) that evoke a sense of foreboding and caution that this victory is not easily won or sustained. The confrontational and conquering language throughout 1 John suggests that there is indeed a battle that the Johannine community must face to achieve their *nikē* of *pistis*. Therefore, like a general to his soldiers, the Johannine teacher writes to his spiritual children to point out the underlying threats and to suggest the proper response when they encounter their opponents.

---

[89] Cf. the recapitulation in the succeeding verse.
[90] Judith Lieu, *I, II, & III John: A Commentary* (Louisville, KY: Westminster John Knox, 2008), 90.
[91] Cf. 3:24; 4:1, 2, 3, 6, 13; 5:6, 8.
[92] Cf. 3:12 (2x), 15 (2x).
[93] Cf. 3:14 (2x); 5:16 (3x), 17.

3

The Conquered

The sense of battle in 1 John is clearly demonstrated through the many opponents that the Johannine community must face: the evil one (2:13, 14; 3:12; 5:18, 19), antichrists (2:18, 22; 4:3; cf. 2 Jn 7), false prophets (4:1), and the world itself (2:15-17; 3:1, 13; 5:4, 5, 19). While the nature of the battle with each opponent differs in the level of physical or spiritual conflict that they have with the Johannine community, all of the opponents appear to be associated with the "world" (κόσμος, 4:1, 3; 5:19), suggesting that the fundamental battle of 1 John is ultimately between the Johannine believers and the world. This chapter will examine the identity of these opponents, the nuances of each fight, and the battle that is taking place overall in 1 John in order to fully understand the nature and implications of the Johannine victory.

3.1 The Evil One

The first named opponent in 1 John is "the evil one" (ὁ πονηρός) who is described in three different chapters as a significant enemy to the Johannine believers (2:13, 14; 3:12; 5:18, 19).[1] The specific identity of the evil one is not readily obvious at first, as the concept of "the evil one" including the Greek article does not appear in many books of the NT,[2] and there are sometimes no definitive referents for clarification.[3] It is possible that the evil one is simply a personification of evil.[4] However, the evil one is likely to be representative of the spiritual archopponent of God, who is part of a long-standing biblical tradition of the devil or Satan operating as a source of opposition (e.g., 1 Chron. 21; Job 1–2; Zech. 3).[5] The First Letter of John has the most frequent references

---

[1] Evil is also mentioned in the context of evil *deeds* in 1 Jn 3:12 and 2 Jn 11.
[2] Πονηρός as a singular substantive with the article occurs sixteen times, of which three are obviously not Satan (Lk. 6:45; Rom. 12:9; 1 Cor. 5:13). Mt. 5:39 suggests a more generic "evil person." The remaining may be referring to Satan or the devil: Mt. 5:37; 6:13; 13:19, 38; Jn 17:15; Eph. 6:16; 2 Thess. 3:3; 1 Jn 2:13, 14; 3:12; 5:18, 19. Cf. Thomas Farrar and Guy Williams, "Diabolical Data: A Critical Inventory of New Testament Satanology," *JSNT* 39, no. 1 (2016): 43–4.
[3] One possible exception might be Mt. 13:38, which is closely aligned with "the devil" (ὁ διάβολος) in v. 39.
[4] Smalley, *1, 2, 3 John*, 75.
[5] Lieu, *I, II, & III John*, 89.

to "the evil one" in the NT, and so the sense of spiritual battle would be prominent if the identity of the opposing figure is indeed the archopponent of God.

Although the words "demon" (δαιμόνιον) and "Satan" (Σατανᾶς) are absent from the Johannine epistles, the references to the "devil" (διάβολος, 1 Jn 3:8, 10) and the Genesis 4 allusion to Cain and his having come from the evil one (3:12) seem to indicate that the identity of the evil one is likely not a human being currently living in the Greco-Roman world. Like the majority of other references to "the evil one," the most likely identity of this enemy in 1 John is the spiritual archopponent known as "the devil." In examining the battle of 1 John, one objective is to determine why the writer feels it necessary to mention this figure multiple times. The analysis below will demonstrate that the writer is warning about the evil one throughout the letter to ensure that the readers are vigilant about the opposing spiritual force that is operating in the world. He does not want them to respond in fear; the author reassures his readers that they are conquerors of the evil one with their *pistis*.

The Young Men Conquer the Evil One

The first clear indication of battle in 1 John is the writer's declaration of decisive victory over the evil one (see Table 1). The Johannine author repeats, "You have conquered the evil one" (νενικήκατε τὸν πονηρόν, 2:13, 14), using the perfect tense, suggesting that the enemy has been defeated already and is therefore no longer any cause for concern. The evil one is not portrayed as a domineering and fearsome figure. On the contrary, there are no details about him here. Instead, the first mention of the evil one seems to function as an assurance that the Johannine believers are already on the victorious side. He repeats, "You have conquered the evil one" (νενικήκατε τὸν πονηρόν) to convey a definitive victory, which is intended to provoke confidence in his readers.

As mentioned in the previous section, the assurance of the conquered evil one is addressed specifically to the "young men" (νεανίσκοι),[6] who are the first conquerors mentioned in the letter, with subsequent named conquerors being the "little children" (τεκνία, 4:4), "everyone who is born of God" (πᾶν τὸ γεγεννημένον ἐκ τοῦ θεοῦ, 5:4), and "the one who believes that Jesus is the Son of God" (ὁ πιστεύων ὅτι Ἰησοῦς ἐστιν ὁ υἱὸς τοῦ θεοῦ, 5:5). The first conquerors of the Johannine letter being the "young men" is appropriate in that the young men would be of military age and would be the ones most associated with fighting if it were a literal battle with the evil one.[7] Despite the specific address, however, the writer is not trying to say that the younger members of the community are the *only* ones who have conquered the evil one. In a three-part rhetorical address (2:12-14), the author uses cyclical and poetic language that acts like a lyrical poem,[8] to build an emphatic recapitulation of having conquered the evil one (vv. 13–14) as a result of knowing Jesus (vv. 12, 13) and knowing the Father (v. 14).

---

[6] In Johannine literature, νεανίσκος appears only at 1 Jn 2:13, 14. Other references occur at Mt. 19:20, 22; Mk 14:51, 16:5 (interestingly in reference to a spiritual figure, an angel at Jesus' tomb); Lk. 7:14; Acts 2:17, 5:10, 23:18, 22. Cf. also νεανίας at Acts 7:58, 20:9, 23:17.
[7] Lieu, *I, II, & III John*, 90. Cf. Herodotus, *The Persian Wars*, 4.72; Plutarch, *Moralia* 237.
[8] Although not technically a poem, the lyrical language prompts many English translations to present the three-part address in verse form (cf. NIV, ESV, NRSV, NLT, NKJV, ISV, CEV).

Table 1 You Have Conquered the Evil One

1 John 2:12-14	
12. I am writing to you, little children, because your sins have been forgiven on account of his name.	Γράφω ὑμῖν, τεκνία, ὅτι ἀφέωνται ὑμῖν αἱ ἁμαρτίαι διὰ τὸ ὄνομα αὐτοῦ.
13. I am writing to you, fathers, because you have known him who is from the beginning. I am writing to you, young men,[9] because you have conquered the evil one.	γράφω ὑμῖν, πατέρες ὅτι ἐγνώκατε τὸν ἀπ' ἀρχῆς. γράφω ὑμῖν νεανίσκοι, ὅτι νενικήκατε τὸν πονηρόν.
14. I wrote to you, children, because you have known the Father. I wrote to you, fathers, because you have known him who is from the beginning. I wrote to you, young men, because you are strong and the word of God remains in you, and you have conquered the evil one.	ἔγραψα ὑμῖν, παιδία, ὅτι ἐγνώκατε τὸν πατέρα. ἔγραψα ὑμῖν, πατέρες, ὅτι ἐγνώκατε τὸν ἀπ' ἀρχῆς. ἔγραψα ὑμῖν, νεανίσκοι, ὅτι ἰσχυροί ἐστε καὶ ὁ λόγος τοῦ θεοῦ ἐν ὑμῖν μένει καὶ νενικήκατε τὸν πονηρόν.

In the first part of the address (v. 12), the relational teacher speaks to his "little children" (τεκνία), a vocative form seen almost exclusively in 1 John,[10] to help explain why he is writing this letter[11] and to draw attention to what he is about to say.[12] At first glance, it appears to be a tripartite address to the children (τεκνία/παιδία), fathers (πατέρες), and young men (νεανίσκοι). However, the address of τεκνία is more likely referring to the entire community as the writer has already utilized it at the start of the chapter (2:1). The specific address to the fathers and young men are speaking to the older and younger generations, respectively. In this series of assurances, the author's first assurance to the general community is that their sins are forgiven because of Christ, which he has already alluded to previously (1:7-9; 2:1-2) and is clearly a

---

[9] Some versions (e.g., NRSV, CEV) translate νεανίσκοι as the more inclusive "young people," and although the writer probably does not intend to exclude female members, "young men" is a better counterpart to "fathers." It also complements the "you are strong" (ἰσχυροί ἐστε, 2:14), reflecting the sense of military conquering (although a literal violent military conquering is not intended by the author).

[10] The vocative τεκνίον occurs only eight times in the NT: seven times in 1 John (2:1, 12, 28; 3:7, 18; 4:4; 5:21) and once when Jesus is addressing his disciples in Jn 13:33. There are notable similarities with 1 John in that the teacher of John's Gospel is speaking with a sense of urgency to his disciples about a new command and of the importance of loving one another (Jn 13:34-5; cf. 1 Jn 2:8, 10). The writer of the letter appears to prefer τεκνίον to παιδίον (child), which is much more common in the NT (appears fifty-two times), but in 1 John appears only twice in the vocative neutral plural (παιδία, 2:14, 18). (Cf. παιδίον in Jn 4:49; 16:21; 21:5). Other relational terms of address in 1 John include ἀδελφοί (brothers) in 3:13 and ἀγαπητοί (beloved) at 1 Jn 2:7; 3:2, 21; 4:1, 7, 11. Cf. 3 Jn 2, 5, 11.

[11] Cf. the references to the present tense "I am writing to you" (γράφω ὑμῖν) in 2:1, 7, 8, 12, 13; and the aorist "I wrote/I have written to you" (ἔγραψα ὑμῖν) in 2:14 (3x), 21, 26; 5:13.

[12] This is especially true in the last verse of the letter (5:21), which starts with the vocative τεκνία to alert the audience to his final warning.

concern later in the letter (3:4-9; 4:10; 5:16-18) because sin is involved in the battle that they face (cf. 3:8; 5:18-19). Just as he addressed his τεκνία in 2:1, the writer wants to remind them to avoid sin, and to recognize that, if they do sin, they are able to be forgiven because of Christ's sacrifice. The forgiveness for sin that they enjoy is not on account of their own efforts but on account of Jesus and his deeds (cf. 3:23; 5:13).

As is often the case with little children, the readers are passive recipients of what has been done for them, and the forgiving in the perfect tense indicates that this is a completed past act.[13] His children can be confident that, because of what Christ has done and because they have entered into a relationship with Christ already through their *pistis*, they can be secure in knowing that their sins are forgiven. Thus, a Johannine believer should not "walk in darkness" (ἐν τῇ σκοτίᾳ περιπατεῖ, 2:11), but walk in the light, behaving like Jesus in their words and actions (2:8-11; cf. 1:5, 7).

When addressing the community for the second time in v. 14, the writer switches from τεκνία (v. 12) to παιδία (v. 14), a common NT term for "children,"[14] further supporting the idea that he is speaking to the community as a whole. This time, he does not address the issue of sin (as v. 12) but chooses instead to say: "You have known the Father" (ἐγνώκατε τὸν πατέρα). The language transitions well as it continues the theme of "knowing" from the previous verse and seamlessly transitions to the recapitulation to the fathers.

When the writer addresses the "fathers" (πατέρες), he says the same phrase (vv. 13, 14): "you have known him who is from the beginning" (ἐγνώκατε τὸν ἀπ' ἀρχῆς). Addressing the fathers separately aligns with the hierarchical values of both Jewish and Greco-Roman culture, which divide communities by age,[15] and he follows the typical household code of addressing the older or more senior group first.[16] It is possible that the "fathers" are a specific group of people, such as the elders (πρεσβύτεροι) of the community.[17] However, the writer has been speaking quite generally throughout the letter to his "little children" (2:1, 28; 3:7, 18; 4:4; 5:21), and the letter does not imply any gradation of seniority and experience (cf. 2:20, 27).[18] Indeed, the word "elder" in the Johannine epistles is only used for the writer himself.[19] Thus, it seems likely that "fathers" is referring to the older members of the Johannine community. The writer does not designate the different age groups to reinforce division and hierarchy as proliferated in the culture and tradition at large. On the contrary, he is trying to promote cohesion by recognizing what would

---

[13] Lieu, *I, II, & III John*, 88.
[14] While the general noun παιδίον appears in several places in the NT (e.g., Mt. 2:13, 20; Mk 5:39, 40; Lk. 1:59, 66; 1 Cor. 14:20; Heb. 2:13, 14), the vocative παιδία appears exclusively in Johannine literature: Jn 21:5; 1 Jn 2:14, 18.
[15] See distinctions between older and younger people in 1 Kgs 12; Ps. 148:12; Prov. 20:29; Lam. 5:14; Ezek. 9:6; Joel 2:28; Zech. 8:4-5. In the NT: Acts 2:17 (quoting Joel 2:28); 1 Tim. 5:1-2; Tit. 2:1-6; 1 Pet. 5:1-5. Cf. Aristotle, *Politics* 1.3; Plutarch, *Moralia* 237D; Cassius Dio, *Roman History* 21.3; Josephus, *War* 1.25.1; Philo, *On the Account of the World's Creation*, 103–5.
[16] Cf. James Rives, *Religion in the Roman Empire*, Blackwell Ancient Religions (Malden, MA: Blackwell Publishing, 2007), 117. Interestingly, some NT writers list the junior group first: Col. 3:18–4:1; Eph. 5:22–6:9.
[17] Cf. elders mentioned in other letters: 1 Tim. 5:17; Tit. 1:5; Jas 5:14; 1 Pet. 5:1, 5.
[18] Lieu, *I, II, & III John*, 87.
[19] Cf. 2 Jn 1; 3 Jn 1.

normally be clear divisions according to cultural background, but seeing them collectively as his children, one community.[20]

The repeated address to the fathers is almost identical (vv. 13, 14) with the only difference being the present tense "I am writing" (γράφω, 2:13), and the aorist tense "I wrote" (ἔγραψα, 2:14) in the recapitulation to emphasize confidence in the knowledge of a secure relationship with "him who is from the beginning" (τὸν ἀπ' ἀρχῆς). The reference to knowing him who is "from the beginning" (ἀπ' ἀρχῆς, vv. 13, 14) hearkens back to the start of the letter (1:1) and the earlier reference to the command that they had from the beginning (2:7), the command to love one another (cf. 3:11), which was given by Jesus at the start of their Johannine *pistis* (Jn 13:34).[21]

The declaration to the fathers is even more personal in using the masculine pronoun (1 Jn 2:13, 14) in contrast to the neuter (1:1) or the command they had from the beginning (2:7). The message that the older generation have definitively known "*him* who is from the beginning" places emphasis on the *person*. That person is likely referencing God or Jesus, but more likely refers to Jesus because the writer has already addressed all of the "children" as having known the Father (v. 14) and then establishes the fathers as knowing Jesus. The verb "you have known" (ἐγνώκατε) in the perfect tense in both verses (vv. 13, 14) underscores the confident possession of this relationship, which is rooted in the past.[22] This is appropriate to the older community who may have had an earlier *pistis* in Jesus as the Son of God, and therefore, have had a longer relationship with him.

To complete the three-part address, the Johannine leader asserts to the young men, the first named victors of 1 John, that they have conquered the evil one (vv. 13, 14). As representatives of the "soldiers" of the Johannine community in their twenties and thirties, they may be the fighters who are "on the front lines of battle" in the sense that they face more conflicts related with the evil one (see more in Section 3.3). Despite the militaristic message, their conquering is not meant to be a physically violent victory. The emphasis is on *knowing*. "You have known" (ἐγνώκατε) is declared three times (once in v. 13, twice in v. 14). Knowing "him who is from the beginning" (τὸν ἀπ' ἀρχῆς, vv. 13, 14), which was addressed to the fathers, and the children *knowing* the Father (v. 14), underlines that the thematic importance has been on relationship with God. The implication here is that this relationship leads to conquering the evil one, and this is addressed to the young men, not because victory can only be achieved by the younger generation but because they are the age group that embodies those who would be soldiers if they were in a literal battle. Later in the letter, we see that every member of the Johannine community, the τεκνία, is addressed in conquering the opposition (4:4 cf. 5:4-5), and thus, the fight is not simply for the "young men." The young men being the initial named conquerors rather reinforces the sense of Johannine battle.[23]

---

[20] Cf. Lieu, *I, II, & III John*, 87.
[21] Marshall, *The Epistles of John*, 129. Cf. later in 1 John when the theme of "sin" and "beginning" also come together in reference to the devil who has been sinning from the beginning (3:8).
[22] Cf. Smalley, *1, 2, 3 John*, 78.
[23] However, there may also be the implication that the young ones face more challenges because of their greater engagement with "the world." See more in Section 3.3.

The author of 1 John does not explain what it means to conquer the evil one. However, the variations in the recapitulation (v. 14) offer some indication of the nature of the battle against him. The variations are more than just for rhetorical interest, as has been suggested.[24] In the final word to the "young men," the author adds that they are "strong" (ἰσχυρός) and that "the word of God remains in you" (ὁ λόγος τοῦ θεοῦ ἐν ὑμῖν μένει). The second variation would be an especially unusual addition to "strong" if it were there to simply avoid tedium.

The writer of 1 John uses the word "strong" only once (v. 14),[25] which seems a little surprising as it might be expected to appear more frequently in a letter that involves Johannine conquerors and several significant adversaries. The word has been used as a title (ὁ ἰσχυρός) for God,[26] and as a reference to Satan (Lk. 11:21, cf. 11:18). Although we cannot definitively say that the Johannine author is trying to convey a specific point with the declaration "you are strong" (ἰσχυροί ἐστε), the reference to the strength of the conquerors may indicate the strength and endurance needed in the spiritual fight against the evil one,[27] who presumably has significant strength of his own, and is therefore not an easy enemy to defeat.[28] In an encouragement appropriate from the Johannine mentor to his spiritual children, he is indicating that it is because of their spiritual strength that they had a decisive victory against the evil one, and the encouraging implication is that they continue to have that strength now for current and future battles (as discussed further below).

The second additional variation, "the word of God remains in you" (ὁ λόγος τοῦ θεοῦ ἐν ὑμῖν μένει), suggests the way in which the Johannine conquerors are able to fight their enemy. They know that the word of God is Jesus, who remains in them (cf. 1:1, 10; 2:24, 27; 3:9, 24; 4:13, 15), and it is through their *pistis* in Jesus that they are able to defeat the evil one. When they embraced *pistis* in Jesus, the word of God remained in them, and they were able to conquer the evil one. There is an inner strength, having internalized the word of God that has allowed them to be victorious.

The Evil One and the Murderer

Although the perfect tense in Chapter 2 (νενικήκατε, 2:13-14) suggests that the evil one has already been conquered, the next reference to this opponent seems to indicate that there is still some sort of threat attached to him. This time, the Johannine believers are not fighting against the evil one, but potentially becoming like him (3:11-12):

---

[24] For example, Lieu, *I, II, & III John*, 90.
[25] The word ἰσχυρός does not appear elsewhere in the Epistles or Gospel, but appears in the NT to refer to physical (e.g., Mt. 12:29; Lk. 11:21, 22) or abstract strength (e.g., Mk 1:7; 2 Cor. 10:10, Heb. 6:18).
[26] In the LXX, ἰσχυρός appears some 160 times to refer to strength and power in nature, people, or armies, and also to describe the might of God (e.g., Deut. 10:17; Josh. 4:24; Neh. 1:5; 2 Macc. 1:24; Dan. 9:4). It is also used substantively as a title for the Lord (ὁ ἰσχυρός, e.g., 2 Sam. 22:31, 32, 33; 23:5; Job 22:13; 33:29; 34:31).
[27] Cf. Yarbrough, *1–3 John*, 122.
[28] Jesus himself did not have easy encounters with the devil (cf. Mt. 4:1-11; Mk 1:12-13; Lk. 4:1-13).

For this is the message you have heard from the beginning, that we should love one another. Not like Cain who was from the evil one and murdered his brother. And why did he murder him? Because his deeds were evil and his brother's righteous.

Ὅτι αὕτη ἐστὶν ἡ ἀγγελία ἣν ἠκούσατε ἀπ' ἀρχῆς, ἵνα ἀγαπῶμεν ἀλλήλους, οὐ καθὼς Κάϊν ἐκ τοῦ πονηροῦ ἦν καὶ ἔσφαξεν τὸν ἀδελφὸν αὐτοῦ καὶ χάριν τίνος ἔσφαξεν αὐτόν; ὅτι τὰ ἔργα αὐτοῦ πονηρὰ ἦν τὰ δὲ τοῦ ἀδελφοῦ αὐτοῦ δίκαια.

The language seems extreme as the writer stresses the importance of loving one another and then gives the severe counterexample of murdering another. This indicates the immense gravity of what the writer is trying to convey to his readers about the Johannine battle in which they are engaged.

The author reminds his audience about what they have heard "from the beginning" (ἀπ' ἀρχῆς, 3:11), language that he used earlier in the letter to refer to their *pistis* (1:1; 2:7, 24) and in relation to their conquering the evil one (2:13, 14). He has also previously alluded to the importance of loving others (2:10; 3:10), but the writer now declares that their loving one another is central to the message of their *pistis*.[29] As a counterexample, he tells the Johannine believers that they should not be like Cain, who "was from the evil one and murdered his brother" (ἐκ τοῦ πονηροῦ ἦν καὶ ἔσφαξεν τὸν ἀδελφὸν αὐτοῦ, 3:12). In other places in the letter, exhortations are followed by positive examples that are introduced with καθὼς (2:6, 27; 3:3, 7; cf. Jn 15:12), but here the writer alludes to the extreme negative example of the Genesis narrative of fratricide (Gen. 4).

The language describing Cain who was "from the evil one" (ἐκ τοῦ πονηροῦ) and doing evil deeds (ἔργα πονηρὰ) parallels the language a few verses before (see Table 2).

Table 2 The Devil and the Evil One

1 John 3:8	1 John 3:11-12
The one who commits sin is from the devil; for the devil has been sinning from the beginning. The Son of God was revealed for this purpose, to destroy the works of the devil.	For this is the message you have heard from the beginning, that we should love one another. Not like Cain who was from the evil one and murdered his brother. And why did he murder him? Because his works were evil and his brother's righteous.
ὁ ποιῶν τὴν ἁμαρτίαν ἐκ τοῦ διαβόλου ἐστιν, ὅτι ἀπ' ἀρχῆς ὁ διάβολος ἁμαρτάνει· εἰς τοῦτο ἐφανερώθη ὁ υἱὸς τοῦ θεοῦ, ἵνα λύσῃ τὰ ἔργα τοῦ διαβόλου.	Ὅτι αὕτη ἐστὶν ἡ ἀγγελία ἣν ἠκούσατε ἀπ' ἀρχῆς, ἵνα ἀγαπῶμεν ἀλλήλους, οὐ καθὼς Κάϊν ἐκ τοῦ πονηροῦ ἦν καὶ ἔσφαξεν τὸν ἀδελφὸν αὐτοῦ καὶ χάριν τίνος ἔσφαξεν αὐτόν; ὅτι τὰ ἔργα αὐτοῦ πονηρὰ ἦν τὰ δὲ τοῦ ἀδελφοῦ αὐτοῦ δίκαια.

The message and personhood of Jesus is "from the beginning" (ἀπ' ἀρχῆς, 3:11, cf. 1:1; 2:7, 13, 14, 24), which contrasts with the devil, who has been sinning "from the beginning" (ἀπ' ἀρχῆς, 3:8). However, Cain who was "from the evil one" (ἐκ τοῦ

---

[29] Cf. John Painter, *1, 2, and 3 John* (SP 18; Collegeville, MN: Liturgical Press, 2002), 233; Yarbrough, *1–3 John*, 197.

πονηροῦ, 3:12), is representative of the sinner who is "from the devil" (ἐκ τοῦ διαβόλου, 3:8, cf. 3:10). Cain committed murder because "his works were evil" (τὰ ἔργα αὐτοῦ πονηρὰ ἦν, 3:12), and this is similar to "the works of the devil" (τὰ ἔργα τοῦ διαβόλου, 3:8). The language suggests that "the evil one" is at least connected to "the devil," and that they are likely to be synonymous with one another.[30]

If the evil one is indeed referring to the devil, the sense of contention between the Johannine community and the evil one is clear (3:10):

> The children of God and the children of the devil are revealed in this way: everyone who does not do what is right is not from God, nor the one who does not love his brother.
>
> ἐν τούτῳ φανερά ἐστιν τὰ τέκνα τοῦ θεοῦ καὶ τὰ τέκνα τοῦ διαβόλου· πᾶς ὁ μὴ ποιῶν δικαιοσύνην οὐκ ἔστιν ἐκ τοῦ θεοῦ, καὶ ὁ μὴ ἀγαπῶν τὸν αδελφὸν αὐτοῦ.

The parallel of the "children of God" (τὰ τέκνα τοῦ θεοῦ) versus the "children of the devil" (τὰ τέκνα τοῦ διαβόλου) not only underscores the relational language that the Johannine teacher uses in addressing his audience as τεκνία (children, 3:7), but also further reinforces the sense of opposition and conflict in the letter. The writer refers to the Johannine readers, who are the children of God, and contrasts them to the children of the devil, which includes Cain who was from the evil one/devil (3:12; cf. 3:8, 10).

God's children are to parallel Cain's brother, who did righteous deeds (3:12). The deeds of Cain's brother being identified as righteous (δίκαιος) acts as a contrasting parallel to the language in the verses prior in which the children of the devil do not do what is righteous (δικαιοσύνη, 3:7-10). This theme of righteousness is evident throughout this section (2:29–3:12) especially, as it starts and ends with the emphasis on what is "right" (δίκαιος). Moreover, the emphasis on "the children" (τὰ τέκνα) of God as distinct from "the children" of the devil simultaneously reminds the audience that children naturally resemble their father. They have a filial likeness and derive their character and values from their parent. If they are truly *children* of God, their actions should reflect God's love and justice (3:7, 10–12, 14–18).

The emphasis of the writer is now clear: the Johannine children should reflect God's character. However, the allusion to Cain specifically is a curious one. Of all possible examples, the writer chooses to mention Cain as the one who is "from the evil one." Certainly, the story about Cain and his brother would have been well-known to those of a Jewish background. However, it was also probably familiar to members of the Johannine community who came from a non-Jewish background as well, considering that the story is one of the first scriptural narratives.[31]

---

[30] Smalley, *1, 2, 3 John*, 168, 184; Marshall, *The Epistles of John*, 189.
[31] Smalley says that the allusion to Cain and Abel is unusual because it is the *only* direct reference to the Jewish scriptures in a work that is so close to the Fourth Gospel where more allusions are apparent. He admits that the reason for this is that there were likely more pagan influences at this time (Smalley, *1, 2, 3 John*, 183–4). Indeed, the sole clear reference to the Jewish scriptures indicates that the Greco-Roman culture is more prevalent, and that this illustration was probably carefully chosen to indicate a specific point about fratricide.

One might expect that the writer of 1 John would take a more victorious stance while mentioning the evil one, as he did in the earlier references (2:12-14), and focus on *Abel* as the righteous one[32] while pointing to Cain as the example of greed or unbelief (cf. Jude 11). However, Abel's name is not mentioned, and thus does not seem to be the primary focus. Instead, Cain who is "from the evil one" and his evil deeds are the center of attention in comparison to his brother's righteous deeds (3:12). Therefore, the writer seems to have chosen this illustration for a specific purpose.

The Johannine author may have thought this to be the ideal narrative for two main reasons: one is that Cain and Abel are literal brothers, and the other is that the "evil" brother chooses to murder. In the context of exhorting the audience to love one another, the counterexample being the murder of a familial brother may seem extreme. However, it may shed some light on the kinds of issues the audience was facing in terms of conflict between family members and what temptations they may have had in resorting to violence.

The writer reinforces the severity of the conflict in the succeeding verse (3:13):

Do not be astonished, brothers, if the world hates you.

μὴ θαυμάζετε, ἀδελφοί, εἰ μισεῖ ὑμᾶς ὁ κόσμος.[33]

The author prepares the readers to expect the world (κόσμος) around them to hate (μισέω) them, and the example of Cain might imply that this hate from the world could include hatred from family members. Yet, the Johannine audience is exhorted not to be like Cain who was from the evil one (3:12). Thus, the emphasis is not that other brothers in the world might hate the Johannine believer. The emphasis is that the Johannine believer may be like the murderous brother.

The writer repeats the issue of hate once more, as a contrast to loving others, to underscore his point (3:14-15):

We know that we have passed from death to life because we love one another. The one who does not love remains in death. Everyone who hates a brother is a murderer, and you know that every murderer does not have eternal life remaining in them.

ἡμεῖς οἴδαμεν ὅτι μεταβεβήκαμεν ἐκ τοῦ θανάτου εἰς τὴν ζωήν, ὅτι ἀγαπῶμεν τοὺς ἀδελφούς· ὁ μὴ ἀγαπῶν μένει ἐν τῷ θανάτῳ. πᾶς ὁ μισῶν τὸν ἀδελφὸν αὐτοῦ ἀνθρωποκτόνος ἐστίν. καὶ οἴδατε ὅτι πᾶς ἀνθρωποκτόνος οὐκ ἔχει ζωὴν αἰώνιον ἐν αὐτῷ μένουσαν.

---

[32] Cf. similarly in other places such as *4 Macc.* 18:11; Mt. 23:35; Heb. 11:4 (Lieu, *I, II, & III John*, 144).
[33] See similar language of the world hating the disciples (Jn 15:18-19), and when Jesus is praying for his disciples: "The world has hated them because they do not belong to the world" (ὁ κόσμος ἐμίσησεν αὐτούς, ὅτι οὐκ εἰσὶν ἐκ τοῦ κόσμου, Jn 17:14). Such anticipation in the NT elsewhere implies eschatological expectation of persecution (e.g., Mt. 10:22; 24:9). However, there is no suggestion of literal persecution from the world in 1 John, except perhaps here from a specific family member (3:11-15). This verse will be further explored in Section 3.3.

What would cause a Johannine reader to hate so much that they might become like Cain, a murderer to his own family member? Because the Johannine members see one another as siblings (3:13), perhaps the author is addressing hatred toward another member of the Johannine community. The example of Cain murdering his brother was rooted in jealousy because the brother's deeds were righteous and received favor from God (3:12, cf. Gen. 4:4-5). This may imply that there could be jealousy in the Johannine community that is so severe that it could even lead someone to violence. Another possibility is that, if the world is inclined to hate them (3:13), a mutual hatred has developed out of the distance felt when Johannine members chose *pistis* in Jesus over the *pistis* of the world around them.

While all of the above could be of concern to the author, the context of the passage seems to suggest still *another* possible answer. The hatred between family members may be related to finances and charitable compassion (3:17):

> But whoever has a worldly livelihood and may see his brother in need and closes his heart against him, how does the love of God remain in him?
>
> ὃς δ' ἂν ἔχῃ τὸν βίον τοῦ κόσμου καὶ θεωρῇ τὸν ἀδελφὸν αὐτοῦ χρείαν ἔχοντα καὶ κλείσῃ τὰ σπλάγχνα αὐτοῦ ἀπ' αὐτοῦ πῶς ἡ ἀγάπη τοῦ θεοῦ μένει ἐν αὐτῷ;

Those who have a "worldly livelihood" (τὸν βίον τοῦ κόσμου, literally "the life of the world") are expected to demonstrate God's love by helping others, and probably referring especially to those within the Johannine community. Earlier in the letter, he had mentioned this worldly life (βίος, 2:16) in reference to the problem of worldly pride, which will be explored in Section 3.3. Both references suggest that money should not be a source of pride or covetousness.

What the Johannine readers are actually expected to do with the livelihood that they have is to extend it graciously to others. Supporting the poor and vulnerable was already deeply ingrained in scriptural tradition (eg., Lev. 25; Deut. 15), and thus, those of a Jewish background would have been familiar with this value. Though most people during the first and second centuries in the Roman Empire were living close to the breadline, it would not require extravagant wealth for someone to help another through finances or food.[34]

A person who did not have *pistis* in Jesus may not have appreciated a Johannine family member giving away their hard-earned food and money to another person. They would likely resent, hate, and maybe even resort to violence against their own family members. The repeated reference to murder (σφάζω, twice in 3:12) or murderers (ἀνθρωποκτόνος, twice in 3:15)[35] underscores the extremity with which the world around them, including family members, might hate the Johannine believers when they act in the love and compassion of God because those who are from the evil one live by a different standard. The Johannine audience might want to be "like Cain" (3:12) and feel inclined to respond to violence with violence.

---

[34] Lieu, *I, II, & III John*, 151.
[35] Cf. similarities with Jn 8:44 in which Jesus accuses the Jews of coming from their father, the devil (cf. 1 Jn 3:8–10), who is a murderer (cf. 1 Jn 3:15) and their choosing to do his desires (cf. 1 Jn 2:16).

However, the author reminds his readers of the countercultural message to love one another (3:11), which is fundamental to their *pistis*. This includes sharing their livelihood. Indeed, they should be willing to lay down their lives for one another (τίθημι τὴν ψυχὴν, 3:16), language that is exclusive to 1 John and the Fourth Gospel.[36] In other Greek usage, it means to put oneself on the line and not sacrifice it,[37] but here we can see that both can apply as one is expected to put themselves on the line to financially sacrifice for others. The Johannine community should almost *expect* the world to hate them (3:13), and some people may even want to kill them, but they are not to retaliate in kind and be like Cain themselves (3:12). Cain is the counterexample of how they are to live, as he is representative of those in the world who are from the evil one and may be inclined to violence. However, the Johannine community is expected to reflect the central message of their *pistis* in Jesus, and reflect God's character with the countercultural response of generosity and love (3:10, 11, 13, 16, 17).

The Evil One Threatens *Pistis*

The evil one is not mentioned again until almost the very close of 1 John. As the writer makes his concluding remarks, he alludes to the evil one, indicating his concerns for the Johannine community. In an emphatic three-fold series of "we know" declarations (5:18-20), the writer appears to use the first-person plural to join in as part of the community of Johannine believers. In a sense of solidarity, he proclaims again what they all know together as part of their victorious *pistis* against the world (cf. 5:4), and against the evil one (cf. 2:13-14).

The reference to the evil one in the concluding chapter is initially presented like the first references in Chapter 2, from a more positive, victorious stance (5:18):

We know that those who are born of God do not sin, but the one who was born of God protects them, and the evil one does not touch them.

Οἴδαμεν ὅτι πᾶς ὁ γεγεννημένος ἐκ τοῦ θεοῦ οὐχ ἁμαρτάνει, ἀλλ' ὁ γεννηθεὶς ἐκ τοῦ θεοῦ τηρεῖ αὐτὸν καὶ ὁ πονηρὸς οὐχ ἅπτεται αὐτοῦ.

The believers are seemingly untouchable by the evil one, but the fact that they need protection indicates that the threat of the evil one is a reality. Their protector is "the one who was born of God" (ὁ γεννηθεὶς ἐκ τοῦ θεοῦ), presumably Jesus himself.[38] Jesus could be directly protecting them with intention, or the evil one is not able to touch them because they remain in God/Christ (2:6, 14, 24, 28; 3:6, 9, 24; 4:13, 15, 16) and the evil one only has power over those of the world (i.e., those who do not have *pistis* in Jesus as the Son of God).

In John's Gospel, the only mention of the evil one is indeed in relation to protecting his disciples; as Jesus prays to the Father, he says in John 17:15: "I am not asking you

---

[36] Cf. Jn 10:11, 15, 17; 13:37, 38; 15:13; 1 Jn 3:16.
[37] Lieu, *I, II, & III John*, 149.
[38] Cf. Smalley, *1, 2, 3 John*, 303; Marshall, *The Epistles of John*, 252.

to take them out of the world, but I ask you to protect them from the evil one" (οὐκ ἐρωτῶ ἵνα ἄρῃς αὐτοὺς ἐκ τοῦ κόσμου, ἀλλ᾽ ἵνα τηρήσῃς αὐτοὺς ἐκ τοῦ πονηροῦ). In a sense, the evil one as the devil (cf. 3:8, 10), and Jesus as "the one born of God," as he is the Son of God (cf. 3:8; 4:15; 5:5), are the counterparts who are in strife.[39] The evil one is part of the opposition toward the Johannine community, but he is also the weaker counterpart to "the one who is born of God" who is protecting them. The evil one may not be able to exert any power directly over the Johannine believers, but the evil one's authority extends over the world itself (5:19), and the Johannine community still has to interact with the world as they are still surrounded by it and living in it. Therefore, the evil one continues to pose a threat, and they still have to contend with this enemy.

The fact that the author brings up the evil one several times throughout the letter indicates that the evil one, who exerts power over the world, is still a concern. More than a literal threat, the evil one is a threat to their *pistis*, as seen through the emphasis of what the Johannine audience "knows" in the second chapter: they know the Father and know Jesus who is "from the beginning" (2:13-14). This emphasis on what they "know" is recapitulated in the final three-fold rhetorical declaration at the conclusion of the letter. As seen above, the first "we know" (οἴδαμεν; 5:18) mirrors the emphasis on sin (cf. 2:12) and offers a sense of assurance to the Johannine community.

The second "we know" then delineates the Johannine community from the rest of the world around them (5:19):

We know that we are God's children, and that the whole world lies under the power[40] of the evil one.

οἴδαμεν ὅτι ἐκ τοῦ θεοῦ ἐσμεν καὶ ὁ κόσμος ὅλος ἐν τῷ πονηρῷ κεῖται.

The writer asserts that the Johannine members are God's children, echoing the battle of the children of God versus the children of the devil (3:10) and Cain who was representative of the devil (3:12). However, this second "we know" is less reassuring than the first (cf. 5:18). The author acknowledges that the whole world lies under the power of the evil one, and this statement serves to caution the Johannine audience and call them to a greater awareness of what separates them from the world. Although the evil one has been conquered through their *pistis* in Jesus (2:13-14), the evil one is not powerless and seems to persist with some authority and control in the world.

The final "we know" reflects the author's central message, that the Johannine believers must hold onto the victory they have already attained over the evil one by holding onto their *pistis* (5:20):[41]

---

[39] Cf. the temptation narrative in which Jesus and the devil are opponents: Mt. 4:1-11; Mk 1:12-13; Lk. 4:1-13.
[40] Translated literally, this could read "the whole world lies in the evil one," but the author is more likely trying to convey the authority and control that the evil one has over the entire world (cf. Yarbrough, *1–3 John*, 317; Lieu, *I, II, & III John*, 231).
[41] Cf. 1 Jn 2:13-14; 5:4-5.

And we know that the Son of God has come and has given us understanding so that we may know him who is **true**; and we are in him who is **true**, in his Son Jesus Christ. He is the **true** God and eternal life.

οἴδαμεν δὲ ὅτι ὁ υἱὸς τοῦ θεοῦ ἥκει καὶ δέδωκεν ἡμῖν διάνοιαν ἵνα γινώσκομεν τὸν **ἀληθινόν**, καὶ ἐσμεν ἐν τῷ **ἀληθινῷ** ἐν τῷ υἱῷ αὐτοῦ Ἰησοῦ Χριστῷ. οὗτός ἐστιν ὁ **ἀληθινὸς** θεὸς καὶ ζωὴ αἰώνιος.

Although the word *pistis* is not used here, the emphasis that the *true* God is Jesus, the Son of God, in contrast to the world around them that does not believe this as true, is something that the writer has reiterated throughout the epistle.[42]

There is a clear sense of battle between truth and lie in the letter (cf. 1:6; 2:27), and a stark sense of division between the two (2:21):

I have written to you not because you do not know the truth, but because you know it, and [know] that every lie is not from the truth.[43]

οὐκ ἔγραψα ὑμῖν ὅτι οὐκ οἴδατε τὴν ἀλήθειαν ἀλλ' ὅτι οἴδατε αὐτὴν καὶ ὅτι πᾶν ψεῦδος ἐκ τῆς ἀληθείας οὐκ ἔστιν.

In contrast to the truth (ἀλήθεια), the words "lie" (ψεύδομαι, 1:6), "liar" (ψεύστης, 1:10; 2:4, 22; 4:20; 5:10), and "deceive, lead astray" (πλανάω, 1:8; 2:26; 3:7) permeate the letter. Indeed, the word "liar" (ψεύστης) is used more frequently in 1 John than elsewhere in the NT,[44] emphasizing that *pistis* in the truth is the writer's main concern, and that he does not want to see his "little children" succumb to the world and its desires, which are under the power of the evil one (cf. 2:15-17; 5:19). The "liar" is the one who does not obey God's commands (2:4), denies that Jesus is the Christ (2:22), does not love their fellow Johannine brothers and sisters (4:20), and is equated with the antichrist (2:22).

The writer draws hard lines in the dichotomy between truth and lie, as they cannot be compromised. He knows what is at stake if the Johannine audience succumbs to the polytheistic culture that subscribes to the fundamental lie, which is that the concept of the "divine son" is more affiliated with the emperor than with Jesus (see more in Sections 5.1 and 5.2). The Johannine community is to retain their *pistis*, which is counter to the world that is under the power of the devil, the evil one. The people who do not have the same *pistis* in Jesus as the Son of God and acknowledge him as the true God may be hostile to them (3:13), but they must not be like Cain and follow the evil one (3:12). As they hold onto the victory that they have already achieved by remaining in the word, that is, Jesus (2:14), he protects them, and they are untouchable to the world and to the powers of the devil (5:20).

---

[42] See "true" (ἀληθινός) at 1 Jn 2:8; 5:20 and "truth" (ἀλήθεια) at 1:6, 8; 2:4, 21; 3:18, 19; 4:6; 5:6; cf. 2 Jn 1-4; 3 Jn 1, 3, 4, 8, 12.
[43] The word in brackets helps to smooth out the translation in English.
[44] Cf. Jn 8:44, 55; Rom. 3:4; 1 Tim. 1:10; Tit. 1:12.

Yet, the Johannine readers should not be complacent as the final warning to "keep themselves from idols" (5:21) suggests. The evil one is still a threat, as they can seemingly still act like Cain, who was from the evil one (3:12). Though the evil one has been conquered through their *pistis* in Jesus (2:13, 14), who protects them (5:18), the Johannine writer throughout his letter indicates that the idols of the world are still under the power of the evil one, and the believers must therefore remain vigilant and contend with this persistent underlying threat in their words and actions of loving others rather than resorting to hate and violence (cf. 3:11-15). The author warns the community not to act like Cain, who was of the evil one and a child of the devil (3:8-10, 12), but to hold onto their *pistis* in Jesus and allow their character to reflect their identity as children of God (3:10).

3.2 The Antichrists and False Prophets

The previous section discussed the first named enemy in 1 John, the evil one, who is the spiritual archopponent pervading the culture and threatening to undermine the *pistis* of the Johannine community. The second opponent is named soon after the first: the antichrist (ἀντίχριστος). The term "antichrist" appears only within the Johannine letters (1 Jn 2:18, 22; 4:3; 2 Jn 7) in the NT,[45] and this enemy is often presumed to be a spiritual figure who may be synonymous with the devil, Satan, and the beast in Revelation 13.[46] Indeed, the reference to "the spirit of the antichrist" (τὸ [πνεῦμα] τοῦ ἀντιχρίστου, 1 Jn 4:3) might seem to support this view; perhaps the antichrist is a spiritual figure embodied in a physical form, an idea that has certainly been proliferated in subsequent writings beyond the NT[47] and has entered the modern-day culture in which political figures are accused of being "the antichrist."[48] However, the contexts around the discussion of the antichrist in 1 John seem to indicate that this opponent is not really a spiritual demon, or even the counterfigure of Jesus Christ. The term "antichrist" might appear to imply that this enemy is somehow at a comparable level to Jesus Christ, and that the battle is between Jesus and the antichrist.[49] However, the way in which the writer is warning about antichrists whom the Johannine audience have

---

[45] Later writers utilized the term "antichrist"; for example, the earliest patristic reference comes from Polycarp, *Letter to the Philippians* 7.1, which depends on 1 John (4:2-3).

[46] Painter, *1, 2, and 3 John*, 210; cf. discussion in Brown, *The Epistles of John*, 333–6. The association of the Revelation beast to the antichrist in the Johannine Epistles can be attributed principally to later writers, Irenaeus and Hippolytus (cf. Craig Koester, "The Antichrist Theme in the Johannine Epistles and Its Role in Christian Tradition," in *Communities in Dispute: Current Scholarship on the Johannine Epistles*, ed. R. Alan Culpepper and Paul N. Anderson [Early Christianity and its Literature 13; Atlanta: SBL Press, 2014], 189).

[47] Cf. *Sib. Or.* 3.63-74; *Asc. Isa.* 4.1-18.

[48] Cf. "One in Four Americans Think Obama May Be the Antichrist," *The Guardian*, April 2, 2013, https://www.theguardian.com/world/2013/apr/02/americans-obama-anti-christ-conspiracy-theories, and Sarah Jones, "Here's How We'd Really Know that Trump is the Antichrist," *New York Magazine*, August 21, 2019, https://nymag.com/intelligencer/2019/08/heres-how-wed-really-know-that-trump-is-the-antichrist.html.

[49] As with the evil one, the relationship between the antichrist and Jesus might appear to be comparable to the confrontations between the devil and Jesus in the Synoptic Gospels (Mt. 4:1-11; Mk 1:12-13; Lk. 4:1-13).

encountered in the past, and may continue to encounter in the future, suggests that these opponents are more likely the human counterfigures to the Johannine believers.

As discussed in the previous section, the writer of 1 John has been concerned that the members of the Johannine community may succumb to the temptations that surround them in the world (see more on the identity of the world in the next section). After the exhortation to not love the world (2:15-17), he writes with even greater urgency, employing the vocative "Children" (Παιδία) once again (cf. 2:14) to call his disciples to attention, and to caution them about another foe in addition to the evil one (2:18):

> Children, it is the last hour! As you have heard that antichrist is coming, so now many antichrists have come. From this we know that it is the last hour.
>
> Παιδία, ἐσχάτη ὥρα ἐστιν καὶ καθὼς ἠκούσατε ὅτι ἀντίχριστος ἔρχεται καὶ νῦν ἀντίχριστοι πολλοὶ γεγόνασιν, ὅθεν γινώσκομεν ὅτι ἐσχάτη ὥρα ἐστίν.

The writer warns that it is the "last hour" (ἐσχάτη ὥρα),[50] a phrase that he repeats, and one that is mentioned only in this verse within the Johannine letters, and indeed, only in the NT with this exact phrasing. Because the "last hour" does not have the definite article, it could be referring to the general character of the period, or perhaps some short period of time. However, given the eschatological associations with "hour" (ὥρα, e.g., Jn 2:4; 4:23; 16:2; cf. Lk 22:53), and the similar associations elsewhere in the NT about the prophesied "last days" (ἐσχάται ἡμέραι, e.g., Acts 2:17 quoting Joel 2:28; cf. Heb. 1:2; 1 Pet. 1:20), many scholars adopt the view that "last hour" is referring to an eschatological period of time.[51] The Johannine leader indicates that his audience is already familiar with the concept of an antichrist coming in the last hour or is at least familiar with the idea that an antichrist exists and that it has been foretold as a figure that will come. The writer confirms that many antichrists have indeed come, and this is considered to be the proof that the last hour is here.

The undertone of the warning is urgent and ominous with the declaration of the last hour and the confirmation that the anticipated antichrists have already come.[52] Because of the reference to the "evil one" a few verses before (2:13, 14), one might assume that the antichrist is either a similar spiritual being or that "antichrist" is perhaps another word to identify "the evil one." However, the word "antichrist" does not always appear with the definite article (2:18), and the succeeding plural of "antichrists" seems to indicate that the anticipated antichrist is not a specific spiritual enemy like the devil or Satan, who could be considered the evil counterpart to Jesus Christ.

---

[50] "The last hour" does not have the article in Greek but could be translated with the definite article; cf. Brooke Foss Westcott, *The Epistles of St. John: The Greek Text with Notes*, 2nd edn, ed. F. F. Bruce (Abingdon: Marcham Manor Press, 1966), 69; Marshall, *The Epistles of John*, 148 n. 1.

[51] Cf. Smalley, *1, 2, 3 John*, 95–6; Marshall, *The Epistles of John*, 148; Lieu, *I, II, & III John*, 99; Ruben Zimmermann, "Eschatology and Time in the Gospel of John," in *The Oxford Handbook of Johannine Studies*, ed. Judith M. Lieu and Martinus C. de Boer (Oxford: Oxford University Press, 2018), 298.

[52] The perfect tense for "have come" (γεγόνασιν), indicates the past completed event. At the time that the author is writing, several antichrists have already appeared.

If there was any confusion about the identity of the antichrists, the writer in the next verse makes clear that the antichrists that he is talking about are not spiritual figures but people who used to be a part of the Johannine community (2:19):

> They went out **from us**, but they were not **from us**; for if they were **from us**, they would have remained with us. But by going out they made known that none of them are **from us**.
>
> **ἐξ ἡμῶν** ἐξῆλθαν ἀλλ' οὐκ ἦσαν **ἐξ ἡμῶν**· εἰ γὰρ **ἐξ ἡμῶν** ἦσαν, μεμενήκεισαν ἂν μεθ' ἡμῶν· ἀλλ' ἵνα φανερωθῶσιν ὅτι οὐκ εἰσὶν πάντες **ἐξ ἡμῶν**.

The sense of conflict is clear as the author draws a line between the believers in Christ and the antichrists, the people who left the Johannine community. The repeated acknowledgment that the antichrists are those who are not "from us" (ἐξ ἡμῶν), which is mentioned four times in the single verse, emphasizes the distinction between the two groups. The antichrists did not remain in the community, and their leaving was evidence that they were fundamentally different from the Johannine community. To designate the people who left as "antichrists" may seem extreme, as they could have been called "deserters" or "abandoners." However, the nomenclature reveals the concerns of the writer, who would deem the title appropriate for those who tout a message that counters the Johannine belief in Jesus as the Son of God. These antichrists may have been friends and perhaps even relatives, but they are no longer simply ex-members of the community. They are the opposition who left because they deny the *pistis* of Jesus as the Son of God. The author of 1 John calls them "*anti*christs"[53] to demonstrate the severity of the difference between these opponents and the Johannine believers: they do not believe in Jesus as the Christ, and they are therefore representative of what is *against* Christ.

The antichrists are not just those who abandoned the group, or those who passively believe in something different. They are described as an active threat against the truth, and therefore a threat to the group, as the writer continues in his concerns about the antichrists (2:20-3):

> But you have an anointing from the Holy One, and all of you have known. I have written to you not because you do not know the truth, but because you know it, and [know] that every lie is not from the truth. Who is the liar but the one who denies that Jesus is the Christ? This is the antichrist, the one who denies the Father and the Son. No one who denies the Son has the Father; the one who confesses the Son has the Father also.
>
> καὶ ὑμεῖς χρῖσμα ἔχετε ἀπὸ τοῦ ἁγίου· οἴδατε πάντες. οὐκ ἔγραψα ὑμῖν ὅτι οὐκ οἴδατε τὴν ἀλήθειαν ἀλλ' ὅτι οἴδατε αὐτὴν καὶ ὅτι πᾶν ψεῦδος ἐκ τῆς ἀληθείας

---

[53] The prefix anti- usually means opposite or against; cf. LSJ s.v. "ἀντί." Other similar examples: speak against or contradict (ἀντιλέγω; cf. Herodotus, *The Persian Wars* 9.42); withstand or resist (ἀντιβαίνω; cf. Demosthenes, *On the Crown* 18.186); and opposing force to force (ἀντίβιος; Homer, *Iliad* 1.304).

οὐκ ἔστιν. Τίς ἐστιν ὁ ψεύστης εἰ μὴ ὁ ἀρνούμενος ὅτι Ἰησοῦς οὐκ[54] ἔστιν ὁ Χριστός; οὗτός ἐστιν ὁ ἀντίχριστος ὁ ἀρνούμενος τὸν πατέρα καὶ τὸν υἱόν. πᾶς ὁ ἀρνούμενος τὸν υἱὸν οὐδὲ τὸν πατέρα ἔχει, ὁ ὁμολογῶν τὸν υἱὸν καὶ τὸν πατέρα ἔχει.

The sense of contention is amplified as the author of 1 John distinguishes the Johannine believers from the antichrists. The believers are those who know the truth while the antichrist is identified as the one who lies (ὁ ψεύστης) and the one who denies (ὁ ἀρνούμενος) that Jesus is the Christ. This time (2:22) the definite article is used to demonstrate the defining character of an antichrist; the antichrist is a title that can be given to anyone who lies and denies the truth about Jesus. "The one who denies" (ὁ ἀρνούμενος) is particularly emphasized, as the designation appears three times within two verses (2:22, 23), demonstrating the writer's concern about the active role that the antichrist can play.

The one who denies Jesus as the Christ is a threat, and the Johannine teacher wants to ensure that his disciples do not succumb to the lies of the antichrists who deny the truth about Jesus. He explains (2:26-8):

> I have written these things to you concerning those who would deceive you. As for you, the anointing that you received from him remains in you, and so you do not need anyone to teach you. But as his anointing teaches you about all things, and is true and is not a lie, and just as it has taught you, remain in him. And now, little children, remain in him, so that when he is revealed we may have confidence and not be put to shame before him at his coming.
>
> Ταῦτα ἔγραψα ὑμῖν περὶ τῶν πλανώντων ὑμᾶς. καὶ ὑμεῖς τὸ χρῖσμα ὃ ἐλάβετε ἀπ' αὐτοῦ, μένει ἐν ὑμῖν καὶ οὐ χρείαν ἔχετε ἵνα τις διδάσκῃ ὑμᾶς, ἀλλ' ὡς τὸ αὐτοῦ χρῖσμα διδάσκει ὑμᾶς περὶ πάντων καὶ ἀληθές ἐστιν καὶ οὐκ ἔστιν ψεῦδος, καὶ καθὼς ἐδίδαξεν ὑμᾶς μένετε ἐν αὐτῷ. Καὶ νῦν, τεκνία, μένετε ἐν αὐτῷ, ἵνα ἐὰν φανερωθῇ σχῶμεν παρρησίαν καὶ μὴ αἰσχυνθῶμεν ἀπ' αὐτοῦ ἐν τῇ παρουσίᾳ αὐτοῦ.

The writer uses yet another participle to underscore the fundamental characteristic of the antichrists: the deceivers (πλανῶντες, v. 26).[55] The central reason for his concern is clear; he is writing because he is worried that the antichrists will deceive the Johannine community into believing a message that is counter to Jesus as the Son of God. Because the antichrists were formerly a part of the community, and the Johannine members may still socialize, work with, or even live with some of the antichrist deceivers, the warning is understandably justified. The Johannine teacher urges his disciples to resist the lies and remain (μένετε, v. 27) in the truth, an imperative which he repeats in verse

---

[54] The literal translation would be "the one who denies that Jesus is not the Christ," but it should be noted that the second clause "Jesus is not the Christ" is an indirect quotation referring to what "the one who denies" is saying. To avoid confusion in English, the verse is translated without the "not" in the latter clause.

[55] The concern over deception is also seen in 1 John (1:8; 3:7), cf. deceivers similarly equated with the antichrist (2 Jn 7).

28 after using the vocative "little children" (τεκνία, cf. 2:1, 12) once again to call them to attention. The contention is clear in the battle of what to believe, and the Johannine believers must maintain an active resolve in keeping in the truth about Jesus and not allowing deceivers to sway them away from Christ and leave the community just as the antichrists did. They must not become antichrists themselves.

The writer mentions the antichrist one final time in the letter with the additional emphasis on the conflict between spirits (4:3):

> And every spirit that does not confess Jesus is not from God. And this is the spirit of the antichrist, of which you have heard that it is coming; and now it is already in the world.
>
> καὶ πᾶν πνεῦμα ὃ μὴ ὁμολογεῖ τὸν Ἰησοῦν ἐκ τοῦ θεοῦ οὐκ ἔστιν· καὶ τοῦτο ἐστιν τὸ τοῦ ἀντιχρίστου, ὃ ἀκηκόατε ὅτι ἔρχεται, καὶ νῦν ἐν τῷ κόσμῳ ἐστὶν ἤδη.

The theme of the "spirit" (πνεῦμα) is woven throughout the letter, but especially in Chapter 4, where it is mentioned eight times.[56] The writer talks about the spirit in different contexts, framed positively in relation to God and the truth (3:24; 4:2, 6, 13; 5:6, 8), negatively in relation to false prophets and deceit (4:1, 3, 6), or more generally as a holistic term (4:1). Seen collectively, the term "spirit" indicates the source of the inspiration,[57] and it is unsurprising that the writer would refer most frequently to the spirit of God because he wants the Johannine believers to be inspired by the truth. At the same time, he does not want them to be naïve.

The reality is that there is also "the spirit of the antichrist" (τὸ [πνεῦμα][58] τοῦ ἀντιχρίστου, 4:3), which could be referring to a specific demon, but because the antichrists are human beings who have left the Johannine community, the reference to the antichrist spirit is likely a more general statement about anything or anyone, which does not inspire the truth about the incarnation and divinity of Jesus. The spirit of the antichrist is the counter to the spirit of God (τὸ πνεῦμα τοῦ θεοῦ)[59] mentioned previously (4:1-2):

> Beloved, do not believe every spirit, but test the spirits to see whether they are from God; for many false prophets have gone out into the world. By this you know the Spirit of God: every spirit that confesses that Jesus Christ has come in the flesh is from God
>
> Ἀγαπητοί, μὴ παντὶ πνεύματι πιστεύετε, ἀλλὰ δοκιμάζετε τὰ πνεύματα εἰ ἐκ τοῦ θεοῦ ἐστιν, ὅτι πολλοὶ ψευδοπροφῆται ἐξεληλύθασιν εἰς τὸν κόσμον. ἐν τούτῳ γινώσκετε τὸ πνεῦμα τοῦ θεοῦ· πᾶν πνεῦμα ὃ ὁμολογεῖ Ἰησοῦν Χριστὸν ἐν σαρκὶ ἐληλυθότα ἐκ τοῦ θεοῦ ἐστιν

---

[56] The word "spirit" (πνεῦμα) appears twelve times in the letter at 3:24; 4:1 (2x), 2 (2x), 3, 6 (2x), 13; 5:6 (2x), 8.
[57] Cf. Marshall, *The Epistles of John*, 204.
[58] The πνεῦμα appears earlier in the verse.
[59] Cf. "the spirit of God" (τὸ πνεῦμα τοῦ θεοῦ) at Mt. 3:16; 1 Cor. 2:11; 3:16 and with the anarthrous πνεῦμα θεοῦ at Rom. 8:9 and 1 Cor. 7:40.

In contrast to the spirit that confesses that Jesus has come in the flesh, the spirit of the antichrist counters this message and denies the incarnation of the divine Jesus (cf. 4:3).

The spirit of the antichrist is identified as already "in the world" (ἐν τῷ κόσμῳ, 4:2), and the writer of the letter emphasizes the importance of discerning between the different spirits, which are "of God" or "of the antichrist" because there is another opponent who is against the truth about Jesus Christ: the false prophets. Although false prophets (ψευδοπροφῆται, 4:1) appears only once among the Johannine letters, the terminology is seemingly more common than the designation of "antichrist," as "false prophets" appear in other NT books, including in the Gospels where Jesus himself warned about them.[60] In 1 John, the "many false prophets" (πολλοὶ ψευδοπροφῆται, 4:1) relates back to the "many antichrists" (ἀντίχριστοι πολλοί) mentioned a couple chapters before (2:18). Just as antichrists "went out" (ἐξῆλθαν, 2:19) from the Johannine community and now operate in the spirit of the antichrist that is already "in the world" (ἐν τῷ κόσμῳ, 4:2), so false prophets have "gone out into the world" (ἐξεληλύθασιν εἰς τὸν κόσμον, 4:1) in a spirit that is not of God and are declaring a message that is not from God. The positioning of the antichrists and false prophets as being out in the world reinforces the negative view of "the world" (κόσμος), which has been alluded to in previous verses (cf. 2:2, 15, 16, 17; 3:1, 13, 17) and builds the sense of tension between the Johannine community and the opponents who are associated with the world (see more on "the world" in Section 3.3).

Conquering the Docetists?

Much scholarly discussion surrounding the antichrists and false prophets has historically presumed that the tension in the Letter reflects an intra-Johannine conflict centered on the issue of heresy. The polemic of 1 John has been seen to be arguing against the dualism of gnostic teaching, which separated the "spiritual" from the realities of the world.[61] Similarly, based on the premise that 1 John presupposes the Gospel of John, the conflict has been assumed to be related to the dispute over the common tradition of the Gospel in which the opponents are reading the Fourth Gospel under gnostic presuppositions; the result is an intra-Johannine schism based on docetic christology,[62] that is, seeing the human figure of Jesus as mere appearance. Raymond Brown in his extensive commentary on the Epistles contributed significantly to this view.[63] He refrained from identifying the antichrists specifically as docetists, and instead referred to them as "secessionists" who caused a schism in the Johannine community because they promoted a dualistic christology that negated the saving significance of Jesus' life and death and the connection between the preexistence and suffering of Jesus as the Christ.[64]

---

[60] "False prophets" appears ten other times in Mt. 7:15; 24:11, 24; Mk 13:22; Lk. 6:26; Acts 13:6; 2 Pet. 2:1; Rev. 16:13; 19:20; 20:10.
[61] Bultmann, *The Johannine Epistles*, 38–41; Schnackenburg, *The Johannine Epistles*, 141–3.
[62] Klaus Wengst, *Der erste, zweite und dritte Brief des Johannes* (Gütersloh: Mohn, 1978), 25; Brown, *Epistles of John*, 69–71.
[63] Regarding his influence, cf. Anderson, "The Community that Raymond Brown Left Behind," 275.
[64] Brown, *Epistles of John*, 75–85.

It is understandable as to why some scholars have supposed the conflict in 1 John to be related to docetism as some of the rhetoric appears to stress the material corporeality of Jesus: "every spirit that confesses that Jesus Christ has come in the flesh is from God" (4:2b). The second letter adds further support: "those who do not confess that Jesus Christ has come in the flesh; any such person is the deceiver and the antichrist" (2 Jn 7). In addition to the references about Jesus' flesh, the initial description of the antichrists is often cited as evidence for the Johannine writer's argument against docetism (2:22-3):

> Who is the liar but the one who denies that Jesus is the Christ? This is the antichrist, the one who denies the Father and the Son. No one who denies the Son has the Father; the one who confesses the Son has the Father also.
>
> Τίς ἐστιν ὁ ψεύστης εἰ μὴ ὁ ἀρνούμενος ὅτι Ἰησοῦς οὐκ ἔστιν ὁ Χριστός; οὗτός ἐστιν ὁ ἀντίχριστος ὁ ἀρνούμενος τὸν πατέρα καὶ τὸν υἱόν. πᾶς ὁ ἀρνούμενος τὸν υἱὸν οὐδὲ τὸν πατέρα ἔχει, ὁ ὁμολογῶν τὸν υἱὸν καὶ τὸν πατέρα ἔχει.

The docetists not only deny that Jesus is the Christ, but they also deny the sacraments of Baptism and the Eucharist,[65] and so the author could be viewed as combatting docetism with references to water and blood toward the end of the letter (5:6-8). Thus, it appears that the Johannine author is among those, including Ignatius, Irenaeus, and others, who were combatting docetic belief in the early centuries.[66]

One challenge to this presumption is that δόξα and δοκέω are not mentioned in the First Letter when docetism is associated with these words.[67] Though they both appear in the Fourth Gospel[68] and could be read to contribute toward docetic belief, δόξα and δοκέω being absent from the Johannine Letters makes it problematic to assume that the antichrists and false teachers are representatives of a specific heresy or that the author's primary purpose in addressing the conflict is to combat the issue of docetism.[69] Moreover, the Gospel and the Letters have been interpreted as both docetic[70] and anti-docetic,[71] suggesting that the evidence in both the Gospel and the Letters may not be so self-evident when examining the texts alone.[72] This also explains why Brown and others are hesitant to identify the opponents as docetists specifically.[73]

---

[65] Cf. Udo Schnelle, *Antidocetic Christology in the Gospel of John* (Minneapolis: Fortress, 1992), 68; Urban C. Von Wahlde, *Gnosticism, Docetism, and the Judaisms of the First Century: The Search for the Wider Context of the Johannine Literature and Why It Matters* (London: Bloomsbury, 2015), 65 n. 10; Georg Strecker, *The Johannine Letters: A Commentary on 1, 2, and 3 John*, tr. Linda M. Maloney, ed. Harold Attridge (Minneapolis: Fortress Press, 1996), 73, 183.

[66] Cf. Ignatius *Smyrn.* 5.2, *Trall.* 10; Irenaeus *Adv. Haer* 1.26.1.

[67] Cf. Strecker, *The Johannine Letters*, 75 n. 74; Stefan Mulder, "Early Christian Christology Contextualised: The Graeco-Roman Context of 'Christian' Docetism" (MA Thesis, University of Groningen, 2016), 7.

[68] δόξα appears at John 1:14 (2x); 2:11; 5:41, 44 (2x); 7:18 (2x); 8:50, 54; 9:24; 11:4, 40; 12:41, 43 (2x); 17:5, 22, 24; δοκέω appears at John 5:39, 45; 11:13, 31, 56; 13:29; 16:2; 20:15.

[69] Strecker, *The Johannine Letters*, 75 n. 74.

[70] Ernst Käsemann, *The Testament of Jesus* (Philadelphia: Fortress, 1968), 26, 66, 70.

[71] Udo Schnelle, *Die Johannesbriefe* (Leipzig: Evangelische Verlagsanstalt, 2010), 138–46.

[72] Wahlde, *Gnosticism, Docetism, and the Judaisms of the First Century*, 61.

[73] For example, Brown, *Epistles of John*, 363–77; Schnackenburg, *The Johannine Epistles*, 22–3.

The confusion over the rhetoric in the Letters, which appears to address some concern over docetism, is resolved when read within the cultural context. A docetic understanding of Jesus is likely a Hellenistic syncretism that has been transmitted into the Johannine community.[74] Particularly for those in the community who came from a non-Jewish background, a docetic inclination would be a default understanding about Jesus as Greco-Roman deities never became incarnate, and they would therefore struggle to imagine the Johannine conception of divine incarnation.[75] The tendency toward docetic thinking would be a natural extension of the more familiar concept of divine epiphany, reflected in Greco-Roman art and literature in which divine beings could appear in forms that they temporarily inhabit.[76] If the antichrists of the First Letter are being labelled as such for their inclination toward docetism, then these antichrists who are "in the world" (4:3) and touting what is "from the world" (4:5) have adapted the understanding of divine epiphany in the surrounding culture and presented a Johannine christology that mirrors the view that is in the Greco-Roman world.[77] Thus, the Johannine writer is using countercultural language to differentiate these opponents from the community and warns his audience to distinguish between truth and error (4:6), the error being the adaptation of the cultural norm from the Greco-Roman world to accept a docetic Jesus.

Reading the "docetic" language of 1 John in light of the Greco-Roman world not only helps explain the reference to Jesus' flesh (4:2) but also helps reveal the true nature of the overall conflict permeating the letter. If the primary conflict in 1 John was an intra-Johannine theological dispute and the antichrists have already left (2:19), then presumably, there should no longer be any concern. Indeed, Paul Anderson's suggestion of what happens to the antichrists after they leave the Johannine community would seem to support this. Assuming the expulsion of Jewish Christians from the synagogue in the Gospel of John,[78] Anderson proposes that the group of seceding antichrists are Jewish family and friends who likely *returned* to the local synagogue out of loyalty to "the Father" and Jewish monotheism and out of a desire to be back among the majority of their ethnic community, which had the appeal of religious certainty over and against the fledgling community of believers in Jesus as the Christ.[79] This explanation, however, would not justify the extreme label of "antichrists" for Jewish family and friends who wanted to return to the synagogue. Moreover, the sense of urgency about the antichrists and false prophets who are "in the world" (4:3) does not appear to be

---

[74] Strecker, *The Johannine Letters*, 70.
[75] See further discussion in George van Kooten, "Bleeding Blood, Not Ichor—Christ the 'Gottmensch,'" in *Über Gott: Festschrift für Reinhard Feldmeier zum 70. Geburtstag*, ed. Jan Dochhorn, Rainer Hirsch-Luipold, and Ilinca Tanaseanu-Doebler (Tübingen: Mohr Siebeck, 2022).
[76] Cf. Verity Platt, *Facing the Gods: Epiphany and Representation in Graeco-Roman Art, Literature and Religion* (Cambridge: Cambridge University Press, 2011).
[77] Cf. George van Kooten, "Christ and Hermes: A Religio-Historical Comparison of the Johannine Christ-Logos with the God Hermes in Greek Mythology and Philosophy," in *Im Gespräch mit C. F. Georg Heinrici: Beiträge zwischen Theologie und Religionswissenschaft*, ed. Marco Frenschkowski and Lena Seehausen (Tübingen: Mohr Siebeck, 2021), 305–6.
[78] Cf. Martyn, *History and Theology in the Fourth Gospel*, 46–66.
[79] Cf. Anderson, "The Community That Raymond Brown Left Behind," 275; Anderson, "Antichristic Crises: Proselytization Back into Jewish Religious Certainty," 217–40.

limited to simply "the Jewish world" or the Jewish ethnic community. The contention, which began *internally* within the community, has clearly shifted *externally* as the Johannine believers continue to encounter their opponents "in the world" and will have to "test the spirits" (4:1) to discern whether they are indeed an opponent who must be "conquered" (4:4). The following section will examine the final opponent, "the world," and how it reflects contention with the Greco-Roman world.

3.3 The World

The final conquered opponent of 1 John is the one that appears most frequently in the letter: the "world" (κόσμος). One may think that "world" is a very general term, and it would therefore not be surprising to find it commonly used. Interestingly, out of the more than 180 occurrences of the word "world" in the NT, more than half are found in the Gospel of John and Johannine letters. In the slight letter of 1 John alone, "world" appears an unexpected twenty-three times within four chapters ("world" does not appear in Chapter 1).[80] Like its usage in the Gospel of John, "world" in 1 John appears in what could be considered positive and neutral contexts (e.g., 4:9, 14, 17). However, the majority of references appear in a predominantly negative context. As noted in previous sections, the world is often aligned with the other named opponents: the evil one, antichrists, and false prophets (e.g., 4:1, 3; 5:19), but especially in the final chapter, the world itself is portrayed as being an opponent, which the Johannine believers must conquer (5:4, 5). This section will now look at the contention with the world itself and investigate the nature and necessity of conquering this opponent.

The Desires of the World

We have previously discussed the young men who were conquerors of the evil one (2:13, 14; see Section 3.1). However, the address to the young men as conquerors is immediately followed by an exhortation not to love the world, suggesting that the address to the young people may also be appropriate as they are those who may interact most with the culture around them. They may need to be strong internally (2:14) to conquer the temptations in the Greco-Roman world (2:15-17):

> Do not love the world or the things in the world. If anyone loves the world, the love of the Father is not in him; for all that is in the world—the desire of the flesh and the desire of the eyes and the pride of life—is not from the Father but from the world. And the world along with its desire is passing away, but the one who does the will of God remains forever.

> Μὴ ἀγαπᾶτε τὸν κόσμον μηδὲ τὰ ἐν τῷ κόσμῳ. ἐὰν τις ἀγαπᾷ τὸν κόσμον, οὐκ ἔστιν ἡ ἀγάπη τοῦ πατρὸς ἐν αὐτῷ· ὅτι πᾶν τὸ ἐν τῷ κόσμῳ, ἡ ἐπιθυμία τῆς σαρκὸς καὶ ἡ ἐπιθυμία τῶν ὀφθαλμῶν καὶ ἡ ἀλαζονεία τοῦ βίου, οὐκ ἔστιν ἐκ τοῦ πατρὸς

---

[80] 1 Jn 2:2, 15 (3x), 16 (2x), 17; 3:1, 13, 17; 4:1, 3, 4, 5 (3x), 9, 14, 17; 5:4 (2x), 5, 19. cf. 2 Jn 7.

ἀλλ' ἐκ τοῦ κόσμου ἐστίν. καὶ ὁ κόσμος παράγεται καὶ ἡ ἐπιθυμία αὐτοῦ, ὁ δὲ ποιῶν τὸ θέλημα τοῦ θεοῦ μένει εἰς τὸν αἰῶνα.

Though the young men have conquered the evil one with their *pistis* in Jesus as the Son of God (2:14), here we see that the world is on the definitively opposing side of the battle, and subsequent references to the world are similarly in a negative context (e.g., 3:13; 4:3-5; 5:4-5, 19).

This contrasts with the typical nuance of the word in the Greco-Roman culture as the root meaning of κόσμος is order and arrangement with positive overtones of coherence, beauty, and structure.[81] For example, Herodotus uses the word κόσμος to refer to people sitting in a particular order:

> When they had sat down in **order** one after another, Xerxes sent Mardonius and put each to the test by questioning him if the Persian ships should offer battle.
>
> ὡς δὲ **κόσμῳ** ἐπεξῆς ἵζοντο, πέμψας Ξέρξης Μαρδόνιον εἰρώτα ἀποπειρώμενος ἑκάστου εἰ ναυμαχίην ποιέοιτο.[82]

In this context, the κόσμος has a nuance of structure and arrangement. Another context of κόσμος could be in relation to ornaments, as seen in Plutarch:

> Accordingly, now that it was completely finished and had received all the **ornaments** that belonged to it, Publicola was ambitious to consecrate it.
>
> ὡς οὖν ἀπείργαστο τελέως καὶ τὸν προσήκοντα **κόσμον** ἀπεῖχεν, ἦν τῷ Ποπλικόλᾳ φιλοτιμία πρὸς τὴν καθιέρωσιν.[83]

Finally, in Josephus, the word κόσμος is seen in reference to items of beauty: "the bearer of women's apparel of great price" (κόσμον τε φέρων γυναικεῖον πολυτελῆ).[84] These examples demonstrate some of the diverse, positive connotations of κόσμος in the culture.

The positive perception of κόσμος may help explain why the author of 1 John may have framed the world as the opposing "other." As he warns (2:15-17), the culture of the Greco-Roman world lives by a different standard of values and desires, which are counter to the values and desires that the Johannine community is meant to adopt. The young people may have been more susceptible and tempted to succumb to these worldly values, and they therefore have to contend "on the front lines" of the Johannine battle with the κόσμος, which appears to have a force and character of its own.[85]

When the author forbids loving the world (2:15), he is not necessarily rejecting a comfortable life or societal success. Rather, he is pointing out that love of the world is

---

[81] Cf. LSJ s.v. κόσμος.
[82] Herodotus, *The Persian Wars*, 8.67 (Godley, LCL).
[83] Plutarch, *Publicola* 14 (Perrin, LCL).
[84] Josephus, *Ant.* 1.250 (Thackeray, LCL).
[85] Lieu, *I, II, & III John*, 93.

incompatible with love of the Father (ἡ ἀγάπη τοῦ πατρὸς). The Greek is ambiguous in that it could be referring to "love from" or "love for" God (cf. ἡ ἀγάπη τοῦ θεοῦ in 2:5). However, most likely it is the objective genitive love for the Father, which parallels loving the world. Unlike John's Gospel, in which the disciples are "in the world" (ἐν τῷ κόσμῳ, 16:33; 17:11) and are meant to go out into the world (cf. Jn 17:18), 1 John tends to be more ambivalent (4:4, 17), recognizing that the Johannine community by necessity needs to have some interaction with the world, but implies that there should also be a level of distance. The writer warns about the dangers of the world and its values so that their *pistis* may not be swayed.

In contrast to the positive three-fold declaration against the evil one (2:12-14), another rhetorical triple is utilized (2:16) with a wholly negative description about what is "in the world" and in direct opposition to the Father. The writer of 1 John explains that what is ἐν τῷ κόσμῳ is "the desire of the flesh, and the desire of the eyes, and the pride of life" (ἡ ἐπιθυμία τῆς σαρκὸς καὶ ἡ ἐπιθυμία τῶν ὀφθαλμῶν καὶ ἡ ἀλαζονεία τοῦ βίου). His description reflects the values that are pursued in the Greco-Roman world. The word "desire" (ἐπιθυμία) itself is not necessarily negative; elsewhere in the NT, it is sometimes seen in a positive context (Lk. 22:15; Phil. 1:23; 1 Thess. 2:17; Tit. 2:12). Far more frequently, however, ἐπιθυμία is seen in a negative context,[86] and sometimes in a more sexual one (e.g., Rom. 1:24; 6:12; 1 Thess. 4:5).

The negative association of ἐπιθυμία was acknowledged in the surrounding culture:[87] Thucydides and Epictetus contrasted acting from desire with doing so by foresight, reflecting the philosophical notion that desire needed to be controlled because it was a threat to the rational mind.[88] Desire, and specifically sexual desire, in the Greco-Roman world was associated with the goddess Aphrodite (Roman: Venus),[89] and the specific designation of the desire of the "flesh" (σάρξ, 1 Jn 2:16) suggests that he is referring to sexual desire as well. This is not definitively the case, as the word σάρξ, like ἐπιθυμία, is not always used in a negative context in the NT,[90] including in John's Gospel (e.g., Jn 1:14; 6:53; 17:2) and even in 1 Jn, which refers to Jesus having come "in the flesh" ἐν σαρκὶ (4:2).

However, σάρξ does appear in a negative context in John's Gospel (6:63) and in the NT in general.[91] One related note is that σάρξ is distinct from the word "body" (σῶμα), which does not appear in the Johannine epistles but does appear in John's Gospel (2:21; 19:31, 38, 40; 20:12), mostly in reference to Jesus's physical body. The different nuances of the words may complicate our understanding of what is being said in 1 John with regard to loving the world (2:15-17), but the combination of ἐπιθυμία and σάρξ in the

---

[86] For example, Mk 4:19; Jn 8:44, Rom. 7:8; Eph. 4:22; Col. 3:5; 1 Tim. 6:9; 2 Tim. 2:22; 3:6; 4:3; Tit. 3:3; Jas 1:14-15; 1 Pet. 1:14; 4:3; 2 Pet. 1:4; 3:3; Jude 1:16, 18.

[87] Cf. also negative Jewish desire: Ps. 106 (LXX 105):14 when the Israelites tested God in the wilderness because of their desire, and the roving desire perverting the innocent mind in Wis. 4:12.

[88] Thucydides 6.13; Epictetus, *Discourses* 2.18.

[89] Cf. Plutarch, *Moralia*, 757B; Apollodorus, *The Library* 3.12; Aristotle, *Nicomachean Ethics* 1149b15–16.

[90] For example, Mt. 16:7; Mk 10:8; Lk. 3:6; 24:39; Acts 2:26; Rom. 1:3; 2 Cor. 4:11; Eph. 2:14; 1 Tim. 3:16; Phlm. 16; Heb. 5:7.

[91] For example, Rom. 7:5; 8:6; 1 Cor. 5:5; Gal. 5:19; 6:8; Phil. 3:3; Jas 5:3; Jude 7-8; Rev. 17:16; 19:18.

NT as "a desire of the flesh" (ἡ ἐπιθυμία τῆς σαρκὸς) demonstrates a clearly negative pattern (e.g., Rom. 13:14; Gal. 5:16; Eph. 2:3; 1 Pet. 2:11; 2 Pet. 2:10, 18).

In addition to his concern about the desire of the flesh, the writer notes the more bemusing "desire of the eyes" (ἡ ἐπιθυμία τῶν ὀφθαλμῶν). It is possible that he may have biblical precedents in mind, for example, when Eve sinfully desired to eat of the fruit that was a delight to her eyes (Gen. 3:6), or it may have a sexual connotation (as in Mt. 5:28; 2 Pet. 2:14). The eyes alone are simply an organ of sense, and does not necessarily imply that a blind person, for example, would not be able to experience a sinful temptation. Instead, the emphasis on the ἐπιθυμία of the eyes suggests that there is a perversion[92] and a selfishness that is not concerned with loving others but is inspired by a love of what they see in the world for the purpose of personal fulfillment.

Finally, the author cautions against the pride of life (ἡ ἀλαζονεία τοῦ βίου), which is interesting, firstly, because the word ἀλαζονεία is seen only in two books of the NT (1 Jn 2:16; Jas 4:16; cf. the adjective in Rom. 1:30; 2 Tim. 3:2).[93] It can mean pride or arrogance, particularly in reference to feigning and giving a false pretension.[94] The implication is that the pride in 1 John is decidedly negative, just like the desires of the flesh and the eyes. This pride is specifically of "life" (βίος), which appears ten times in the NT,[95] of which two are in 1 John (2:16; 3:17). It is significant that βίος, used with a negative nuance in association with the world, is not the same as the ζωή of 1 John (1:1-2; 2:25; 3:14, 15; 5:11-13, 16, 20), which is affiliated with eternal life in Christ. Specifically, the pride of life (ἡ ἀλαζονεία τοῦ βίου) seems to suggest the love of possessions and wealth. It is a challenge to interpret because it may be misunderstood in light of the world's livelihood (τὸν βίον τοῦ κόσμου, 3:17). However, the Johannine believers still need to survive and earn money for their livelihood (see more below). At the same time, they should not adopt the world's perspective in having pride in their finances and valuing money in the same manner as the culture.

The writer of 1 John may not be indicating precisely that the desire of the flesh is sexual, that the desire of the eyes is covetousness, and that the pride of life is wealth. However, it is reasonable to say that these were all related to the Greco-Roman culture. The fact that ἐπιθυμία and ἀλαζονεία appear only once (2:16) while the words "flesh" (σάρξ), "eyes" (ὀφθαλμοι), and "life" (βίος) appear elsewhere[96] further highlights the focus on the "desire" and "pride," which are a part of the opposition to the world. The writer makes clear that such desire (and pride) "is not from the Father but from the world" (οὐκ ἔστιν ἐκ τοῦ πατρὸς ἀλλ' ἐκ τοῦ κόσμου ἐστίν), and they are therefore supposed to avoid them if they are to truly remain a part of the Johannine community.

---

[92] Smalley, *1, 2, 3 John*, 84.
[93] Similar words might be "haughtiness" (ὑπερηφανία, Mk 7:22), or perhaps the more popular "boasting" (καύχησις, e.g., Rom. 3:27; 1 Cor. 15:31; 2 Cor. 1:12; 1 Thess. 2:19; Jas 4:16), which can be seen in a positive context as well.
[94] LSJ s.v. ἀλαζονεία. In the LXX, it appears as a boastful display of power and success (2 Macc. 9:8; 15:6), of wisdom (Wis. 17:7; *4 Macc.* 8:19), and of wealth (Wis. 5:8).
[95] Cf. Mk 12:44; Lk. 8:14, 43; 15:12, 30; 21:4; 1 Tim. 2:2; 2 Tim. 2:4.
[96] Besides 1 Jn 2:16, the word "σάρξ" appears (in reference to Jesus coming in the flesh) in 4:2, cf. 2 Jn 7; "ὀφθαλμοι" appears at 1 Jn 1:1; 2:11 and "βίος" appears at 3:17.

The world (as a collective entity) along with its desires "is passing away" (παράγεται, 2:17), a parallel echo of the darkness passing away (ἡ σκοτία παράγεται, 2:8). These are values reflective of a temporary world with fleeting desires, while one who does the will (θέλημα) of God remains forever (2:17). One can see the dichotomy presented in the choice of the θέλημα of God versus the ἐπιθυμία of the world (cf. similar dichotomy in 1 Pet. 4:2). The writer seems to redirect the focus, to remind his readers not to dwell on the worldly, selfish, and temporary ἐπιθυμία that is passing away (παράγεται), but to focus on the will (θέλημα) of God and remain forever (μένει εἰς τὸν αἰῶνα). This reinforces the sense of division between the Father and the world (2:15) and underlines the sense of conflict between the young men and the evil one (2:13-14), which the writer then expands in subsequent references to the opposing enemy (3:12; 5:19).

By framing the world as an "other" that is full of temptation and pride that leads to sin, the author of 1 John is demonstrating his countercultural message against the world around the Johannine community. He emphasizes that this polytheistic world that indulges in temporary fulfillment of their desires is separate and distinct from the Johannine God and those of the Johannine community who are meant to reflect his will (2:17). Thus, the writer warns his readers not to covet the Greco-Roman world (2:15) lest they begin to reflect the love of the culture rather than the Johannine love of God.

Contention with the World

While the temptations of the Greco-Roman world may seem attractive, the writer also indicates that the world is not simply a passive object of desire. The Johannine believers may expect to face active contention and conflict with the world (3:13):

> Do not be astonished, brothers, if the world hates you.
>
> μὴ θαυμάζετε, ἀδελφοί, εἰ μισεῖ ὑμᾶς ὁ κόσμος.

The world is personified as having an emotion and hating (μισέω) the Johannine believers. "Hate" appears elsewhere in the letter, but in the other three occurrences (2:11; 3:15; 4:20), the emphasis is on the believer, who should not hate, and is instead called to love (see also Section 3.1). Here, the world itself is doing the hating (3:13), conveying a hostility that could even lead to murdering one's brother (3:12, 14).

The writer seems to prepare the believers for the world to hate them. As discussed above, the false prophets, antichrists, and the evil one are all associated with the world, and thus, the Johannine community should not be surprised when they face contention with this world of people who do not have the same *pistis*. The writer suggests that hostility may even come from a family member who does not have a *pistis* in Jesus as the Son of God (cf. 3:12 and the discussion in Section 3.1), and the Johannine believers should not be surprised if they experience hatred from them as well.

In the following chapter, we see another personification of the world in which the world is portrayed as part of the opposition (4:5):

They are from the world; therefore what they say is from the world, and the world listens to them.

αὐτοὶ ἐκ τοῦ κόσμου εἰσὶν, διὰ τοῦτο ἐκ τοῦ κόσμου λαλοῦσιν καὶ ὁ κόσμος αὐτῶν ἀκούει.

The personified world listens (ἀκούω)[97] to "them," which is referring to the antichrists and false prophets who are not a part of the Johannine community (cf. 4:1-4). The world is once again portrayed as an enemy who is not only the source of opponents who are "from the world" (ἐκ τοῦ κόσμου) but "what they say is from the world" (τοῦτο ἐκ τοῦ κόσμου λαλοῦσιν), and the broader community of the general public is swayed by the words of the antichrists and false prophets. This Greco-Roman world listens to those who actively tout a different *pistis* that is false and against Christ (anti-Christ; see also Section 3.2). The author is reinforcing his point that the Greco-Roman world and its *pistis* are separate from the Johannine community, and it should therefore not be surprising when anyone from this world not only hates the Johannine believers (3:13) but also does not listen to them (4:6).

In the final chapter, the writer of 1 John depicts the Greco-Roman world as the conquered adversary to the Johannine believers (5:4-5):

For everyone who is born of God conquers the world. And this is the victory that has conquered the world, our faith. Who is the one who conquers the world except the one who believes that Jesus is the Son of God?

ὅτι πᾶν τὸ γεγεννημένον ἐκ τοῦ θεοῦ νικᾷ τὸν κόσμον· καὶ αὕτη ἐστὶν ἡ νίκη ἡ νικήσασα τὸν κόσμον, ἡ πίστις ἡμῶν. τίς ἐστιν δὲ ὁ νικῶν τὸν κόσμον εἰ μὴ ὁ πιστεύων ὅτι Ἰησοῦς ἐστιν ὁ υἱὸς τοῦ θεοῦ;

In the climax of the letter, which proclaims victory over the world, the Johannine believers who are born of God and believe that Jesus is the Son of God are the conquerors, and the world of antichrists, false prophets, and nonbelievers is the defeated enemy. Central to this victory is the difference of *pistis,* of faith, or what is believed. *Pistis* in Jesus as the divine Son of God (5:5) is not only what distinguishes the Johannine community from the world, but *pistis* itself seems to conquer the world (5:4).

The world as the conquered enemy makes particular sense if we acknowledge the polytheistic culture of the Greco-Roman world that prevailed at the time of this letter in the first and second centuries CE. The Johannine community would have been a very small minority in this culture, and one can imagine how members might have struggled in their daily lives at work or even at home to remain in their belief of Jesus as the Son of God when the culture touted the emperor as the divine son and acknowledged multiple gods and goddesses in every aspect of life. The sense of battle against several opponents, including the world itself, which the writer has described throughout

---

[97] The verb (ἀκούω) is often translated "to hear," but in English, the word "listens" offers a deeper connotation of paying attention to what is heard. This verb in 1 John occurs at 1:1, 3, 5; 2:7, 18, 24 (2x); 3:11; 4:3, 5, 6 (2x); 5:14, 15; cf. 2 Jn 6; 3 Jn 4.

Table 3 Conquering the World

John 16:33	1 John 5:4-5
I have said this to you, so that in me you may have peace. In the world you face persecution. But take courage; I have conquered the world!	For everyone who is born of God conquers the world. And this is the victory that has conquered the world, our faith. Who is the one who conquers the world except the one who believes that Jesus is the Son of God?
ταῦτα λελάληκα ὑμῖν ἵνα ἐν ἐμοὶ εἰρήνην ἔχητε· ἐν τῷ κόσμῳ θλῖψιν ἔχετε· ἀλλὰ θαρσεῖτε, ἐγὼ νενίκηκα τὸν κόσμον.	ὅτι πᾶν τὸ γεγεννημένον ἐκ τοῦ θεοῦ νικᾷ τὸν κόσμον· καὶ αὕτη ἐστὶν ἡ νίκη ἡ νικήσασα τὸν κόσμον, ἡ πίστις ἡμῶν. τίς ἐστιν δὲ ὁ νικῶν τὸν κόσμον εἰ μὴ ὁ πιστεύων ὅτι Ἰησοῦς ἐστιν ὁ υἱὸς τοῦ θεοῦ;

1 John, becomes clear when one considers the level with which the Johannine believers had to contend with the tendencies, temptations, and beliefs of the culture.

Conquering the World in John's Gospel

To better understand the contention between "the world" (κόσμος) and the Johannine believers, it is helpful to look at John's Gospel, which is often referenced by scholars in relation to 1 John[98] because of the close similarities in the language of conquering the world (1 Jn 5:4-5; Jn 16:33 [see Table 3]). The victory proclamations are prominent within the texts because the verb for "conquer" (νικάω), only appears once in John's Gospel (16:33) and the distinct substantive for "victory" (νίκη) appears only once in 1 John (5:4).

In John's Gospel, Jesus is speaking to his disciples, foretelling his impending suffering and death. In the preceding chapters, Jesus has also alluded to the persecution that the disciples will face,[99] and he tells them that some will even kill the disciples as part of their worship to God (16:2). Now Jesus mentions their suffering again (v. 33), telling them that they will face persecution in the world. Jesus may have been concerned with the future failure of faith by the disciples when they fled at his capture.[100] He knew that they would despair and perhaps assume failure when their teacher was crucified and when they themselves would face persecution. The disciples could easily assume

---

[98] Cf. Yarbrough, *1–3 John*, 276; Smalley, *1, 2, 3 John*, 270; Marshall, *The Epistles of John*, 229; Lieu, *I, II, & III John*, 207 n. 132; Jörg Frey, "Dualism and the World in the Gospel and Letters of John," in *The Oxford Handbook of Johannine Studies*, 285.

[99] Cf. Jn 14:27 and 15:20. In 15:20, the verb for "persecute" (διώκω) is akin to "pursuit," which is different from the noun for "persecution" (θλῖψις) in 16:33, which is more akin to "pressure." However, the overall message of needing peace when facing difficulty is consistent. Cf. LSJ s.v. "διώκω" and "θλῖψις."

[100] Mt. 26:56 and Mk 14:50-2 explicitly refer to the disciples fleeing when Jesus is captured. Lk. 22:54 cites Peter following at a distance. Unlike the Synoptic Gospels, however, the Gospel of John does not explicitly mention the fleeing of the disciples. In John 18, Simon Peter and "another disciple" are noted as following Jesus, and Jesus does say that the disciples will be scattered and leave him alone (Jn 16:32), but as with much of John's Gospel, the main focus is on Jesus himself.

defeat if Jesus had not foretold what would happen. They had already been questioning Jesus's divinity (16:30), and it would have appeared that he was definitely not from God if he were captured by the Jewish leaders and Roman soldiers and killed on the cross. It would seem that Jesus had been defeated by the Jews and the Romans, and that he was not truly the Christ. Thus, Jesus tells them that he is saying all of these things (his discourse, not just the things from the previous verse) so that they would have peace when encountering their troubles (v. 33). Though it seems that Jesus has been defeated, they could be confident that he has achieved victory. Much like in 1 John, the purpose of such warnings is not to scare the disciples; on the contrary, Jesus is trying to reassure them. He tells his disciples to take courage, knowing that he has "conquered the world."

The context of John's Gospel is of literal persecution, but as we have seen in previous sections, the believers of 1 John face their own form of persecution from the evil one, antichrists, and false prophets who are in the world. The tension between the two factions can be so intense that it may even result in murderous violence (1 Jn 3:12, 15). In John's Gospel, Jesus is certain of a murderous outcome that is prompted by certain Jewish leaders who are angry of his claim that he is the Son of God (Jn 19:7), and that will be carried out by the Roman soldiers who are under the authority of the emperor (see more on this below). The persecution against the *disciples* would also likely involve Roman soldiers. Thus, when Jesus talks about having peace while facing literal persecution, and taking courage in knowing that he has conquered the world, this opposition that he is conquering must include the Roman imperial world. Rome is the ultimate power in the culture and would be a primary source of fear for Jesus' followers.

The Ruler of This World

One indication that the conquered κόσμος includes the immediate Greco-Roman world is with the references to "the ruler of this world" (ὁ ἄρχων τοῦ κόσμου τούτου) in John's Gospel (12:31; 14:30; 16:11).[101] Many scholars equate this ruler with "the devil," or "Satan,"[102] and indeed the comparison is understandable given that the words "devil" (διάβολος) and "Satan" (Σατανᾶς) are also mentioned in the Gospel of John

---

[101] Technically, the construction in 14:30 is slightly different (ὁ τοῦ κόσμου ἄρχων) as it does not include "this." However, many English translations (e.g., NIV, NLT, ESV, CEV, NRSV, NKJV) tend to keep "the ruler of *this* world" in 14:30 for the sake of consistency with the other two occurrences.

[102] For example, Lieu, *I, II, & III John*; George Raymond Beasley-Murray, *John* (WBC; Waco, TX: Word Books, 1987); Raymond Brown, *The Gospel of John I–XII* (AB; Garden City, NY: Doubleday, 1966); Craig Keener, *The Gospel of John: A Commentary* (Peabody, MA: Hendrickson Publishers, 2010); Richard Bauckham, *Gospel of Glory: Major Themes in Johannine Theology* (Grand Rapids: Baker Academic, 2015). David Rensberger seems to avoid discussing the ruler even though he himself writes about politics in John because of the overwhelming majority at the time that identified the ruler exclusively with Satan. However, he does identify Pilate as a likely representation of the hostile Roman state. Cf. David Rensberger, *Overcoming the World: Politics and Community in the Gospel of John* (London: SPCK, 1989), 90; N. T. Wright and J. P. Davies, "John, Jesus, and 'The Ruler of This World': Demonic Politics in the Fourth Gospel?," in *Conception, Reception, and the Spirit: Essays in Honor of Andrew T. Lincoln*, ed. J. Gordon McConville and Lloyd K. Pietersen (Eugene, OR: Cascade Books, 2015), 76 n. 21.

("devil" in 6:70; 8:44; 13:2; "Satan" in 13:27). However, there are no direct encounters with the devil or with evil spirits in the Fourth Gospel;[103] all references to Jesus performing exorcisms is omitted,[104] and the temptation narrative is missing in the Gospel of John in comparison to each of the Synoptic Gospels, which not only include the confrontation (Mt. 4:1-11; Mk 1:12-13; Lk. 4:1-13) but also mention "the devil" or "Satan" more frequently than in the Gospel of John.[105]

If "the ruler" (ὁ ἄρχων) was meant to primarily refer to the devil or Satan, the temptation narrative would be the ideal inclusion in John's Gospel to demonstrate the tension and ultimate loss of the ruler to Jesus. Instead, the references to the devil and Satan in John's Gospel are in relation to people: to Judas Iscariot (6:70; 13:2, 27) or in relation to the Jews (8:44). Thus, "the ruler of this world" may perhaps be *influenced* by the devil, just as with Judas Iscariot and the Jews, but is more likely referring directly to a human being and specifically a representation of the ruler of the Greco-Roman world. The emperor, as the literal ruler over the Greco-Roman world in which Jesus and his disciples live, is the likely conquered counterpart to the kingdom rule of Jesus.[106]

Three times Jesus makes reference to "the ruler of this world" (ὁ ἄρχων[107] τοῦ κόσμου τούτου) (12:31; 14:30; 16:11), who is evidently a part of the κόσμος that Jesus is conquering (as we shall see later in 16:33). In all three instances, Jesus is speaking in the context of internal and external conflict, in which the

---

[103] Cf. Lieu, *I, II, & III John*, 136.

[104] The word "demon" (δαιμόνιον) is used in John in the context of Jews accusing Jesus of being possessed by a demon (7:20; 8:48, 49, 52; 10:20). In 10:21, δαιμόνιον appears in the context of those who believe that Jesus does not have a demon. The word "demon" does not appear in the Johannine epistles showing further consistency between the Gospel and Letters that conflict between the conquering Jesus and evil spirits is not the focus, but rather the more literal conflict with the Greco-Roman world.

[105] Matthew mentions "the devil" or "Satan" a total of 10 times ("διάβολος" at Mt. 4:1, 5, 8, 11; 13:39; 25:41; "Σατανᾶς" at 4:10; 12:26 (2x); 16:23), Mark six times ("διάβολος" does not appear, "Σατανᾶς" at 1:13; 3:23 (2x), 26; 4:15; 8:33), and Luke ten times ("διάβολος" at 4:2, 3, 6, 13; 8:12; "Σατανᾶς" at 10:18; 11:18; 13:16; 22:3, 31) in comparison to four times in the Gospel of John ("διάβολος" at 6:70; 8:44; 13:2; "Σατανᾶς" at 13:27). Cf. the Johannine epistles where the word "Σατανᾶς" does not appear, but "διάβολος" appears four times at 1 Jn 3:8 (3x), 10, as noted in the previous section.

[106] Cf. also those who identify "the ruler of this world" as the emperor: Tom Thatcher, *Greater than Caesar: Christology and Empire in the Fourth Gospel* (Minneapolis: Fortress, 2009), and George van Kooten, "*Bildung*, Religion, and Politics in the Gospel of John: The Erastic, Philhellenic, Anti-Maccabean, and Anti-Roman Tendencies of the Gospel of 'the Beloved Pupil,'" in *Scriptural Interpretation at the Interface between Education and Religion*, ed. Florian Wilk (Themes in Biblical Narrative 22; Leiden: Brill, 2019), 171. Wright and Davies, "John, Jesus and 'The Ruler of This World'" identify the ruler with Satan and the emperor. Carter views Pilate as the ruler of the world (Warren Carter, *John and Empire: Initial Explorations* [London: T&T Clark, 2008], 290–9), but Pilate himself is obviously not a powerful ruler who needs to be conquered. He seems to be swayed by the crowds (Jn 19:12-16) rather than being a strong ruler over them. Pilate *represents* the ruler, who is the emperor and the more likely counterpart to Jesus.

[107] The word ἄρχων can refer to "ruler," "authority," or "official." Cf. LSJ s.v. "ἄρχων." Some scholars prefer to translate ἄρχων as "prince" (e.g., Beasley-Murray, *John*, 213; Brown, *The Gospel of John, I–XII*, 468), and draw comparisons to "the rulers of this age" (τῶν ἀρχόντων τοῦ αἰῶνος τούτου) seen for example, in 1 Corinthians (2:6, 8). Cf. the "authorities" (Jn 3:1, 7:26, 48; 12:42) being obvious human authorities, giving even more support to "the ruler of this world" in the Gospel of John as referring to a human being. Cf. Francis Moloney, who views the Jews as the representatives and slaves of a "prince of evil" (*The Gospel of John* [SP 4; Collegeville, MN: Liturgical Press, 1998], 354–5).

ruler is the embodiment of the opposition. When Jesus first mentions "the ruler of this world" (12:31), he is speaking to a crowd while admittedly experiencing his own internal conflict about his impending death. He says that his "soul is troubled" (12:27),[108] and he seems tempted to ask God to save him from his future suffering.[109]

Despite his troubled soul, however, Jesus proclaims his first declaration of the ruler's defeat (12:31):

Now is the judgment of this world; now the ruler of this world will be driven out.

νῦν κρίσις ἐστὶν τοῦ κόσμου τούτου, νῦν ὁ ἄρχων τοῦ κόσμου τούτου ἐκβληθήσεται ἔξω·

Modern readers familiar with NT texts might assume that the ἄρχων being "driven out" is Satan falling from heaven in Luke (10:18) or the great dragon "who is called the Devil and Satan" being thrown down to the earth in the book of Revelation (12:9).[110] Indeed, there seems to be some overlap between Luke and Revelation as "the Satan" (ὁ Σατανᾶς) is clearly named in both cases. However, in Luke, Jesus is responding to some of his disciples who are amazed that demons submit to them (10:17), and the aorist participle for "fall" (πεσόντα, 10:18) seems to indicate that Jesus watched Satan fall in the past.

By contrast, in John's Gospel, the verb ἐκβληθήσεται (will be driven out) is in the future tense; the ruler is about to be driven out. Thus, it seems presumptive to equate "the ruler of this world" in John with the Satan of Luke and Revelation. Jesus in John's Gospel says that the ruler is *about* to be driven out (12:31) because Jesus anticipates his suffering and death at the hands of the Romans. Yet, he knows that his death is the reason that he came (12:27), and that this is all a part of the judgment of the world, with its culture of polytheism and the emperor as the divine son (*divi filius*)[111] (this will be discussed further in Section 5.1). The dominant culture, which promotes a *pistis* in the emperor as the divine ruler of the world will be driven out by Jesus, the true divine son, who supersedes the ruler of the Greco-Roman world with his own kingship.[112]

When Jesus mentions the ruler for a second time, it is a part of the Farewell Discourse (chs 14–17) in which Jesus is giving his final words to his disciples. He has previously washed his disciples' feet (13:1-19), and foretold Judas Iscariot's betrayal

---

[108] When Jesus says that his soul is "troubled," the verb here (ταράσσω) literally means "to stir" or "disturb" (cf. LSJ s.v. "ταράσσω"). It is used in four other instances in the Gospel of John to reference Jesus or the disciples being troubled by their current or impending circumstances (11:33; 13:21; 14:1, 27). (The verb ταράσσω also occurs in reference to water being "stirred up" [5:7]) Death is related to all of these "disturbances," whether it is Lazarus' death (11:33), Jesus' death (12:27; 13:21), or the disciples' deaths (or possibly a combination of both Jesus and the disciples' deaths) (14:1, 27). See also Beasley-Murray, *John*, 249.

[109] In the Synoptic Gospels, Jesus in Gethsemane *does* ask the Father for his impending suffering and death to be taken away (Mt. 26:36-46; Mk 14:32-42; Lk. 22:39-46).

[110] Cf. Beasley-Murray, *John*, 213.

[111] Cf. Beard, North, and Price, *Religions of Rome*, 208–10.

[112] Jesus' kingly entry into Jerusalem occurs just before (12:12-19) in which the Pharisees were concerned that the culture was already shifting toward Jesus.

(13:21-30) and Peter's denial (13:36-8), but knowing that his time with them is limited, Jesus says (14:30-1):

> I will no longer talk much with you, for the ruler of this[113] world is coming. He has no claim over me; but I do as the Father has commanded me, so that the world may know that I love the Father. Rise, let us be on our way.
>
> οὐκέτι πολλὰ λαλήσω μεθ' ὑμῶν, ἔρχεται γὰρ ὁ τοῦ κόσμου ἄρχων· καὶ ἐν ἐμοὶ οὐκ ἔχει οὐδέν, ἀλλ' ἵνα γνῷ ὁ κόσμος ὅτι ἀγαπῶ τὸν πατέρα καὶ καθὼς ἐντολὴν ἔδωκεν μοι ὁ πατήρ, οὕτως ποιῶ. ἐγείρεσθε ἄγωμεν ἐντεῦθεν.

Jesus tells his disciples that their conversation will shortly come to an end because the ruler of this world is "coming." The use of the verb "to come" (ἔρχομαι) gives the sense that there is something tangible on its way, which is underlined in the fact that Jesus says immediately after, "rise, let us be on our way" (ἐγείρεσθε ἄγωμεν ἐντεῦθεν, 14:31).[114] Jesus knows that his arrest is imminent, and these captors who are "coming" will include the Roman σπεῖρα (Jn 18:3, 12), the tactical unit or cohort of soldiers,[115] along with their officer, the χιλίαρχος, who together represent the authority of the emperor, the ruler of the Greco-Roman world.[116] The Roman soldiers are necessary because the Jewish leaders are not able to arrest Jesus without the approval of the ruling government. The soldiers not only capture Jesus but actively mock and torture him (Jn 19:1-3; cf. Mt. 27:27-31; Mk 15:16-20). The Roman soldiers also cast lots for Jesus's clothing, just as they might with the spoils of war (Jn 19:23-5).

Despite the threat of the coming ruler represented by the Roman soldiers, Jesus does not mention his opposition to incite his disciples to military violence.[117] Jesus knows that the disciples feel troubled over what their teacher is saying (14:1, 27) and that it may seem as though the ruler of the world is conquering Jesus as he is captured, tortured, and killed by the Romans. However, the disciples can be reassured that the ruler may have power and authority over the current Greco-Roman world but has no power or authority over Jesus (14:30). Instead of being fearful and intimidated, the disciples can respond with peace; this peace is not "as the world gives" (14:27). Jesus's clarification makes sense if he is speaking about the conception of peace in Greco-Roman culture, which would associate εἰρήνη (Greek) or *pax* (Latin) with an absence of fear, a treaty of peace, or the goddess of peace.[118] In contrast to the peace

---

[113] The τούτου does not appear here in comparison to the other references to the ruler, but for the sake of consistency, I will retain the "this" in the translation.

[114] Cf. Wright and Davies, "John, Jesus, and 'The Ruler of This World,'" 81.

[115] LSJ s.v. "σπεῖρα."

[116] In comparison to the Synoptic Gospels, John's Gospel portrays the Romans with an indifference that demonstrates an anti-Roman sentiment (Kooten, "*Bildung*, Religion, and Politics in the Gospel of John," 171–2).

[117] Peter later foolishly reacts violently by cutting off the right ear of the high priest's slave in the presence of the Roman soldiers, their officer, and the Jewish police (18:10-12). He could have easily started a full riot. Cf. Wright and Davies, "John, Jesus, and 'The Ruler of This World,'" 85.

[118] Cf. LSJ s.v. "εἰρήνη." Eirene/Pax is the goddess of peace, the daughter of Zeus and Themis (Hesiod, *Theogony* 902). The senate was commissioned to erect an *Ara Pacis*, an altar of peace, in Rome to celebrate the establishment of the age of peace, which was completed in 9 BCE. It still remains today

that they might see in the world around them, Jesus offers a peace that they may retain even when they are without their teacher (cf. 14:3, 18-19, 28) and even as they face persecution themselves (16:33).

When Jesus mentions the ruler of this world for the third and final time in John (16:11), he is describing the events after he "goes away" and "the Advocate" (παράκλητος) comes (16:7). At that time, the ruler will have already been condemned (16:11) and judgment will have been executed against the ruler. Jesus is foretelling the victorious results so that, as they face imminent conflict from those in the culture around them, the disciples will not despair. Jesus offers encouragement through his conquering message (16:33):

> I have said this to you, so that in me you may have peace. In the world you face persecution. But take courage; I have conquered the world!
>
> ταῦτα λελάληκα ὑμῖν ἵνα ἐν ἐμοὶ εἰρήνην ἔχητε. ἐν τῷ κόσμῳ θλῖψιν ἔχετε· ἀλλὰ θαρσεῖτε, ἐγὼ νενίκηκα τὸν κόσμον

Jesus is acknowledging that the time that he has been describing is coming and has already begun (16:32) in which the persecution of both Jesus and his disciples is imminent. The ruler may appear to win as Jesus is tortured and killed by the Romans and his disciples face persecution from their surrounding culture. However, Jesus wants his disciples to remember that, as they face persecution, they can have peace knowing that Jesus has actually conquered the world and the ruler of it through his death on the cross, which is a part of the judgment that overthrows the current kingdom ruled by the emperor.

The Jews may be considered the instigators of this persecution, but the actual executors are the Romans, who act under the power and authority of the emperor.[119] The Jewish leaders were certainly aware of who was ruling their world. They were already concerned that the Romans would come and destroy the Jews and their temple because Jesus was causing so much commotion by performing miracles (11:48). They acknowledge the emperor as the ultimate authority in the process of their trying to condemn Jesus. When Pilate, as another representative of the emperor, and the only one with the power to allow for Jesus' crucifixion, does not find any legal case against Jesus, the Jews assert (19:12b):

> If you release this man, you are no friend of the emperor. Everyone who claims to be a king sets himself against the emperor.
>
> Ἐὰν τοῦτον ἀπολύσῃς, οὐκ εἶ φίλος τοῦ Καίσαρος· πᾶς ὁ βασιλέα ἑαυτὸν ποιῶν ἀντιλέγει τῷ Καίσαρι.

---

with its own museum at the *Museo dell'Ara Pacis* in Rome. Cf. Stefan Weinstock, "Pax and the 'Ara Pacis,'" *Journal of Roman Studies*, no. 50, Parts 1 and 2 (1960): 44–58.

[119] For more on Roman persecution, see Richard J. Cassidy, *John's Gospel in the New Perspective: Christology and the Realities of Roman Power* (Maryknoll, NY: Orbis Books, 1992), 56–9.

Pilate sees the impending riot and questions the crowd again about whether Jesus should really be killed, to which the chief priests answer: "We have no king but the emperor" (οὐκ ἔχομεν βασιλέα εἰ μὴ Καίσαρα, 19:15). Even the Jews recognize the authority of the emperor as he is the ruler and king over the Greco-Roman world. They too have chosen to submit to the Roman imperial ideology of the world and proclaim their loyalty to the Roman emperor.[120]

Despite immense opposition, Jesus points out in all three instances of his mentioning the "ruler" that he is not threatened, and in fact, the only reason why the Romans have any authority or power is because it has been granted to them from above (19:11). "The ruler of this world" is the lesser counterpart to Jesus, who overrules and supersedes the *divi filius* as the true Son of God,[121] and the Savior of the World (4:42 cf. 1 Jn 4:14), another title used for Roman rulers.[122] For the Gospel writer, the use of such monikers that were used for the emperor is a bold political statement[123] while simultaneously underlining the difference between the rule of the emperor in the Greco-Roman world versus the rule of Jesus Christ over all of creation (see more in Section 5.1).

Jesus entered into Jerusalem in a kingly manner,[124] which was the counterpoint to the culture of triumphant Roman conquerors who would enter the city through the Triumphal Gate to the cheers of Roman people.[125] In the everyday Greco-Roman world, all would see the emperor as the ruler of the world, but Jesus shows through his kingly entry and declaration of conquering the current world that he is the ruler who will uproot (12:31), overpower (14:30), and supplant (16:11) the current ἄρχων. As Jesus clarifies to Pilate, the emperor may rule the current world, but his kingdom is not derived from the Greco-Roman world, and thus, his followers do not need to fight against the ruler in the same way that the Romans might conquer others (18:36). Like the conquering of the Greco-Roman world in 1 John, the conquering of the world and its ruler in John's Gospel is one that counters the prevailing culture with a distinct Johannine *pistis*.

As we have seen, "the ruler of this world" being identified with the emperor in John's Gospel indicates that the conquering of the world (16:33) is a contention against the polytheistic world under the Roman Empire. We shall see that the contention against the Greco-Roman world persists in the First Letter of John as well, and that the Johannine author presents a consistent countercultural narrative to his audience because of his concern over their *pistis*.

---

[120] Cf. Gerhard van den Heever, "Finding Data in Unexpected Places (or: From Text Linguistics to Socio-rhetoric): Towards a Socio-Rhetorical Reading of John's Gospel," *Neot* 33, no. 2 (1999): 358.
[121] Cf. "The Son of God" (ὁ υἱὸς τοῦ θεοῦ) in Jn 1:34, 49; 3:18; 5:25; 11:4, 27; 19:7; 20:31.
[122] "Savior of the World" (ὁ σωτὴρ τοῦ κόσμου) was not a common first-century Jewish or Samaritan messianic designation, but it was a title used for Roman rulers from Julius Caesar to Hadrian and later emperors. Craig R. Koester, "'The Savior of the World' (Jn 4:42)," *JBL* 109, no. 4 (1990): 666–7.
[123] Cf. Thatcher, *Greater than Caesar*, 136.
[124] Jn 12:12-19; cf. Mt. 21:1-11; Mk 11:1-11; Lk. 19:28-40.
[125] Cf. Beard, North and Price, *Religions of Rome*, 44.

4

A Countercultural Letter

Having determined that the conquering language in both 1 John and the Gospel of John reflect a contention against the "world," and that the "world" in the Gospel is clearly an allusion to the polytheistic world under the Roman Empire, this chapter will now examine further the contention with the world in 1 John and demonstrate that the author is also making allusions to the Greco-Roman world and its polytheistic beliefs that dominated the culture of the time. The concern about the prevailing culture continues to be evident throughout the brief letter particularly in the reference to fear that is incompatible with love (4:18), and in the concluding exhortation to the readers to keep themselves from idols (5:21). Through his acknowledgement of the culture, the writer is not only demonstrating his awareness of the culture but also framing a countercultural narrative against it. The Johannine teacher wants to convey to his spiritual children that they should not be naïve or complacent in their *pistis* and that conquering the world also means contending against the polytheistic culture that surrounds them in the Greco-Roman world.

4.1 Against the Culture of Fear

In the earlier chapters of his letter, the writer of 1 John alludes to some concern about the culture when he exhorts his disciples to resist the desires of the Greco-Roman world (2:15-17), and clarifies that this resistance is not to be a violent one, which might be an expected response in the culture when facing conflict (3:11-15).[1] He emphasizes instead the importance of responding with love (1 Jn 3–4),[2] which is especially apparent in his discourse in Chapter 4 as the cognates of "love" (i.e., ἀγαπητός, ἀγαπάω, ἀγάπη) appear more than thirty times within the few verses (4:7-21). Amid this exhortation to love, the author then suddenly and prominently addresses the issue of fear (4:18):

> There is no fear in love, but perfect love casts out fear; for fear has to do with punishment, and whoever fears has not been perfected in love.

---

[1] See also Section 3.1.
[2] The importance of love is alluded to previously in 1 Jn 2:5, 10.

φόβος οὐκ ἔστιν ἐν τῇ ἀγάπῃ ἀλλ' ἡ τελεία ἀγάπη ἔξω βάλλει τὸν φόβον, ὅτι ὁ φόβος κόλασιν ἔχει, ὁ δὲ φοβούμενος οὐ τετελείωται ἐν τῇ ἀγάπῃ.

The reference to fear stands out because it is mentioned four times and only in this sole verse in all of the Johannine epistles. Moreover, it is declared as an antithesis in which fear cannot exist in love and is instead forcefully cast out in the presence of love, evoking more of the contentious language that permeates the letter.

Positive Jewish Fear?

The author offers little explanation as to what he means by placing fear as the incompatible antithesis to love, but the lack of explanation would make sense if the issue of fear was obvious to the audience of the letter. In the case of 1 John, love is associated with God; indeed, twice he says that "God *is* love" (ὁ θεὸς ἀγάπη ἐστίν, 4:8, 16). However, fear being placed in opposition to love seems to indicate that this is not the same sort of fear seen often in the New Testament and in the LXX, which has positive connotations.

The reverential fear of God, which appears several times in the New Testament,[3] is seen in the Gospel of Luke, in which Mary, the pregnant mother of Jesus, sings a song of praise (1:49-50):

> For the Mighty One has done great things for me, and holy is his name.
> His mercy is for those who fear him from generation to generation.
>
> ὅτι ἐποίησέν μοι μεγάλα ὁ δυνατός. καὶ ἅγιον τὸ ὄνομα αὐτοῦ,
> καὶ τὸ ἔλεος αὐτοῦ εἰς γενεὰς καὶ γενεὰς τοῖς φοβουμένοις αὐτόν.

In her song, Mary does not appear to suggest that generations of people are terrified of God. On the contrary, earlier on, she says, "my spirit rejoices in God my savior" (καὶ ἠγαλλίασεν τὸ πνεῦμά μου ἐπὶ τῷ θεῷ τῷ σωτῆρί μου, v. 47). Her song is out of extreme joy, and she is thankful for the "great things" (v. 49) God has done for her and for the mercy he has shown to generations of people who have demonstrated their reverence for him (v. 50).

In a few instances in the New Testament, there is the sense of serving God "with fear and trembling" as seen in Philippians (2:12-13):[4]

> Therefore, my beloved, just as you have always obeyed me, not only in my presence, but much more now in my absence, work out your own salvation with fear and trembling; for it is God who is at work in you, enabling you both to will and to work for his good pleasure.
>
> Ὥστε ἀγαπητοί μου, καθὼς πάντοτε ὑπηκούσατε, μὴ ὡς ἐν τῇ παρουσίᾳ μου μόνον ἀλλὰ νῦν πολλῷ μᾶλλον ἐν τῇ ἀπουσίᾳ μου, μετὰ φόβου καὶ τρόμου τὴν ἑαυτῶν

---

[3] Cf. Acts 10:2, 22, 35; 13:16, 26; 2 Cor. 7:1; Eph. 5:21; 6:5; Col. 3:22; 1 Pet. 1:17.
[4] Cf. 2 Cor. 7:15; Eph. 6:5.

σωτηρίαν κατεργάζεσθε· θεὸς γάρ ἐστιν ὁ ἐνεργῶν ἐν ὑμῖν καὶ τὸ θέλειν καὶ τὸ ἐνεργεῖν ὑπὲρ τῆς εὐδοκίας.

This could be misunderstood to mean that God is like a scary, demanding dictator and that the people need to be trembling in fear when they serve him. However, the same phrasing is used in 2 Corinthians (7:15-16):

> And his heart goes out all the more to you, as he remembers the obedience of all of you, and how you welcomed him with fear and trembling. I rejoice, because I have complete confidence in you.
>
> καὶ τὰ σπλάγχνα αὐτοῦ περισσοτέρως εἰς ὑμᾶς ἐστιν ἀναμιμνῃσκομένου τὴν πάντων ὑμῶν ὑπακοήν, ὡς μετὰ φόβου καὶ τρόμου ἐδέξασθε αὐτόν. χαίρω ὅτι ἐν παντὶ θαρρῶ ἐν ὑμῖν.

This is referring to the way in which the Corinthians received Titus. They were welcoming him, and both Paul and Titus are happy about this. Thus, this "fear and trembling" does not appear to be a negative fear, but instead suggests the humility with which people serve others.

In the Septuagint, "fear and trembling"[5] appears in a Psalm (55:5):

> Fear and trembling come upon me, and horror overwhelms me.
>
> φόβος καὶ τρόμος ἦλθεν ἐπ' ἐμέ καὶ ἐκάλυψέν με σκότος

In this context, the "fear and trembling" is indeed a negative sentiment. However, this is not about fear and trembling because of a negative fear of God. The psalmist is fearful because of wicked enemies who are bringing trouble against him (cf. vv. 2, 12). The psalmist is not fearful of God in a negative sense; he actually cries out to God for help, and he has confidence that God will save him (v. 16).

Fear in relation to God in the LXX often uses the same Greek cognates (φόβος, φοβέω, φοβέομαι) as the fear of 1 John, but the fear of God in the Jewish context is continually presented as a positive reverential fear of the Lord. This type of fear is so significant to the Jewish community that it is mentioned in almost every book of the LXX.[6] For example, in the final chapter of Joshua, all of the tribes of Israel gather together, and Joshua says to them (24:14):

> Now therefore fear the Lord, and serve him in sincerity and in righteousness; put away the foreign gods that your ancestors served beyond the River and in Egypt, and serve the Lord.

---

[5] Cf. Judg. 7:3.
[6] Some of the many examples include: Gen. 22:12; Exod. 9:30; Deut. 6:24; 2 Sam. 23:3; 1 Chron. 16:25; Prov. 1:7; Eccl. 8:12; Isa. 50:10. Verses such as Gen. 20:11 and Exod. 18:21 further support the positive fear of the divine with the use of the Greek word, θεοσέβεια, which can be translated as "fear of God" or "reverence toward God." See Georg Bertram, "θεοσεβής, θεοσέβεια," *TDNT*, 3:123–8.

καὶ νῦν φοβήθητε κύριον καὶ λατρεύσατε αὐτῷ ἐν εὐθύτητι καὶ ἐν δικαιοσύνῃ καὶ περιέλεσθε τοὺς θεοὺς τοὺς ἀλλοτρίους οἷς ἐλάτρευσαν οἱ πατέρες ὑμῶν ἐν τῷ πέραν τοῦ ποταμοῦ καὶ ἐν Αἰγύπτῳ καὶ λατρεύετε κυρίῳ

The allusion to serving God with sincerity and righteousness indicates the positive context in which Joshua is calling the people to serve God.

Fearing God is affiliated with wisdom and insight into knowing and understanding him,[7] and experiencing his love and mercy. Rather than placing fear and love in contrast to one another as 1 John does, the positive Jewish concept of fearful reverence actually aligns fear with love, as in Deuteronomy (10:12):

So now, O Israel, what does the Lord your God require of you? Only to fear the Lord your God, to walk in all his ways, to love him, to serve the Lord your God with all your heart and with all your soul

καὶ νῦν Ισραηλ τί κύριος ὁ θεός σου αἰτεῖται παρὰ σοῦ ἀλλ' ἢ φοβεῖσθαι κύριοντὸν θεόν σου πορεύεσθαι ἐν πάσαις ταῖς ὁδοῖς αὐτοῦ καὶ ἀγαπᾶν αὐτὸν καὶ λατρεύειν κυρίῳ τῷ θεῷ σου ἐξ ὅλης τῆς καρδίας σου καὶ ἐξ ὅλης τῆς ψυχῆς σου

While the Johannine letter places fear and love in conflict with one another, the verbal forms of fear and love are placed in parallel with one another in Deuteronomy because fearing God from a Jewish perspective is affiliated with loving God and serving him. For the Jews, fear of the divine denotes a reverence and respect for the God to whom they belong.

One possible outlier among the plethora of verses that present a positive fear of God in the LXX is Ps. 119:120 (118:120 LXX). Initially, the psalmist seems to have a negative fear of God and divine judgment:

My flesh trembles for fear of you, and I am afraid of your judgments.

καθήλωσον ἐκ τοῦ φόβου σου τὰς σάρκας μου ἀπὸ γὰρ τῶν κριμάτων σου ἐφοβήθην

Like many other psalms, however, the speaker is discursive with his emotions; in prior verses, the psalmist says that he loves God's law but hates double-minded people and the wicked of the earth.[8] His overall attitude toward God continues to be one of reverence and respect, not negative, overwhelming fear. Though the psalmist may feel a momentary flash of negative fear regarding God's judgment, he still loves God and honors his law. Thus, this psalm is yet another example of the positive Jewish association of fear and love.

In contrast to the psalmist who experiences a simultaneous love and fear of God, the writer of 1 John asserts that they are mutually exclusive (4:18).

---

[7] Cf. Prov. 9:10.
[8] Ps. 119:113, 119 (118:113, 119 LXX).

There is no fear in love, but perfect love casts out fear; for fear has to do with punishment, and whoever fears has not been perfected in love.

φόβος οὐκ ἔστιν ἐν τῇ ἀγάπῃ ἀλλ' ἡ τελεία ἀγάπη ἔξω βάλλει τὸν φόβον, ὅτι ὁ φόβος κόλασιν ἔχει, ὁ δὲ φοβούμενος οὐ τετελείωται ἐν τῇ ἀγάπῃ.

The negative fear in the first Johannine epistle cannot be the positive, fearful reverence for God seen so frequently in the Jewish context. If the Jewish conception of divine fear was applicable to 1 John, then the "fear of God" would actually be a discordant "fear of *love*" because 1 John says that God *is* love (4:8, 16). Fear of love could arguably make sense in a Jewish context if the author of 1 John were addressing a fearful reverence of the God who embodies, reflects, and expresses love. However, the positive Jewish conception of fear cannot be the same negative fear of divine judgment in 1 John (4:18) that is cast out in the presence of love and is instead a marker of someone who has not been perfected in love. Because the writer of 1 John asserts to the Johannine community that fear is "cast out" (ἔξω βάλλω) when they remain in the perfect love of God, he is more likely addressing the fear of the divine that was well-entrenched in the Greco-Roman culture.

Fearing the Gods in the Greco-Roman World

The reference to fear being cast out (4:18) is more readily understandable when viewed in light of the Greco-Roman culture because the writer of 1 John discusses love and fear in the context of divine judgment (4:16b-17):

> God is love, and those who remain in love remain in God, and God remains in them. Love has been perfected among us in this: that we may have boldness on the day of judgment, because as he is, so are we in this world.
>
> Ὁ θεὸς ἀγάπη ἐστίν, καὶ ὁ μένων ἐν τῇ ἀγάπῃ ἐν τῷ θεῷ μένει καὶ ὁ θεὸς ἐν αὐτῷ μένει. ἐν τούτῳ τετελείωται ἡ ἀγάπη μεθ' ἡμῶν, ἵνα παρρησίαν ἔχωμεν ἐν τῇ ἡμέρᾳ τῆς κρίσεως, ὅτι καθὼς ἐκεῖνός ἐστιν καὶ ἡμεῖς ἐσμεν ἐν τῷ κόσμῳ τούτῳ.

The idea of having boldness on the day of judgment would have been a radical statement (which will be addressed below) for those living in the Greco-Roman world, which tended to fear divine judgment and retribution.

The earliest writers of Greek tragedies presented divine judgment in the context of moral law, in which the human being would receive divine retribution based on how they acted on earth. For example, Aeschylus presents the story of Agamemnon, who becomes fearful when his wife Clytemnestra spreads extravagant cloths for Agamemnon to walk on. He says that the gods alone deserve such honors, and he hopes that the gods will not strike him from afar for accepting honor for himself.[9] Agamemnon was fearful of the divine judgment that he would receive for his actions.

---

[9] Aeschylus, *Agamemnon* 921, 946–7.

In *Eumenides,* divine judgment is portrayed even more directly as the goddess Athena appears as the president of the court of Athenian citizens and administers her judgment over the people.[10] The goddess offers her judgment before a literal courtroom context, which evokes a clear visual image of the authority of the deity.

Among the most fearsome representatives of divine judgment in Greco-Roman culture were the Erinyes, sometimes called the Furies or Eumenides, who were based on the theater of Aeschylus, but remained popular in Greek, Etruscan, and Roman art and were mentioned well into the second and third centuries CE.[11] They were often portrayed as terrifying divine beings dressed in black with snakes in their hair who would torment convicted criminals even in the afterlife in Hades.[12] One could easily understand why these beings would promote a culture of fear in the Greco-Roman world and how they would contribute to a fear of divine judgment in general.

Fear itself was personified in the god Phobos (Roman: Timor or Pavor), who is often mentioned alongside his brother Deimos (Roman: Formido or Metus), the personification of terror and dread.[13] As their names suggest, they are fearsome deities, considered to be the sons of Ares, the war god,[14] and they are described as participants in battle, hitching up their father's horses[15] and driving his chariot.[16] The association with battle seems to suggest that fear and terror are useful forces in intimidating opponents; the reactions that they evoke lead to victory in war. The Spartans tried to ally themselves with fear by honoring Phobos and creating a cult, which is well attested at Sparta from as early as the seventh or sixth century BCE.[17] The fear god had a sanctuary there,[18] and he was institutionalized, not only to curry his favor in war but also to reinforce the fear that citizens were supposed to have of the law, scaring them into obedience.[19]

War heroes were noted as honoring Phobos. According to Plutarch, Alexander the Great sacrificed to Phobos before his victory at the Battle of Guagamela in 331 BCE, just as Theseus had done before his victory against the Amazons.[20] By sacrificing to

---

[10] Aeschylus, *Eumenides* 582–4, 794–807.
[11] Pausanias 8.25, 42; Quintus Smyrnaeus 8, 243.
[12] Aeschylus, *Choephoroe* 1048–50; *Eumenides* 48–56, 175–8, 339–40; Pausanias 1.28.6. Cf. Herbert Jennings Rose, B. C. Dietrich, and Alan A. D. Peatfield, "Erinyes" in *OCD*.
[13] Cf. Homer, *Iliad* 4.440; 11.37; Hesiod, *The Shield* 195, 463; Dionysius of Halicarnassus, *On Literary Composition* 16.46, 64; Philostratus of Athens, *Heroicus* 25.7.6. In the LCL, Phobos is sometimes translated as "Fear" or "Rout" in English, and Deimos is translated as "Dread" or "Terror."
[14] Homer, *Iliad* 4.440; in Hesiod, *Theogony* 933–5, they are the sons of Ares and Aphrodite.
[15] Homer, *Iliad* 15.119.
[16] Hesiod, *The Shield* 463.
[17] Nicholas Richer, "Personified Abstractions in Laconia: Suggestions on the Origins of Phobos," in *Personification in the Greek World*, ed. Emma Stafford and Judith Herrin (Aldershot: Ashgate, 2005), 112; Maria Patera, "Reflections on the Discourse of Fear in Greek Sources," in *Unveiling Emotions II: Emotions in Greece and Rome: Texts, Images, Material Culture*, ed. Angelos Chaniotis and Pierre Ducrey (Stuttgart, Germany: Franz Steiner Verlag, 2013), 113. Interestingly, the Spartans were also known for their athleticism, which may have been related to their wanting to stay in shape for war. Cf. Nigel Jonathan Spivey, *The Ancient Olympics*, 2nd ed. (Oxford: Oxford University Press, 2012), 26–7.
[18] Plutarch, *Agis and Cleomenes* 8.3.
[19] Patera, "Reflections," 113–14.
[20] Plutarch, *Alexander* 31.9; *Theseus* 27.2.

Phobos on the eve of battle, the leaders hoped to divert any force that could destroy their soldiers while directing spiritual forces toward their enemies.[21] In Selinus, a fifth-century BCE inscription commemorates a victory in which Phobos is thanked alongside Zeus and Athena for saving the city.[22] Fear in this sense could therefore be viewed positively, as association with Phobos had the potential for victory. Unlike the Jewish association of reverential fear of God, however, Phobos is not beloved. He is only beneficial in the sense that he is useful in his function of assisting his father Ares in battle and intimidating the enemy camp.

The references to the physical descriptions of Phobos indicate that he is not a revered deity of beauty, but a terrifying figure meant to repulse those who see him. He is described in various forms, but he is said to be the least beautiful of the gods,[23] and is often depicted as part of a shield motif. He is a dragon-like figure with bright eyes of fire on the shield of Heracles[24]; he resembles a lion on the shield of Agamemnon;[25] and he is described as crowning the aegis of Athena, another deity associated with warfare.[26] Phobos was probably depicted on shields as a way to harness his power of fear and to intimidate any opponents.[27] The imagery on the shields that are meant to protect soldiers would simultaneously induce fear and intimidation to the enemy camp, as if Phobos was a force that had chosen one side in the battle.

In addition to the descriptions of Phobos represented on shields, other extant material culture offers some insight into the perception of fear in the Greco-Roman culture. An inscription on an oenochoe (wine jug) from Berlin dating to around 530 BCE identifies Phobos, who is shown in anthropomorphic form driving Ares's chariot. The inscription is helpful in cases of other similar imagery in which the charioteers are not named, and may suggest that the unnamed figures are Phobos as well.[28] If they are indeed representations of the fear god, then it would further demonstrate his cultural significance and potential influence. Although some of the figures in material culture cannot be verified, the relevance of Phobos seems to have persisted for several centuries. Not only does he appear in Greco-Roman literature (as indicated above), but he is also mentioned, for example, in a second-century CE funerary inscription from Cilicia. Phobos is named alongside Atë (goddess of ruin and folly)[29] and Moira (goddess of fate and destiny),[30] probably to indicate that they are guardians of the tomb and to ward off those who might try to rob the site.[31] The naming of the deities serves as a warning of the dire consequences that would befall any tomb raiders.

---

[21] Cf. Patera, "Reflections," 114–15.
[22] *Syll.*³ 1122.
[23] Sextus Empiricus, *Against the Physicists* 1.188.
[24] Hesiod, *The Shield* 144, 195.
[25] Pausanias 5.19.4.
[26] Homer, *Iliad* 5.739.
[27] Cf. Stephen Scully, "Reading the Shield of Achilles: Terror, Anger, Delight," *Harvard Studies in Classical Philology* 101 (2003): 32.
[28] Cf. Harvey A. Shapiro, *Personifications in Greek Art: The Representation of Abstract Concepts, 600–400 B.C.* (Zurich: Akanthus, 1993), 210–12.
[29] Atë is the daughter of Zeus who was expelled from Olympus to bring harm to men (Homer, *Iliad* 19.90–4, 126–31; cf. Hesiod, *Theogony* 230).
[30] Cf. Homer, *Iliad* 19.87; Hesiod, *Theogony* 217, 904; Aeschylus, *Prometheus Vinctus* 516.
[31] Patera, "Reflections," 113 n. 24.

Phobos and the other gods and goddesses of the Greco-Roman world were feared because they were thought to have supernatural power and authority, which they would exert in the human world. People were therefore simultaneously motivated to seek their favor and intimidated into living a moral life so that they might avoid divine judgment as a consequence. Yet the deities were also believed to be capricious, and they were sometimes portrayed as interfering in human affairs without a clear rationale or sense of moral justice.[32] Herodotus, for example, demonstrates divine determinism in which the gods are recognized as those who decide what is just[33]; at the same time, they are described as interfering on a whim, just as the god Apollo intervenes so that his favorite Croesus can avoid just punishment for his actions.[34]

In Plutarch, the *Lives* are meant to be case histories of crime and punishment in which humans bring about their own punishment or receive just punishment through supernatural means.[35] However, Plutarch also mentions the role of *tychē* (τύχη, "fate" or "fortune")[36] several dozen times in his writings, even writing an entire essay on the subject.[37] Fortune is personified in the goddess Tyche (Roman: Fortuna), perhaps the most capricious of all the gods.[38] She is believed to govern human affairs,[39] and therefore has significant power, even being attributed with the hegemony of Rome.[40] Although she can bring about good fortune, she is also known for suddenly bringing bad fortune, and subsequently, Tyche is viewed as dangerous and unpredictable.[41] Given her unpredictability, it is understandable as to how she might contribute to the fear of the gods.

The Greco-Roman Response to Fear

Because the culture of the Greco-Roman world consisted of capricious gods inducing fear through their unpredictable divine judgment, it may have prompted a desire for human beings to have some semblance of control over their lives. Different attempts seem to have been made in response to the culture of divine fear so that human beings might try to reduce the unknown and unpredictable. Thucydides, for example, seems to exert some level of control or rationality in his account of the Peloponnesian War, in which the gods are more conspicuous because they are largely absent.[42] On the surface,

---

[32] Cf. J. Gwyn Griffiths, *The Divine Verdict: A Study of Divine Judgement in the Ancient Religion* (Studies in the History of Religions 52; Leiden: Brill, 1990), 70.
[33] Herodotus 8.106.
[34] Herodotus 1.87, 91.
[35] Frederick E. Brenk, *In Mist Apparelled: Religious Themes in Plutarch's Moralia and Lives* (Mnemosyne, Bibliotheca Classica Batava, Supplementum 48; Lugduni Batavorum: Brill, 1977), 256–75.
[36] LSJ, s.v. "τύχη."
[37] For example, Plutarch, *Pyrrhus* 13.1; *Dion* 26.7, 51.4; *Caesar* 9.1; *Lucullus* 29.5; *Brutus* 50.5; *Crassus* 21.1; *Otho* 13.3. He wrote an entire essay on the subject of *tychē* in *Moralia* 97C–100.
[38] Cf. Griffiths, *The Divine Verdict*, 87–8; Noel Robertson and B. C. Dietrich, "Tyche" in *OCD*.
[39] Cf. Angelos Chaniotis, "Empathy, Emotional Display, Theatricality, and Illusion in Hellenistic Historiography," in *Unveiling Emotions II*, 57.
[40] Plutarch, *Moralia* 316C–326C; cf. Polybius 1.63.9.
[41] For example, Thucydides 6.11.6; Polybius 15.6.8, 30.10.1, 39.8.2.
[42] Cf. Hugh Lloyd-Jones, *The Justice of Zeus* (Sather Classical Lectures 41; Berkeley: University of California Press, 1971), 137.

his history appears to be more "scientific" without the input of the spiritual beings.[43] However, Thucydides does mention the role of *tychē* in his writings (6.11.6), which may suggest that he still reflects some of the culture of divine intervention.

The sense of divine fear in the culture instigated different aversive responses. The Stoics ironically exerted control with their sense of determinism, which negated the idea of free will in a person's life, and so the idea of divine punishment or reward was not a major concern.[44] They were able to ease their fears by accepting aforehand that they did not determine whatever happened to them. Epictetus reflects this strategy:

> When you see someone weeping in sorrow, either because a child has gone on a journey, or because he has lost his property, beware that you be not carried away by the impression that the man is in the midst of external ills, but straightway keep before you this thought: "It is not what has happened that distresses this man (for it does not distress another), but his judgment about it."
>
> Ὅταν κλαίοντα ἴδῃς τινὰ ἐν πένθει ἢ ἀποδημοῦντος τέκνου ἢ ἀπολωλεκότα τὰ ἑαυτοῦ, πρόσεχε μή σε ἡ φαντασία συναρπάσῃ ὡς ἐν κακοῖς ὄντος αὐτοῦ τοῖς ἐκτός, ἀλλ᾽ εὐθὺς ἔστω πρόχειρον ὅτι "τοῦτον θλίβει οὐ τὸ συμβεβηκός (ἄλλον γὰρ οὐ θλίβει), ἀλλὰ τὸ δόγμα τὸ περὶ τούτου."[45]

Epictetus says that it is the *perspective* that is of greater concern than the event itself. If people have the right judgment or perspective, then they will experience tranquility. The Stoic philosophy views life as a cycle of material recurrence: referring to the lives of men, Seneca says, "Born from nothingness, they go back to nothingness."[46] The Stoics are able to find peace in knowing that there is nothing to look forward to but also nothing to fear, including any fear of the gods.

The Epicureans, by contrast, developed a different perspective. They tried to allay their fears by rejecting the idea that the gods exerted any influence and by rejecting the concept of the afterlife for human beings. They rewrote the cultural norm and believed gods to be calm and placid beings who would not conceive of anger against humans or a desire to harm them.[47] One can understand the appeal of the Epicurean perspective. Rather than being fearful of the gods, who could not be controlled, and being fearful of death and divine judgment in the afterlife, which could not be avoided, one could adopt the idea that the gods were pleasant beings and that they would not interfere with human life. People could enjoy their lives without the fear of the divine.

However, the Epicurean ideals were criticized as a reaction to *deisidaimonia* (δεισιδαιμονία), an extreme fear of the gods, often translated as "superstition" in

---

[43] Thucydides was at one time considered more "scientific" by some scholars in comparison to the history of Herodotus, who seemed to have distorted or invented some of his material, but Thucydides is also suspected of fabricating his history. Cf. Virginia J. Hunter, *Thucydides: The Artful Reporter* (Toronto: Hakkert, 1973).
[44] The Old Stoics, however, did view punishment from retribution as a warning to others. Cf. John M. Rist, *Stoic Philosophy* (Cambridge: Cambridge University Press, 1969), 83.
[45] Epictetus, *Encheiridion* 16 (Oldfather, LCL).
[46] Seneca the Younger, *De Tranquillitate Animi* 15.4 (Basore, LCL).
[47] Lucretius, *De Rerum Natura* 6.68–79.

English, which was significant enough in the culture for both Greek and Roman writers to comment on it. Plutarch devoted an essay to *deisidaimonia*, admonishing those who took their fear of the divine to the extreme:

> Superstition, as the very name (dread of deities) indicates, is an emotional idea and an assumption productive of a fear which utterly humbles and crushes a man, for he thinks that there are gods, but that they are the cause of pain and injury.
>
> τὴν δεισιδαιμονίαν δὲ μηνύει καὶ τοὔνομα δόξαν ἐμπαθῆ καὶ δέους ποιητικὴν ὑπόληψιν οὖσαν ἐκταπεινοῦντος καὶ συντρίβοντος τὸν ἄνθρωπον, οἰόμενον μὲν εἶναι θεούς, εἶναι δὲ λυπηροὺς καὶ βλαβερούς.[48]

Plutarch denigrated superstition as emotional rather than rational, and he was critical of those who adopted the perspective of the gods as the source of pain.[49] Simultaneously, he disapproved of the other extreme, the Epicurean response of rejecting the fear of the gods entirely and presuming that divine judgment did not exist.

In the essay, *That Epicurus Actually Makes a Pleasant Life Impossible*, Plutarch addresses the Epicurean view:

> For Epicurus supposes that fear of punishment is the only motive to which we can properly appeal in deterring from crime. It follows then that we should cram them even fuller of superstitious dread and bring to bear on them the joint array of celestial and terrestrial terrors and chasms and alarms and apprehensions if they are to be shocked by all this into a state of greater honesty and restraint. For they are better off avoiding crime for fear of the next world than committing crimes and spending their lives in insecurity and apprehension.
>
> οὐ γὰρ Ἐπίκουρος ἄλλῳ τινὶ τῆς ἀδικίας οἴεται δεῖν ἀπείργειν ἢ φόβῳ κολάσεων. ὥστε καὶ προσεμφορητέον ἐκείνοις τῆς δεισιδαιμονίας καὶ κινητέον ἐπ' αὐτοὺς ἅμα τὰ ἐξ οὐρανοῦ καὶ γῆς δείματα καὶ χάσματα καὶ φόβους καὶ ὑπονοίας εἰ μέλλουσιν ἐκπλαγέντες ὑπὸ τούτων ἐπιεικέστερον ἔχειν καὶ πρᾳότερον. λυσιτελεῖ γὰρ αὐτοῖς τὰ μετὰ τὸν θάνατον φοβουμένοις μὴ ἀδικεῖν ἢ ἀδικοῦσιν ἐπισφαλῶς ἐν τῷ βίῳ διάγειν καὶ περιφόβως.[50]

Although Plutarch did not approve of the extreme fear of the gods, he said that superstitious dread was preferable to the opposite Epicurean extreme of negating divine judgment entirely. Plutarch would actually promote superstitious dread in those who adopted the Epicurean response. He encouraged a more negative fear of the gods because he thought that it was better to avoid crime for fear of divine punishment rather than living in the insecurity of not believing in an afterlife. Plutarch believed that Epicurean

---

[48] Plutarch, *Moralia* 165C (Babbitt, LCL).

[49] Peter van Nuffelen argues that Plutarch is trying to correct the misconception of the divine world among the superstitious: instead of worshiping the gods as tyrants, the people should recognize the benevolence of the gods who desire to grant peace and wealth. Nuffelen expands on Plutarch's idea of benevolent hierarchy in Peter van Nuffelen, *Rethinking the Gods: Philosophical Readings of Religion in the Post-Hellenistic Period* (Cambridge: Cambridge University Press, 2011), 157–75.

[50] Plutarch, *Moralia* 1104B (Einarson and De Lacy, LCL).

ideals promoted atheism, but he was wrong because the Epicureans did believe in the existence of the gods; they just tried to discount the *fear* of the gods that prevailed in the culture.[51] Plutarch indicates that both responses of *deisidaimonia* and the Epicurean view do not reflect the majority,[52] but they seem to have gained enough popularity for Plutarch to write his critical essays to correct those who might wish to adopt either view.

Plutarch was not alone in his criticisms of the extreme responses to divine fear in the culture. Cicero, a few decades earlier, was similarly critical of the Epicureans and their response to superstition in his *De Natura Deorum* (On the Nature of the Gods):

> For the doctrines of all these thinkers abolish not only superstition, which implies a groundless fear of the gods, but also religion, which consists in piously worshipping them.
>
> Horum enim sententiae omnium non modo superstitionem tollunt in qua inest timor inanis deorum, sed etiam religionem quae deorum cultu pio continetur.[53]

Cicero condemned the Epicureans for rejecting the fear of the gods because the rejection of this fear was essentially rejecting the gods themselves. Like Plutarch, he acknowledged that the fear could develop into an extreme, fearful superstition, but it did not mean that the fear should be rejected completely.[54]

Cicero confronted Epicurus's claim that he could detach himself from such fears:

> Epicurus however does actually think that the gods exist, nor have I ever met anybody more afraid than he was of those things which he says are not terrible at all, I mean death and the gods.
>
> Ille vero deos esse putat, nec quemquam vidi qui magis ea quae timenda esse negaret timeret, mortem dico et deos.[55]

According to Cicero, Epicurus may have purported to be free from superstition and fear, but in actuality, Epicurus himself suffered from a severe fear of the gods. In response, Epicurus developed a philosophy that promoted the absence of divine judgment to allay his own extreme fear of death. Cicero's explanation is plausible because fear of the divine was indeed a part of the culture and was likely promoted in Athens, where Epicurus may have been raised. According to Diogenes Laertius, who passionately defended Epicurean thought, Epicurus was a citizen of Athens,[56] which

---

[51] For most of antiquity, Epicureans were considered to be "the atheists," but Epicurus himself was actually fiercely critical of atheists. Cf. Tim Whitmarsh, *Battling the Gods: Atheism in the Ancient World* (London: Faber and Faber, 2016), 173–7.

[52] Plutarch, *Moralia* 1104B–C.

[53] Cicero, *De Natura Deorum* 1.117–18 (Rackham, LCL).

[54] It should be noted that *superstitio* is not considered to be completely synonymous with *deisidaimonia*. While both terms did refer to the excessive and demeaning behavior toward the gods, *deisidaimonia* did not usually include magic or the practices of foreigners. Cf. Beard, North, and Price, *Religions of Rome*, 225. Cicero, however, is clearly similar to Plutarch in that he is criticizing the Epicurean perspective on the fear of the gods.

[55] Cicero, *De Natura Deorum* 1.86 (Rackham, LCL).

[56] Diogenes Laertius, *Lives of Eminent Philosophers* 10.1.

was known for its cult worship including a prominent cult of the war god Ares,[57] who, as seen above, was also closely affiliated with his son Phobos, the god of fear. Epicurus probably noticed that some, including himself, were consumed by the fear of death and the fear of divine wrath, and, in a countercultural response, determined that no one had to fear the gods because man did not exist after death.

The Johannine Response to Fear

With this background of fear in mind, we now turn back to the fear in the First Letter of John (4:18):

> There is no fear in love, but perfect love casts out fear; for fear has to do with punishment, and whoever fears has not been perfected in love.
>
> φόβος οὐκ ἔστιν ἐν τῇ ἀγάπῃ ἀλλ' ἡ τελεία ἀγάπη ἔξω βάλλει τὸν φόβον, ὅτι ὁ φόβος κόλασιν ἔχει, ὁ δὲ φοβούμενος οὐ τετελείωται ἐν τῇ ἀγάπῃ.

As we have established, this fear is not the Jewish conception of divine reverence that aligns love with fear for God. More likely, the First Letter is referring to the culture of fear in the Greco-Roman world, which included the extreme of superstitious *deisidaimonia*.

While the Stoics and Epicureans offered their responses to the fear of the divine in the culture, the writer of 1 John proclaims another countercultural response,[58] which embraces love and results in boldness on the day of judgment (4:17):

> Love has been perfected among us in this: that we may have boldness on the day of judgment, because as he is, so are we in this world.
>
> ἐν τούτῳ τετελείωται ἡ ἀγάπη μεθ' ἡμῶν, ἵνα παρρησίαν ἔχωμεν ἐν τῇ ἡμέρᾳ τῆς κρίσεως, ὅτι καθὼς ἐκεῖνός ἐστιν καὶ ἡμεῖς ἐσμεν ἐν τῷ κόσμῳ τούτῳ.

The writer explains that those who embrace the perfect love[59] of God may have "boldness" (παρρησία), a word that he uses three other times in the letter in having boldness before Jesus or God (2:28;[60] 3:21), and in making requests to him (5:14). The

---

[57] Pausanias 1.8.4.
[58] Philosophizing on death and afterlife in the Gospel of John also suggests some competition with Stoic and Epicurean ideals, cf. Jamie Clark-Soles, *Death and Afterlife in the New Testament* (New York: T&T Clark, 2006), 135–49.
[59] The idea of perfect love or being perfected in love is seen at 1 Jn 2:5; 4:12, 17, 18. The complexities of this love being "perfect" or "completed," and its implications in relation to the Johannine community loving one another and loving God are discussed in David Rensberger, "Completed Love: 1 John 4:11–18 and the Mission of the New Testament Church," in *Communities in Dispute: Current Scholarship on the Johannine Epistles*, ed. R. Alan Culpepper and Paul N. Anderson, 237–71 (Early Christianity and its Literature 13; Atlanta: SBL Press, 2014).
[60] In 2:28, Jesus is not named, and the verse simply says, "before him at his coming" (ἀπ' αὐτοῦ ἐν τῇ παρουσίᾳ αὐτοῦ), but this is likely a reference to Jesus' second coming. Cf. παρουσία at Mt. 24:27, 37, 39; 1 Cor. 15:23; 1 Thess. 2:19; 3:13.

idea of boldness "on the day of judgment" (ἐν τῇ ἡμέρα τῆς κρίσεως), a phrase that appears only once (1 Jn 4:17) in Johannine literature,[61] would have been a radical idea in the context of the culture because, as we have seen, judgment in the culture was often perceived as belonging to the gods who had supernatural powers.

One was not supposed to be bold before the gods in the Greco-Roman world because it operated in a culture of honor and shame.[62] The cultural expectation would be honor or shame before the gods based on a person's behavior. The writer of 1 John seems to allude to this aspect of the culture in his initial reference to boldness, in which he contrasts boldness to being ashamed (αἰσχύομαι)[63] before Jesus (2:28):

And now, little children, remain in him, so that when he is revealed we may have boldness and not be put to shame before him at his coming.

Καὶ νῦν, τεκνία, μένετε ἐν αὐτῷ, ἵνα ἐὰν φανερωθῇ σχῶμεν παρρησίαν καὶ μὴ αἰσχυνθῶμεν ἀπ' αὐτοῦ ἐν τῇ παρουσίᾳ αὐτοῦ.

In this verse, the author had called his spiritual disciples to attention again with the vocative "little children" (τεκνία, cf. 2:1, 12), and he had exhorted them to remain "in him" (ἐν αὐτῷ), referring to their *pistis* in Jesus.

The writer of 1 John wants the Johannine believers to know that if they remain in Jesus, they can have boldness (παρρησία) and not be put to shame (μὴ αἰσχυνθῶμεν) when they stand before him on the eschatological day of divine judgment. Although the "day of judgment" (ἡμέρα κρίσεως) only appears once in 1 John (4:17), the similar language of boldness (παρρησία) and the Johannine believers being "before him at his coming" (ἀπ' αὐτοῦ ἐν τῇ παρουσίᾳ αὐτοῦ) indicates that the day of divine judgment is likely being referenced in Chapter 2 as well (2:28).[64] This further supports that the writer has the culture in mind in Chapter 4 as he delineates the differences between the Johannine community and the world around them, and the subsequent contention that results from their differences. While much of the Greco-Roman culture is fearful of divine punishment (4:18), the Johannine believers who remain in God may be bold before him on the day of judgment (2:28; 4:17).

The writer of 1 John refers to a future eschatology multiple times in the letter (cf. 2:18, 28; 3:2; 4:17),[65] and he offers an explanation as to why the Johannine believers may have boldness on the day of judgment: "because as he is, so are we in this world," (ὅτι καθὼς ἐκεῖνος ἐστιν καὶ ἡμεῖς ἐσμεν ἐν τῷ κόσμῳ τούτῳ, 4:17). As the believers

---

[61] References to a "day of judgment" appear elsewhere in the NT at Mt. 10:15; 11:22, 24; 12:36; 2 Pet. 2:9; 3:7; cf. Jude 6. Jewish apocalyptic literature contains the concept of a judgment day (cf. Schnackenburg, *The Johannine Epistles*, 246), but as demonstrated above, the fear of the divine being incompatible with love (1 Jn 4:18) indicates that the allusion to fear is more likely a reference to the Greco-Roman culture of fear of divine judgment.
[62] Cf. Zeba Crook, "Honor, Shame, and Social Status Revisited," *JBL* 128, no. 3 (Fall 2009): 591–611; John G. Peristiany, ed., *Honour and Shame: The Values of Mediterranean Society*, The Nature of Human Society (London: Weidenfeld and Nicolson, 1966).
[63] Cf. αἰσχύομαι at Lk. 16:3; 2 Cor. 10:8; Phil. 1:20; 1 Pet. 4:16.
[64] Cf. Yarbrough, *1–3 John*, 169.
[65] Cf. Smalley, *1, 2, 3 John*, 258.

remain in the perfect love of God (4:18), they are "as he is" (καθὼς ἐκεῖνος ἐστιν), meaning they resemble the life of Jesus, being bold and unafraid of the temptations and intimidations of the Greco-Roman world (4:18 cf. 2:15-17).[66] While most others in the culture fear authorities on earth and in the heavens, the Johannine writer asserts that his disciples do not have to fear. They do not have to be afraid of coming before God on the day of judgment when they are remaining in God (2:28; 4:15, 16), and they can be like Jesus, who was bold on earth and be fearless of whatever tries to intimidate them in the Greco-Roman culture.

We have discussed Phobos who was representative of the fear in the culture and how he often appeared in the context of military battle. The writer of 1 John offers a counter to this as well, as he is alluding to a different kind of battle with the world in which fear has no place within the perfect love of God. Declaring fear as incompatible with love in 1 John (4:18) makes sense if the author is alluding to the conception of divine fear in Greco-Roman culture. The writer draws a contrast between fear of punishment and perfection in love, and the aspect of fear especially as the antithesis to love demonstrates that he is referring to the fear of the divine, which was a regular part of the Greco-Roman world. Because the members of the Johannine community are living and working in the broader society, it is not surprising that the writer of 1 John would allude to this fear-based culture. The declaration of fear being cast out in the love of God may have resonated especially for those who were raised in this social norm of divine fear before they became members of the Johannine community.

Through the allusion to the negative fear of the gods, the Johannine author demonstrates his countercultural narrative in which the Johannine audience is contending against the ideals of the Greco-Roman culture. He assures his readers that they do not have to dwell on the fear that prevails in the world around them; as they remain in the love of God (3:17; 4:16), respond with love (e.g., 3:11, 14, 23; 4:7, 11, 12), and allow themselves to be perfected in love (4:12, 17, 18), that fear from the culture will be cast out.

4.2 Avoiding the Idols

A Confusing Ending?

In addition to commenting on the negative fear of the divine, the Johannine writer most clearly indicates his awareness and concern for the culture in the way that he concludes his letter. Chapter 5 is triumphant in that it proclaims the victory over the world (5:4) and the assurance of eternal life for the Johannine believers (5:11, 13, 20), but the ending statement is not a note of cheer; it is a final warning (5:21):

> Little children, keep yourselves from idols.
>
> Τεκνία, φυλάξατε ἑαυτὰ ἀπὸ τῶν εἰδώλων.

---

[66] Cf. παρρησία of Jesus at Jn 7:26; 10:24; 16:25, 29; 18:20. See also Section 3.3 and Marshall, *The Epistles of John*, 223.

The writer of 1 John tells his spiritual children to keep themselves, literally, "from the idols" (ἀπὸ τῶν εἰδώλων), and the use of the definitive article suggests that both the writer and the readers knew what "the idols" meant.[67] Many scholars interpreting the letter, however, have found the ending to be confusing, arguing that it seems abrupt and discordant with the previous material.[68]

For many modern readers, the ending to 1 John is confounding because it does not have the standard formal doxology or concluding farewell that is present in the other two Johannine letters (cf. 2 Jn 13; 3 Jn 15). Some scholars have postulated over why the author would have chosen to end the First Letter in this manner when they read the epilogue quite positively.[69] Having given such encouraging declarations that God hears the requests of the Johannine community (5:14-15), and that they are protected from the evil one (5:18), the writer seems to end his pastoral letter in an unexpectedly negative tone with a warning about idols.

From a dramatical standpoint, it would have made more sense to end with the assertion proclaimed just before (5:20):[70]

> And we know that the Son of God has come and has given us understanding so that we may know him who is true; and we are in him who is true, in his Son Jesus Christ. He is the true God and eternal life.
>
> οἴδαμεν δὲ ὅτι ὁ υἱὸς τοῦ θεοῦ ἥκει καὶ δέδωκεν ἡμῖν διάνοιαν ἵνα γινώσκομεν τὸν ἀληθινόν, καὶ ἐσμεν ἐν τῷ ἀληθινῷ ἐν τῷ υἱῷ αὐτοῦ Ἰησοῦ Χριστῷ. οὗτός ἐστιν ὁ ἀληθινὸς θεὸς καὶ ζωὴ αἰώνιος.

The verse would end a sequence of three declarations of what "we know" (vv. 18-20), asserting the shared convictions and intentions of the Johannine community. Some choose to interpret the ending statement itself (5:21) in a positive light, stating that it encourages the readers to go out and implement the message of 1 John, and that it is also an encouragement to embrace the true God while rejecting the false idols.[71]

The central debate regarding the final statement of 1 John is determining what is meant by "the idols" (τά εἴδωλα). Identifying its referent would help explain why the author would have chosen to end his letter with this warning. However, the difficulty is that "the idols" (τά εἴδωλα) appears only once (1 Jn 5:21) among John's Gospel and

---

[67] Brown, *The Epistles of John*, 627.
[68] Marshall, *The Epistles of John*, 255; Lieu, *I, II, & III John*, 234; Brown suggests ten different possibilities, but himself believes that the reference to idols is referring to those who left the Johannine community (Brown, *The Epistles of John*, 627–9).
[69] Many scholars view the epilogue (5:13-21) positively, as a section on "Christian certainties" or "assurances of faith." Cf. Marshall, *The Epistles of John*, 242; R. Alan Culpepper, *The Gospel and Letters of John* (Nashville, TN: Abingdon Press, 1998), 273. Lieu interestingly separates out 5:4-13 from 5:14-21 and entitles the latter section "Exercising the Privileges of Life" to argue that it is not an awkward epilogue or appendix but a summation and exhortation of faithful adherence to what has preceded (Lieu, *I, II, & III John*, 220).
[70] Lieu, *I, II, & III John*, 234.
[71] Cf. Strecker, *The Johannine Letters*, 214; Daniel Akin, *1, 2, 3 John* (NAC 38; Nashville, TN: Broadman & Holman Publishers, 2001), 215.

the Johannine Letters and only a few times elsewhere in the New Testament.[72] Thus, it is challenging for modern readers to discern precisely what the Johannine teacher is trying to caution against.

Scholars have suggested a myriad of possibilities. The use of the aorist imperative with the definite article for "idols" might suggest that there is a specific issue that the writer of 1 John is trying to address rather than a general problem of idols. If that were the case, then perhaps the εἴδωλα could be a shorthand for the food sacrifices (εἰδωλόθυτα, cf. 1 Cor. 8:1, 4, 7, 10; Rev. 2:14, 20), which are addressed as a problem in other New Testament texts.[73] Another suggestion is that the warning has a specific political focus with regard to enforced apostasy in the Empire, and that the Johannine author is writing his letter to encourage the community to face the possibility of martyrdom.[74] A third possibility is a metaphorical interpretation, which would understand "the idols" as a reference to sin, either in general or specifically in relation to the sin of apostasy.[75]

The vast majority of commentators on 1 John have chosen to take a conceptual view of τὰ εἴδωλα, assuming its referent to be existent only in the mind, such as false teachings, false beliefs, and false conceptions of God.[76] Even though all other occurrences of the term εἴδωλον in the New Testament relate to the polytheistic religion of the Greco-Roman culture, these scholars regard "the idols" of 1 John to be an anomaly because they do not detect any cultural allusions in the letter. Thus, a concluding warning about Greco-Roman gods would seem sudden and out of place. Instead, the scholars who hold a conceptual view of the idols tend to read 1 John as a letter focused entirely on the internal ecclesial issues of the Johannine community, and they see "the idols" as a graphic expression of "false gods" in antithesis to the "true God" emphasized three times in the verse before (5:20).[77]

With this conceptual interpretation, "the idols" would be identified with christological heresies that are assumed in the letter (2:22; 4:2-3, 15; 5:1, 5, 6), and the "antichrist," for example, would be considered an "idolater" who is promoting a heretical christology.[78] Some scholars like J. N. Suggit try to appeal to a classical Greek meaning of εἴδωλον (as we shall see further below) as a "phantom," and interpret the

---

[72] The word εἴδωλον appears at Acts 7:41, 15:20; Rom. 2:22; 1 Cor. 8:4, 7; 10:19; 12:2; 2 Cor. 6:16; 1 Thess. 1:9; and Rev. 9:20.

[73] Cf Painter, *1, 2, and 3 John*, 328-30.

[74] Cf. M. J. Edwards, "Martyrdom and the 'First Epistle' of John," *NovT* 31, Fasc. 2 (April 1989): 164-71.

[75] Cf. Wolfgang Nauck, *Die Tradition und der Charakter des ersten Johannesbriefes: zugleich ein Beitrag zur Taufe im Urchristentum und in der alten Kirche* (Tübingen: Mohr, 1957), 136-8; Schnackenburg, *The Johannine Epistles*, 263-4.

[76] Terry Griffith, *Keep Yourselves from Idols a New Look at 1 John* (JSNTSup 233; London: Sheffield Academic Press, 2002), 14. Examples of scholars who hold this view: F. F. Bruce, *The Epistles of John: Introduction, Exposition and Notes* (London: Pickering & Inglis, 1978), 128; Rudolf Bultmann takes εἴδωλα in the sense of false gods (1 Cor. 8:4, 7; 1 Thess. 1:9) (*The Johannine Epistles*, 90ff.); William Loader, *The Johannine Epistles* (EC; London: Epworth, 1992), 80; David Rensberger, *1 John, 2 John, 3 John* (Nashville, TN: Abingdon, 1997), 144-5; Colin Kruse, *The Letters of John* (PNTC; Grand Rapids: Eerdmans, 2000), 202; Marianne Meye Thompson, *1-3 John* (IVP New Testament Commentary Series; Downers Grove, IL: InterVarsity Press, 1992), 38; Marshall, *The Epistles of John*, 255-6; Smalley, *1, 2, 3 John*, 309-10; Brown, *The Epistles of John*, 628.

[77] Griffith, *Keep Yourselves from Idols*, 14.

[78] Griffith, *Keep Yourselves from Idols*, 15.

final warning of 1 John (5:21) to be about the heresy of docetism. The concluding statement could then be equated to "keep yourselves away from ghosts."[79] The difficulty with the conceptual interpretation of idols is that it is driven by general theological interpretation, and there is no evidence that the idols are "untrue mental images."[80] If the term εἴδωλον is indeed in opposition to "the true God" in the penultimate verse (5:20), then the primary referent would need to be a Greco-Roman image to bridge the interpretation between "idols" and "false teachings."[81]

A line of interpretation that is frequently acknowledged but also frequently set aside is the interpretation of the "idols" as graven images of the Greco-Roman gods. This interpretation has rightly been reconsidered.[82] It is very plausible that the "idols" of 1 John are referring to the material culture that displayed ubiquitous images of the gods in public, commercial, and domestic areas of life. This section will examine the concept of the "idol" (εἴδωλον) in the culture and in biblical literature to demonstrate that the concluding warning of 1 John (5:21) is consistent with the conquering language against the many opponents outlined in his letter. Just as the reference to divine fear alludes to the conception of fear in the culture (4:18), the final warning against idols at the end of the letter (5:21) is another indication that the writer of 1 John is presenting a countercultural narrative to his audience.

The Greco-Roman "Idol"

The term εἴδωλον within the Greco-Roman world itself did not have the negative sense that is apparent in 1 John. This is unsurprising as worshipping other gods was not an issue within the polytheistic culture replete with statues and man-made artifacts. The statues were not considered to be the gods and goddesses themselves, but material culture did identify with the deities, who could come down temporarily to embody statues and even animals in an epiphanic form.[83] Because devotion to one deity was not required, no one would have been bothered by anyone worshipping multiple gods or even adding to the polytheistic culture (cf. Acts 17:23). Thus, the Greco-Roman nuance of εἴδωλον is not the same type of Johannine εἴδωλον that clearly relates with some negative form of idolatry. Instead, the Greco-Roman εἴδωλον tends to have a more neutral connotation in relation to a soul, phantom, or image.

In some earlier Greek usage, the word εἴδωλον appears to represent an unsubstantiated form.[84] For example, Aeschylus called the loyalty of friends "a shadowy phantom" (εἴδωλον σκιᾶς).[85] However, εἴδωλον often appears to represent a phantom

---

[79] J. N. Suggit, "1 JOHN 5:21: ΤΕΚΝΙΑ, ΦΥΛΑΞΑΤΕ ΕΑΥΤΑ ΑΠΟ ΤΩΝ ΕΙΔΩΛΩΝ," *JTS* 36 no. 2 (October 1985): 389.
[80] Griffith, *Keep Yourselves from Idols*, 15.
[81] Griffith, *Keep Yourselves from Idols*, 17.
[82] See Julian Hills, "'Little children, keep yourselves from idols': 1 John 5:21 Reconsidered," *CBQ* 51, no. 2 (1989): 285–310.
[83] See Platt, *Facing the Gods*.
[84] LSJ s.v. "εἴδωλον."
[85] Aeschylus, *Agamemnon* 839 (Sommerstein, LCL).

that is similar to a soul or a ghost.[86] In the *Odyssey*, for example, εἴδωλον is used in reference to the souls of men:

> Son of Laertes, sprung from Zeus, Odysseus of many devices, stubborn man, what deed yet greater than this will you devise in your heart? How did you dare to come down to Hades, where dwell the unheeding dead, the *eidōla* of men outworn?
>
> διογενὲς Λαερτιάδη, πολυμήχαν᾽ Ὀδυσσεῦ, σχέτλιε, τίπτ᾽ ἔτι μεῖζον ἐνὶ φρεσὶ μήσεαι ἔργον; πῶς ἔτλης Ἀϊδόσδε κατελθέμεν, ἔνθα τε νεκροὶ ἀφραδέες ναίουσι, βροτῶν εἴδωλα καμόντων;[87]

In this context, the rhetorical questions from Achilles to Odysseus might suggest a negative undertone. However, the word εἴδωλον itself does not have a negative nuance, and is instead simply representative of the men who now live in the realm of the dead. In the writings of Pindar, the word εἴδωλον similarly appears in reference to the soul:

> The body of all men is subject to overpowering death, but a living *eidōlon* of life still remains, for it alone is from the gods. It slumbers while the limbs are active, but to men as they sleep, in many dreams it reveals an approaching decision of things pleasant or distressful.
>
> σῶμα μὲν πάντων ἕπεται θανάτῳ περισθενεῖ, ζωὸν δ᾽ ἔτι λείπεται αἰῶνος εἴδωλον· τὸ γάρ ἐστι μόνον ἐκ θεῶν· εὕδει δὲ πρασσόντων μελέων, ἀτὰρ εὑδόντεσσιν ἐν πολλοῖς ὀνείροις δείκνυσι τερπνῶν ἐφέρποισαν χαλεπῶν τε κρίσιν.[88]

However, Pindar adds the dimension of a "living *eidōlon*" (αἰῶνος εἴδωλον), referring to a "living image" that resembles an eternal soul. The living *eidōlon* continues to remain active while men sleep, and it can contribute to both positive and negative encounters in dreams.

The sense of a negative εἴδωλον could be argued in Platonic discourse, in which the concept of the εἴδωλον is applied to the subordinate designation of "unreal" objects:

> While the body is a semblance which attends on each of us, it being well said that the bodily corpses are *eidōla* of the dead, but that which is the real self of each of us, and which we term the immortal soul, departs to the presence of other gods.
>
> τὸ δὲ σῶμα ἰνδαλλόμενον ἡμῶν ἑκάστοις ἕπεσθαι, καὶ τελευτησάντων λέγεσθαι καλῶς εἴδωλα εἶναι τὰ τῶν νεκρῶν σώματα, τὸν δὲ ὄντα ἡμῶν ἕκαστον ὄντως, ἀθάνατον εἶναι ψυχὴν ἐπονομαζόμενον, παρὰ θεοὺς ἄλλους ἀπιέναι δώσοντα λόγον[89]

---

[86] Cf. Homer, *Iliad* 5.451; *Odyssey* 4.796.
[87] Homer, *Odyssey* 11.476 (Murray and Dimock, LCL).
[88] Pindar, *Fragments* 131.3 (Race, LCL); cf. Plutarch, *Letter of Consolation to Apollonius* 35.120C.
[89] Plato, *Laws* 959b (Bury, LCL).

The physical world contrasts with the "real" world of ideas, which reflects absolute truth and beauty. The immortal soul (ἀθάνατος ψυχή) is considered to be the "true self" that is separated from the body (σῶμα), and the body later becomes a phantom image (εἴδωλον) of the dead.[90]

Some writings use εἴδωλον for a reflected image, as in a mirror or when reflected in the water.[91] Aristotle says:

> The most skillful judge of dreams is the man who possesses the ability to detect likenesses; for anyone can judge the vivid dream. By likenesses I mean that the mental pictures are like *eidōlois* in water, as we have said before. In the latter case, if there is much movement, the reflection is not like the original, nor the *eidōla* like the real object.
>
> Τεχνικώτατος δ' ἐστὶ κριτὴς ἐνυπνίων ὅστις δύναται τὰς ὁμοιότητας θεωρεῖν· τὰς γὰρ εὐθυονειρίας κρίνειν παντός ἐστιν. λέγω δὲ τὰς ὁμοιότητας, ὅτι παραπλήσια συμβαίνει τὰ φαντάσματα τοῖς ἐν τοῖς ὕδασιν εἰδώλοις, καθάπερ καὶ πρότερον εἴπομεν. ἐκεῖ δέ, ἂν πολλὴ γίνηται ἡ κίνησις, οὐδὲν ὁμοία γίνεται ἡ ἔμφασις καὶ τὰ εἴδωλα τοῖς ἀληθινοῖς.[92]

Like Pindar above, Aristotle talks about the εἴδωλον in the context of dreams, and like Plato, he suggests the distinction between what is real and what is a reflection of the real.

Cassius Dio seems to adopt a similar use of the word εἴδωλον with regard to phantom figures. He refers to several supernatural events after the Battle of Alexandria in 30 BCE:

> Meanwhile comets were seen and dead men's *eidōla* appeared, the statues frowned, and Apis bellowed a note of lamentation and burst into tears.
>
> κἂν τούτῳ καὶ ἀστέρες κομῆται ἑωρῶντο, καὶ νεκρῶν εἴδωλα ἐφαντάζετο, τά τε ἀγάλματα ἐσκυθρώπασε, καὶ ὁ Ἆπις ὀλοφυρτικόν τι ἐμυκήσατο καὶ κατεδάκρυσε.[93]

Dio frequently uses εἴδωλον to refer to ghosts or phantoms in his writings,[94] and this may suggest that both Greeks and Romans commonly understood the term in this way. However, the word εἴδωλον does seem to be used in reference to literal images as well, as seen in Herodotus:

> Along with these Croesus sent, besides many other offerings of no great mark, certain round basins of silver, and a golden female *eidōlon* three cubits high, which the Delphians assert to be the statue of the woman who was Croesus' baker.

---

[90] Cf. similarly Plato, *Phaedo* 66c.
[91] Cf also Plato, *Sophist* 266b.
[92] Aristotle, *On Prophecy in Sleep* 464ᵇ9 (Hett, LCL).
[93] Cassius Dio, *Roman History* 51.17.5 (Cary and Foster, LCL).
[94] For example, Cassius Dio, *Roman History* 37.25.2; 63.16.2; 67.19.2.

> ἄλλα τε ἀναθήματα οὐκ ἐπίσημα πολλὰ ἀπέπεμψε ἅμα τούτοισι ὁ Κροῖσος, καὶ χεύματα ἀργύρεα κυκλοτερέα, καὶ δὴ καὶ γυναικὸς εἴδωλον χρύσεον τρίπηχυ, τὸ Δελφοὶ τῆς ἀρτοκόπου τῆς Κροίσου εἰκόνα λέγουσι εἶναι.[95]

Interestingly, a golden female statue called an εἴδωλον is among the offerings given to Delphi. This would have interesting implications for the εἴδωλα in 1 John if the worshippers of the polytheistic culture also called the statues "εἴδωλα." The Johannine author could simply be using the term that was also used in the culture to refer to the representations of the gods.

A similar type of εἴδωλον appears in the writings of Dionysius of Halicarnassus:

> And lest the people should feel any scruple at having neglected their traditional sacrifices, he [Hercules] taught them to appease the anger of the god by making *eidōla* resembling the men they had been wont to bind hand and foot and throw into the stream of the Tiber, and dressing these in the same manner, to throw them into the river instead of the men, his purpose being that any superstitious dread remaining in the minds of all might be removed, since the semblance of the ancient rite would still be preserved. This the Romans continued to do every year even down to my day a little after the vernal equinox.

> ἵνα δὲ μηδὲν εἴη τοῖς ἀνθρώποις ἐνθύμιον, ὡς πατρίων ἠλογηκόσι θυσιῶν, διδάξαι τοὺς ἐπιχωρίους ἀπομειλιττομένους τὴν τοῦ θεοῦ μῆνιν ἀντὶ τῶν ἀνθρώπων, οὓς συμποδίζοντες καὶ τῶν χειρῶν ἀκρατεῖς ποιοῦντες ἐρρίπτουν εἰς τὸ τοῦ Τεβέριος ῥεῖθρον, εἴδωλα ποιοῦντας ἀνδρείκελα κεκοσμημένα τὸν αὐτὸν ἐκείνοις τρόπον ἐμβαλεῖν εἰς τὸν ποταμόν, ἵνα δὴ τὸ τῆς ὀττείας ὅ τι δή ποτε ἦν ἐν ταῖς ἁπάντων ψυχαῖς παραμένον ἐξαιρεθῇ τῶν εἰκόνων τοῦ παλαιοῦ πάθους ἔτι σῳζομένων. τοῦτο δὲ καὶ μέχρις ἐμοῦ ἔτι διετέλουν Ῥωμαῖοι δρῶντες ὀσέτη μικρὸν ὕστερον τῆς ἐαρινῆς ἰσημερίας.[96]

When Dionysius refers to the εἴδωλα, he is talking about the effigies of men, which are given to Saturn (Greek: Cronus) instead of real human sacrifices to appease the anger of the god and to release the superstitious dread they have in their minds (see also the culture of fear in Section 4.1). According to Dionysius, the Romans do this every year, even in his time when the Roman Empire is in its nascent stages. The εἴδωλα here are not images of the gods, but they are related to the worship of the gods.

In the final example, we see that Dionysius does indeed use the term εἴδωλα to refer to statues of the gods:

> We have seen many other *eidōla* also of these gods in ancient temples and in all of them are represented two youths in military garb.

---

[95] Herodotus, *The Persian Wars* 1.51 (Godley, LCL).
[96] Dionysius of Halicarnassus, *Roman Antiquities* 1.38.2–3 (Cary, LCL).

πολλὰ δὲ καὶ ἄλλα ἐν ἱεροῖς ἀρχαίοις εἴδωλα τῶν θεῶν τούτων ἐθεασάμεθα, καὶ ἐν ἅπασι νεανίσκοι δύο στρατιωτικὰ σχήματα ἔχοντες φαίνονται.[97]

The examples of Herodotus and Dionysius demonstrate that the term εἴδωλα could be used not only of man-made effigies but also in reference to the statues of the gods in Roman temples. It is notable that Dionysius's description about the εἴδωλα in the temples also includes the description of the young men who are military guards. The Greek word for "young men" (νεανίσκοι) is the same term that the author of 1 John uses to address the first Johannine conquerors who defeat the evil one (2:13, 14, see also Section 3.1). This further supports that the Johannine author is alluding to the culture with his usage of εἴδωλα and νεανίσκοι, which are terms related to polytheistic worship.

As we have seen, the word εἴδωλον in the Greco-Roman culture seems to be applied often to the intangible, such as a phantom or soul, but it can also refer to tangible, man-made images. These εἴδωλα would not have been seen negatively among Greeks and Romans in the same way that Jews and Christians might view them, but there seems to have been some overlap in the terminology in that εἴδωλα could be applied to the material culture of worship in the Greco-Roman world.

Jewish Idolatry

Because the warning about idols at the end of 1 John is decidedly more negative than the Greco-Roman usage of εἴδωλον, we should now consider the Jewish sense of εἴδωλον which seems to align with the sentiments of the Johannine author.[98] In the Septuagint, the word εἴδωλον appears ninety-one times,[99] which suggests that there is a Semitic influence to the idols of 1 John.[100] Taken on its own, the contrast between "the true God" (5:20) and the idols would not be surprising because the term "idol" (εἴδωλον) was a standard Jewish and subsequently Christian way of referring to the deities other than the one God they worshipped.[101]

The fundamentally negative notion of an idol in the Jewish context is exemplified in the second commandment of the Decalogue (Exod. 20:4; cf. Deut. 5:8):

> You shall not make for yourself an idol, whether in the image of anything that is in heaven above, or that is on the earth beneath, or that is in the water under the earth.
>
> οὐ ποιήσεις σεαυτῷ εἴδωλον οὐδὲ παντὸς ὁμοίωμα ὅσα ἐν τῷ οὐρανῷ ἄνω καὶ ὅσα ἐν τῇ γῇ κάτω καὶ ὅσα ἐν τοῖς ὕδασιν ὑποκάτω τῆς γῆς.

---

[97] Dionysius of Halicarnassus, *Roman Antiquities* 1.68.2 (Cary, LCL). Dionysius also refers to bronze statues of animals as εἴδωλα (1.59.5), and like other writers, he refers to the more ghostly figures (cf. 1.77.2; 6.13.4; 7.68.4; 10.2.3).
[98] For a more Jewish interpretation of the idols of 1 John (5:21), cf. Griffith, *Keep Yourselves from Idols*, and Hills, "Little Children, Keep Yourselves from Idols."
[99] For example, Gen. 31:19; Lev. 19:4; Num. 33:52; 2 Kgs 23:24; 1 Chron. 16:26; 2 Chron. 34:7; Ps. 135:15 (LXX 134:15); Isa. 30:22; Jer. 16:19; Hos. 8:4.
[100] Painter, *1, 2, and 3 John*, 327; Yarbrough, *1–3 John*, 323.
[101] Lieu, *I, II, & III John*, 234.

As with the first commandment, which forbids associating with other gods (Exod. 20:3), the second commandment underlines the relationship between Yahweh and the people of Israel by delineating specifications of how Yahweh *is* to be worshipped.[102] The prohibition in worship to Yahweh is in the use of man-made idols that reflect the image of anything in creation on earth, and also anything "in the heaven above" (ἐν τῷ οὐρανῷ ἄνω) suggesting celestial objects such as stars, as well as spiritual or mythopoeic creatures, such as a deity or angelic figure. Using crafted images to provide a concrete center for worship was a common practice to all of Israel's neighbors,[103] and so the commandment against these "idols" demonstrates the distinction of worship between the people of Israel and the other nations.

In Numbers, the word εἴδωλον seems to underscore the gods being from other nations (25:2):

> They invited the people to the sacrifices of their idols, and the people ate of their sacrifices and bowed down to their idols.
>
> καὶ ἐκάλεσαν αὐτοὺς ἐπὶ ταῖς θυσίαις τῶν εἰδώλων αὐτῶν καὶ ἔφαγεν ὁ λαὸς τῶν θυσιῶν αὐτῶν καὶ προσεκύνησαν τοῖς εἰδώλοις αὐτῶν.

The Israelites in this context are having sexual relations with Moabite women and the Moabite gods are labelled "idols." In Hebrew, אֱלֹהִים reflects the general term for "gods,"[104] but in Greek, the use of εἴδωλον makes it clear that this is a foreign god, and that the Israelites are engaged in the worship of a god who is not the Israelite god. Moreover, this worship of a foreign idol is encouraged through interaction with others who were not a part of their community. The Moabite women are instigators toward the worship of the idols.

A similar narrative is presented with respect to King Solomon whose downfall is the result of foreign women who worshipped idols (1 Kgs 11:2):

> From the nations concerning which the Lord had said to the sons of Israel, "You shall not enter into marriage with them, neither shall they with you; lest they incline your heart to follow their idols"; Solomon clung to these in love.
>
> ἐκ τῶν ἐθνῶν ὧν ἀπεῖπεν κύριος τοῖς υἱοῖς Ισραηλ οὐκ εἰσελεύσεσθε εἰς αὐτούς καὶ αὐτοὶ οὐκ εἰσελεύσονται εἰς ὑμᾶς μὴ ἐκκλίνωσιν τὰς καρδίας ὑμῶν ὀπίσω εἰδώλων αὐτῶν εἰς αὐτοὺς ἐκολλήθη Σαλωμων τοῦ ἀγαπῆσαι.

Like the Israelite men who had sexual relations with the Moabite women, King Solomon falters in his relationship with the God of Israel because of his relationships with foreign women. These women lead the Israelite men into worshipping their gods,

---

[102] Cf. John I. Durham, *Exodus* (WBC 3; Waco, TX: Word Books, 1987), 285.
[103] Durham, *Exodus*, 286.
[104] HALOT s.v. "אֱלֹהִים."

which are labelled "idols." The designation of "idol" underscores the negative sense that these are "other" gods and not the "true" God.

There are several scripture references that allude to "idols" that are a part of material culture. For example, in the book of Genesis (31:19):

> Now Laban had gone to shear his sheep, and Rachel stole her father's idols.
>
> Λαβαν δὲ ᾤχετο κεῖραι τὰ πρόβατα αὐτοῦ· ἔκλεψεν δὲ Ραχηλ τὰ εἴδωλα τοῦ πατρὸς αὐτῆς.

The εἴδωλα here are the small statues of the household gods that Rachel steals, presumably for inheritance or headship rights for her husband or for protection on her journey to Canaan.[105]

In Leviticus, the Israelites are forbidden from *making* "idols" (19:4):

> Do not pursue idols or make cast images for yourselves: I am the Lord your God.
>
> οὐκ ἐπακολουθήσετε εἰδώλοις καὶ θεοὺς χωνευτοὺς οὐ ποιήσετε ὑμῖν ἐγὼ κύριος ὁ θεὸς ὑμῶν.

This verse reflects the sentiment that the Israelites should not make any idols of their own because the only true god is the God of Israel. The neighboring nations may have man-made images to represent the gods, but the Israelites should not covet these images and make such idols of their own. The idols that are made by man are not considered to be gods because they are from material that has no spiritual power or authority, as seen in Isaiah (37:19):

> And have hurled their idols into the fire, though they were no gods, but the work of human hands—wood and stone—and so they were destroyed.
>
> καὶ ἐνέβαλον τὰ εἴδωλα αὐτῶν εἰς τὸ πῦρ οὐ γὰρ θεοὶ ἦσαν ἀλλὰ ἔργα χειρῶν ἀνθρώπων ξύλα καὶ λίθοι καὶ ἀπώλεσαν αὐτούς

The idols are the work of human hands, and therefore not really gods at all, and they can be destroyed without consequence.

Outside of the LXX, we see other Jewish writers demonstrate a similar sentiment regarding the εἴδωλα. Josephus, in his *Jewish Antiquities* reflects a negative view of the idols as he writes about wicked Israelite kings:

> This king was shockingly arrogant and lawless in his conduct toward God, worshipping idols and adopting many unseemly foreign practices, but to the people of Israel he was the cause of innumerable benefits.

---

[105] Victor P. Hamilton, *The Book of Genesis: Chapters 18–50* (NICOT; Grand Rapids: Eerdmans, 1995), 292.

οὗτος ὁ βασιλεὺς τὰ μὲν εἰς τὸν θεὸν ὑβριστὴς καὶ παράνομος δεινῶς ἐγένετο εἴδωλά τε σεβόμενος καὶ πολλοῖς ἀτόποις καὶ ξένοις ἐγχειρῶν ἔργοις, τῷ δὲ λαῷ τῶν Ἰσραηλιτῶν μυρίων ἀγαθῶν αἴτιος ὑπῆρξε.[106]

Josephus criticizes the wickedness of Jeroboam (cf. 2 Kgs 14:23) and includes his worshipping of foreign idols as one indication of his failure to be a faithful king of Israel. His designation of the idols is consistent with the LXX passages that identify the foreign gods as "idols."

Interestingly, Philo seems to reflect a Jewish sentiment specifically against the Greco-Roman sentiment of the idols:

> But not only wealth and glory and the like are idols and unsubstantial shadows, but also all those personages, which the myth-makers have invented and spread delusion therewith, building up their false imaginations into a stronghold to menace the truth, and staging as by machinery new gods, in order that the eternal and really existing God might be consigned to oblivion.

> Ἀλλ᾽ οὐ μόνον πλοῦτος καὶ δόξα καὶ τὰ τοιοῦτα εἴδωλα καὶ ἀμενηναὶ σκιαί, ἀλλὰ καὶ πάντες, οὓς οἱ μυθογράφοι διαπλάσαντες ἐξετύφωσαν ἐπιτειχίσαντες τὰς ψευδεῖς δόξας κατὰ τῆς ἀληθείας, θεοὺς καινοὺς ὥσπερ ἀπὸ μηχανῆς εἰσαγαγόντες ἕνεκα τοῦ τὸν ἀίδιον καὶ ὄντα ὄντως θεὸν λήθη παραδοθῆναι.[107]

By referring to the εἴδωλα in relation to unsubstantial shadows (εἴδωλα καὶ ἀμενηναὶ σκιαί), Philo is alluding to the Greco-Roman conceptions of idols as shadows (as discussed above), and he reflects the negative Jewish conception of worshipping an idol that is not the true God. Philo as a Jew in the Greco-Roman world reflects a similar perspective to the Johannine author. The warning about the idols at the end of 1 John (5:21) resembles the negative Jewish conception of idols because he is making a countercultural argument *against* the polytheistic culture of the Greco-Roman world.

Warning against the Idols in 1 John

The writer of 1 John is consistent with both the Jewish conception of the idols and many New Testament texts that reflect a countercultural perspective against the idols of the Greco-Roman culture. The admonition at the end of the First Letter of John is not unusual, as many New Testament writers similarly offer words of caution before they conclude their letter.[108] The caution against the "idols" in 1 John would have

---

[106] Josephus, *Ant.* 9.205 (Marcus, LCL). Cf. 9.99; 9.243; 9.273; 10.50; 10.65; 10.69. Josephus does, however, use the Greco-Roman concept of εἴδωλον as well (cf. Josephus, *War* 5.513).

[107] Philo, *On the Special Laws* 1.28 (Colson, LCL).

[108] Other NT epistles that similarly address concerns and offer admonition in the final lines: for example, Rom. 16:17-20; 1 Cor. 16:13-14; 2 Cor. 13:5, 10; Gal. 6:17; Eph. 6:10-20; Col. 4:5; 1 Thess. 5:22; 2 Thess. 3:6-15; 1 Tim. 5:20; Tit. 3; Phlm. 21; Heb. 13:9, 22; Jas 5; 1 Pet. 5:8; 2 Pet. 3:17; 2 Jn 10–11; 3 Jn 11; Jude 17–23.

become commonplace as it had been a part of Christian polemic, and converts from non-Jewish backgrounds would have internalized the vocabulary of "idols" as well (cf. 1 Cor. 12:2).[109]

In the New Testament in general, εἴδωλον seems to refer to deities worshipped by Gentile nations, appearing most frequently in 1 Corinthians with regard to food offered to idols (8:4, 7; 10:19; 12:2), that is, food offered to Greco-Roman deities.[110] The exception is Stephen in the book of Acts, who refers to the ancient Israelites making a sacrifice to an "idol" (7:41; cf. Exod. 32).[111] This is referring to a golden statue of a calf, which may have been related to the widespread fertility cult of bull worship in the ancient Near East.[112] The other references to idols are clearly related to Greco-Roman worship:[113] the book of Acts makes a clear reference to Gentile Christians abstaining from what is "polluted by idols" (15:20),[114] the letter to the Romans includes a reference to abhorring idols and robbing temples (2:22),[115] 1 Thessalonians lauds the turning away from idols (1:9),[116] and the final reference in Revelation alludes to idolatry in the form of material culture, worshipping statues made of metal, stone, or wood (9:20). The general New Testament usage of "idol" further suggests that the writer of 1 John may also be referring to man-made idols, such as the representations of the deities seen ubiquitously in the material culture of the Greco-Roman world.

In the epilogue of 1 John (5:13-21), the writer recapitulates the concern over sin, which is mentioned in every chapter of the letter,[117] and he reminds the readers of

---

[109] Lieu, *I, II, & III John*, 235.
[110] Cf. Gordon D. Fee, "Εἰδωλόθυτα Once Again: An Interpretation of 1 Corinthians 8–10," *Bib* 61, no. 2 (1980): 183.
[111] The demand from the Israelites to "make gods for us" (ποίησον ἡμῖν θεοὺς) in Acts 7:40 is an indication of explicit participation in polytheism, which violated the first commandment (Exod. 20:3-4). Notably, Josephus omits discussion of the golden calf incident in his history of the nation, probably because his primary readers were polytheists. Cf. Darrell L. Bock, *Acts* (BECNT; Grand Rapids: Baker Academic, 2007), 298.
[112] Moses Aberbach and Leivy Smolar, "Aaron, Jeroboam, and the Golden Calves," *JBL* 86, no. 2 (Jun 1967): 135; cf. T. Worden, "The Literary Influence of the Ugaritic Fertility Myth on the Old Testament," *VT* 3, Fasc. 3 (Jul 1953): 273–97.
[113] Cf. Griffith, *Keep Yourselves from Idols*, 14.
[114] It is likely that the limitations are to keep relations from becoming strained between Jews and Gentiles, and the prohibition relates to participating in Greco-Roman cult worship. Cf. Bock, *Acts*, 506; Ben Witherington, *The Acts of the Apostles: A Socio-rhetorical Commentary* (Grand Rapids: Eerdmans, 1998), 462–5.
[115] Jewish religion in the first century was threatened by Hellenism, particularly because the dispersion of Jews throughout pagan society led to increased need to avoid pagan practices. It is unclear what is meant by robbing temples, but usage of the cognate ἱερόσυλος occurs in Acts 19:37 in reference to Paul not being a temple robber and in the LXX at 2 Maccabees referring to the robbing of the Jerusalem Temple. Cf. Douglas Moo, *The Epistle to the Romans* (NICNT; Grand Rapids: Eerdmans, 1996), 163. Stealing, adultery, and idolatry in Rom. 2:21-2 relate to the Decalogue (Exod. 20:4-5, 14, 15; Deut. 5:8-9, 18, 19) and may have been part of a Jewish polemic against idolatry (cf. Rom. 1:23). Cf. James D. G. Dunn, *Romans 1–8* (WBC 38A; Dallas, TX: Word Books, 1988), 114.
[116] Cf. F. F. Bruce, *1 & 2 Thessalonians* (WBC 45; Waco, TX: Word Books, 1982), 17–18; Leon Morris, *The First and Second Epistles to the Thessalonians: The English Text with Introduction, Exposition and Notes* (NICNT; Grand Rapids: Eerdmans, 1970), 62–3.
[117] In Chapter 5, sin is mentioned seven times within three verses: the noun ἁμαρτία at 5:16 (2x), 17 (2x) and verbal forms of ἁμαρτάνω at 5:16 (2x), 18. The word ἁμαρτία also occurs at 1 Jn 1:7, 8, 9 (2x); 2:2, 12; 3:4 (2x), 5 (2x), 8, 9; 4:10; see also ἁμαρτάνω at 1:10; 2:1 (2x); 3:6 (2x), 8, 9.

their opponent, the evil one who is operating in the world and has power over the "whole world" (5:18-19, cf. 2:13-14; 3:12).[118] Thus, the author is not entirely positive at the end of his letter, as other scholars have suggested,[119] and it is unsurprising that he would choose to conclude with a strong warning. The exhortation to keep away from idols (5:21) is consistent with the tone of contention against the world outside the Johannine community (see Section 3.3), which permeates throughout the letter. Moreover, it emphasizes the primary pastoral concern about conquering the beliefs of the Greco-Roman polytheistic culture, which undermines and threatens their *pistis* in the incarnate Jesus.

The writer of 1 John calls the readers to attention a final time with the vocative "little children" (Τεκνία), an address he has used six times before to indicate his relational but also instructional tone.[120] The address might also be a reminder of their being born of God (cf. 2:29; 3:9; 4:7; 5:1, 4, 18) and being God's children (τέκνα θεοῦ).[121] After the encouraging first-person plural (5:18-20), in which the author affirmed what "we know" as a collective Johannine community protected by God, the vocative address of "little children" now distances the readers, snapping them to attention to receive the final injunction that reveals his main concern.[122]

The pastoral leader tells them to "keep yourselves" (φυλάξατε ἑαυτὰ), which could also be translated "guard yourselves,"[123] or perhaps more helpfully for modern audiences, "keep away" (as in the NLT).[124] The imperative is one of a handful of imperatives from the teacher (cf. 2:15, 28; 3:1, 7, 13; 4:1), most of which exhort the readers to be mindful of potential threats to the community. The use of the reflexive pronoun (5:21) places the emphasis on the personal action of the Johannine readers;[125] each member of the community has their own responsibility, and the concluding injunction is to keep away from a threat, "the idols," which, like the other named threats in the letter, is presumably not a threat that is within the Johannine community. Just as they were warned to not love the world (2:15) and to not believe the false prophets (4:1), the final statement warns against the attraction or power of idols.[126] The Johannine believers need to avoid and guard against the idols in the Greco-Roman culture of the time.

In the Dead Sea Scrolls, sin and idolatry are closely linked and therefore, "keep yourselves from idols" may appear to be synonymous with "keep yourselves from

---

[118] See also Section 3.1.
[119] Cf. the positive perspectives in Marshall, *The Epistles of John*, 242; Culpepper, *The Gospel and Letters of John*, 273.
[120] See τεκνία at 1 Jn 2:1, 12, 28; 3:7, 18; 4:4. Cf. the similar vocative, παιδία, at 2:14, 18.
[121] The word τέκνον appears in the Johannine letters in different contexts (such as God's children, the children of the devil, or the elect lady's children) in 1 Jn 3:1, 2, 10 (2x); 5:2; 2 Jn 1, 4, 13; 3 Jn 4.
[122] Lieu, *I, II, & III John*, 234.
[123] LSJ s.v. "φυλάσσω." For φυλάσσω ἀπό, cf. Lk. 12:15; 2 Thess. 3:3; *T. Reub.* 4:8.
[124] The verb φυλάσσω appears only in 5:21 in the Johannine letters (cf. Jesus's disciples being guarded in the world at Jn 12:25, 47; 17:12). The verb is synonymous with τηρέω, which also occurs with the preposition ἀπό (Jas 1:27), but it may be significant that τηρέω with ἀπο in the LXX occurs only at Prov. 7:5, while φυλάσσω with ἀπο appears several times, often warning against contact with dangerous or defiling objects or people (Deut. 23:9 [23:10 LXX]; Josh. 6:18; 1 Sam. 21:4 [21:5 LXX]; Ps. 18:23 [17:24 LXX]; Ezek. 33:8). Cf. Yarbrough, *1-3 John*, 323 n. 2.
[125] Westcott, *The Epistles of St. John*, 197.
[126] Cf. Lieu, *I, II, & III John*, 234.

sin."[127] Indeed, this is a tempting conclusion as "sin" (ἁμαρτία) has been mentioned before this final warning (1 Jn 5:16-18). However, the association of sin and idolatry does not mean that idolatry is a synonym for sin. The adoption of false gods or false conceptions of God is usually associated with sin, and so the writer could be urging his readers to have nothing to do with false ideas of God and the accompanying sins. While the writer of 1 John does express concern about sin and the false understandings of God, he seems to mention idols as his final statement because it reinforces his broader concern: the things in the world that threaten their *pistis*. The focus at the end of 1 John is about knowing the true God, who is Jesus Christ, the Son of God (especially 5:1, 5, 6, 9, 10, 11, 12, 13, 20). What is at stake is eternal life (vv. 11, 13, 20), and the writer wants them to remember that the idols out there in the world are not the true Son of God. In that regard, "keep yourselves from idols" could be synonymous with "keep yourselves from the world," but he uses the word "idols" to emphasize the point that they are not the true God (ὁ ἀληθινὸς θεὸς, 5:20).

In the surrounding culture, the readers of 1 John would see purported deities in their daily lives in the forms of statues, images on buildings, and imprints on their coins, and the majority of people in the Greco-Roman world would not believe what they believe. However, that belief (*pistis*) is precisely what separates them from the rest of the world, and by the very nature of believing in Jesus as the Son of God, they are overcoming the prevailing culture full of idols that demand their attention on a regular basis. There is a battle of *pistis* between the Johannine community and the *pistis* in the culture, and conquering the world would involve a battle in which the Johannine believer was constantly fighting against the overwhelming majority of polytheistic worshippers.

I. Howard Marshall says, "Nowhere in the letter has John spoken of the danger of worship of the material images and false gods whose cults flourished in the world of his readers."[128] Indeed, the writer does not directly mention material culture or speak of worshipping other deities as in other places in the New Testament.[129] However, the warning would not necessarily have to *negate* the inclusion of Greco-Roman deities of the culture as some scholars have suggested.[130] The writer does not have to address the deities directly because it is an obvious part of the culture. His primary concern is not about the ubiquitous images of the gods and goddess in the surrounding culture; the main issue is about ensuring that the readers keep their victorious *pistis* in Jesus and that they do not allow it to be swayed by any idol in their surroundings, including the culture of worship that they see at the markets, temples, and neighbors' houses in their everyday life.

Endings of letters are important, as they are often the most memorable, and it is the final opportunity to convey the writer's message.[131] In the case of 1 John, the author wants the final word to be about idols and to emphasize that his disciples should

---

[127] Marshall, *The Epistles of John*, 255.
[128] Marshall, *The Epistles of John*, 256.
[129] For example, Acts 17:29; Rom. 1:23; 1 Cor. 8:5ff, 10:14; 1 Thess. 1:9; Rev. 13:15.
[130] Marshall, *The Epistles of John*, 255. Other scholars admit the possibility of the community being warned against the idols that were so common in first-century religion in the culture: for example, Culpepper, *The Gospel and Letters*, 273; Yarbrough, *1–3 John*, 324; Painter, *1, 2, and 3 John*, 329–30.
[131] Cf. Morna D. Hooker, *Endings: Invitations to Discipleship* (London: SCM Press, 2003), 2.

avoid them. This could be warning about idols in general, that is, anything that would detract them away from acknowledging Jesus as the true God (cf. 5:20). However, the conquering language and the allusions to the culture throughout the letter suggest that he may be referring more specifically to the Greco-Roman deities represented in material culture.

To end the letter with a cautionary exhortation indicates that the ultimate concern for the writer is about the culture and its influences that would sway the Johannine audience from their victorious *pistis* (5:4-5). The injunction to keep themselves from these idols places an urgency on what the readers should avoid. The concluding warning about the idols (5:21) offers even greater support that the Johannine writer is crafting a countercultural narrative because he is concerned about the dominant culture of the time that did not share the core *pistis* of the Johannine community. He gives this concluding warning to ensure that they continue to resist the influences of the Greco-Roman world, and to continue to conquer the culture through their *pistis* in Jesus as the incarnate Son of God.

5

Conquering the World with *Pistis*

As we have seen, the author of 1 John frames his letter in a countercultural narrative because of his concern about the *pistis* of his readers. The sections below will examine the associations of *pistis* in the culture, including the *pistis* that led to Roman victory and the expected *pistis* of the people to the emperor, who was known as the *divi filius*, the divine son. Then the study will turn to the *pistis* language of 1 John to demonstrate that the author deliberately frames his letter in a countercultural narrative that subjugates the Greco-Roman culture to the victorious Johannine *pistis*.

5.1 *Pistis* and Greco-Roman Victory

Pistis of the Romans

The writer of 1 John portrays the Johannine believers as the conquerors of his letter (2:13, 14; 5:4, 5), but in the culture of the Roman Empire, the soldiers operating under the authority of the emperor would have been representative of the conquerors of the time[1]; it was the clout of military victories that allowed Rome to come into power. The domination of the Empire was actually the fruit of a consistent rise to power that escalated during the Middle Republic, and the Roman military was able to achieve some of its victories through a strategy that involved a *pistis* to the Romans.

The Greek historian Polybius was fascinated that Rome had come to dominate the Mediterranean in such a short period of time, and he wrote his *Histories* to help explain the phenomenon. In his accounts, he notes that the "*pistis* of the Romans" (εἰς τὴν Ῥωμαίων πίστιν) was a vital and practical element of their achieving victory. In this *pistis*, other nations subjugated themselves, entrusting their nation to their Roman conquerors. Polybius's narratives include battles that demonstrate that the culture of Roman military victory was, in part, established through *pistis*.

In the account of the Illyrian campaign, Polybius describes the Romans setting sail with 200 ships in 229 BCE.[2] Gnaeus, one of the Roman consuls, stops at the island of Corcyra, and, according to Polybius:

---

[1] As we have seen in Section 2.2, the soldiers and the emperor also looked to the goddess Nike to achieve their military victories.
[2] Polybius 2.11.1–8. Cf. Erich Gruen, "Greek Πίστις and Roman *Fides*," *Athenaeum* NS 60 (1982): 62.

The Corcyreans were much relieved to see the Romans arrive, and they gave up the Illyrian garrison to them with the consent of Demetrius. They unanimously accepted the Romans' invitation to place themselves under their protection, considering this the sole means of assuring for the future their safety from the violence of the Illyrians. The Romans, having admitted the Corcyreans to their friendship, set sail for Apollonia, Demetrius in future acting as their guide.

οἱ δὲ Κερκυραῖοι τὴν παρουσίαν τῶν Ῥωμαίων ἀσμένως ἰδόντες, τήν τε φρουρὰν παρέδοσαν τῶν Ἰλλυριῶν μετὰ τῆς τοῦ Δημητρίου γνώμης, αὐτοί τε σφᾶς ὁμοθυμαδὸν ἔδωκαν παρακληθέντες εἰς τὴν τῶν Ῥωμαίων πίστιν, μίαν ταύτην ὑπολαβόντες ἀσφάλειαν αὑτοῖς ὑπάρχειν εἰς τὸν μέλλοντα χρόνον πρὸς τὴν Ἰλλυριῶν παρανομίαν. Ῥωμαῖοι δὲ προσδεξάμενοι τοὺς Κερκυραίους εἰς τὴν φιλίαν ἔπλεον ἐπὶ τῆς Ἀπολλωνίας, ἔχοντες εἰς τὰ κατάλοιπα τῶν πραγμάτων ἡγεμόνα τὸν Δημήτριον.[3]

The Corcyreans were supposedly relieved to see the Romans arrive because they wanted to have protection from the violence of the Illyrians, and the Corcyreans therefore unanimously accepted the invitation to the "*pistis* of the Romans" (εἰς τὴν Ῥωμαίων πίστιν),[4] and the Romans, having admitted them "to their friendship" (εἰς τὴν φιλίαν),[5] set sail for Apollonia, where the next people group is also received into their *pistis*.

One may wonder to what extent the Corcyreans were truly relieved to see the Romans, but Polybius suggests that the Corcyreans were actively encouraged to give themselves into the "*pistis* of the Romans," which is translated above[6] as "to place themselves under their protection." This *pistis* relationship is seemingly not a demand for the Corcyreans to completely subjugate themselves to the Romans and surrender everything in their possession.[7] Instead, it is portrayed in a positive light, albeit an obviously asymmetrical one, in which there is a form of mutual benefit: the Corcyreans gain military security against the Illyrians, and the Romans gain "friendship" (φιλία), that is, assistance for future battles in the area.[8] The Romans subsequently take other communities into their *pistis* including Epidamnus and Issa.[9]

Though Polybius describes such abovementioned events in which the *pistis* to the Romans appears to be more positive and mutually beneficial, he also includes accounts in which the Romans appear to take a harsher tone with those who refuse their *pistis*, as described in the narrative of the Roman leader Flaminius lecturing the Aetolians in 197 BCE:

---

[3] Polybius 2.11.5–7 (Paton, Walbank, and Habicht, LCL).
[4] Polybius 2.11.5.
[5] Polybius 2.11.7. Cf. another association of φιλία and πίστις at 3.100.3.
[6] As noted in the introduction, all translations of classical texts are from the digital LCL with minor adjustments where appropriate.
[7] Cf. Gruen, "Greek Πίστις and Roman *Fides*," 62.
[8] Demetrius, who gave up Corcyra, later guides the Romans in conquering other cities (Polybius 2.11.3–7).
[9] Polybius 2.11.10, 12.

Flamininus said that they ought not to take any of the other towns, but only Phthiotic Thebes. For the Thebans, when on approaching the town with his army he demanded that they should submit to Rome, had refused. So that, now that they had been reduced by force of arms, he had a right to decide as he chose about them.

ὁ δὲ Τίτος τῶν μὲν ἄλλων οὐκ ἔφη δεῖν οὐδεμίαν, Θήβας δὲ μόνον τὰς Φθίας· Θηβαίους γὰρ ἐγγίσαντος αὐτοῦ μετὰ τῆς δυνάμεως καὶ παρακαλοῦντος σφᾶς εἰς τὴν Ῥωμαίων πίστιν οὐ βουληθῆναι· διὸ νῦν, κατὰ πόλεμον ὑποχειρίων ὄντων, ἔχειν ἐξουσίαν ἔφη βουλεύεσθαι περὶ αὐτῶν ὡς ἂν προαιρῆται.[10]

On the one hand, the cities that have accepted the *pistis* of the Romans seem to receive beneficence and guardianship, and they are considered untouchable by any other group that might threaten them lest the intruders come under the wrath of the Romans as well.[11] On the other hand, those who refuse the *pistis* of the Romans appear to be left extremely vulnerable, as they are subject to utter destruction, not only from the Romans but also from any other potential conqueror. Thus, receiving the *pistis* of the Romans seems to be an almost unavoidable choice for the smaller nations and is clearly an effective strategy for the Roman conquerors, who can achieve military victory with little to no loss of life or resources.

In one of the most well-known accounts to modern scholars from Polybius, there is an added dimension to the *pistis* of the Romans. Polybius presents what he interprets as a cultural misunderstanding between Greek *pistis* and Roman *fides* during Rome's campaign against the Aetolians in 191 BCE.[12] After the battle of Thermopylae in which the Seleucid king, Antiochus III, had to return to Asia, the Aetolians were left in Greece to battle against the Romans, who went on to another victory at Heraclea Trachinia.[13] Phaeneas, the military commander of the Aetolians, decides that a delegation should go to Manius Acilius Glabrio, the Roman general, to beg for an armistice. The Aetolian leaders including Phaeneas himself attempt to discuss with Glabrio at length, but Polybius says that they are cut short because Glabrio claimed to be too busy dealing with the plunder from Heraclea. Glabrio agrees to a temporary ten-day armistice and sends them back accompanied by Lucius Valerius Flaccus to oversee the process.

Flaccus is unsympathetic to the Aetolians who try to speak about former alliances with the Romans. He blames the Aetolians for their current situation and advises them to place themselves in the *pistis* of the Romans, but the whole situation is misunderstood, Polybius claims, because of a different understanding between Greek *pistis* and Roman *fides*:

> The Aetolians, after some further observations about the actual situation, decided to refer the whole matter to Glabrio, committing themselves "to the faith" of the

---

[10] Polybius 18.38.5–6 (Paton, Walbank, and Habicht, LCL).
[11] Cf. Polybius 18.38.9.
[12] Polybius 20.9, cf. Livy 36.27. Cf. Gruen, "Greek Πίστις and Roman *Fides*," 50; Morgan, *Roman Faith and Christian Faith*, 97.
[13] Heraclea Trachinia was a colony founded by the Spartans in 426 BCE that was forced to join the Aetolian Confederacy in 280 (cf. Paus. 10.20.9). For the siege by the Romans, see Livy 36.22.5–24.12.

Romans,[14] not knowing the exact meaning of the phrase, but deceived by the word "faith" as if they would thus obtain more complete pardon. But with the Romans to commit oneself to the faith of a victor is equivalent to surrendering at discretion.

οἱ δ' Αἰτωλοὶ καὶ πλείω λόγον ποιησάμενοι περὶ τῶν ὑποπιπτόντων ἔκριναν ἐπιτρέπειν τὰ ὅλα Μανίῳ, δόντες αὑτοὺς εἰς τὴν Ῥωμαίων πίστιν, οὐκ εἰδότες τίνα δύναμιν ἔχει τοῦτο, τῷ δὲ τῆς πίστεως ὀνόματι πλανηθέντες, ὡς ἂν διὰ τοῦτο τελειοτέρου σφίσιν ἐλέους ὑπάρξοντος. παρὰ <δὲ> Ῥωμαίοις ἰσοδυναμεῖ τό τ' εἰς τὴν πίστιν αὑτὸν ἐγχειρίσαι καὶ τὸ τὴν ἐπιτροπὴν δοῦναι περὶ αὑτοῦ τῷ κρατοῦντι.[15]

Polybius presents the situation as a case of cultural misunderstanding, explaining that *pistis* to the Greeks and *fides* to the Romans had different connotations. Polybius explains that, because they had been allies in the past, the Greeks believed that committing "to the *pistis* of the Romans" would engender more sympathy and mercy because of their humility in submitting to the Romans. However, the Romans equated *pistis/fides* to unconditional surrender, and the misunderstanding between Greek *pistis* and Roman *fides* led to the subjugation of the Aetolians in which Glabrio did not hesitate in making harsh demands and threatening to put the Aetolian ambassadors in chains.[16]

There has been significant debate from modern scholars about this interaction, particularly regarding the issue of whether Greeks and Romans actually understood *pistis* and *fides* differently and whether *pistis/fides* to the Romans was equal to *deditio* (unconditional surrender). Erich Gruen in his well-known article, "Greek Πίστις and Roman *Fides*," was especially influential to later scholarship, as he pointed out that there is seemingly no other author, earlier or later, who questions the mutual intelligibility of *pistis/fides* between Greek and Latin speakers.[17] Moreover, Polybius himself indicates at other points of his *Histories* that *pistis* to the Romans implied some mutual expectation of leniency.[18] One of these interactions involved the same Phaeneas who, six years prior, had been informed by Flaminius regarding Roman obligations toward cities that entered into Rome's *pistis/fides*.[19] Thus, Phaeneas would have already known the implications of surrendering to the Romans, and he likely would have discussed these at length with Flaccus before agreeing to do so.[20]

---

[14] It is interesting that the LCL translation for εἰς τὴν Ῥωμαίων πίστιν here is "'to the faith' of the Romans" when other sections have been translated as "to place themselves under their protection" (2.11.5), "submit to Rome" (18.38.5), or "surrendered to the Romans" (18.38.9). The use of the word "faith" may be related to Polybius' emphasis on the cultural misunderstanding of the word *pistis/fides*, as "faith" itself can have different nuances.

[15] Polybius 20.9.10–12 (Paton, Walbank, and Habicht, LCL); cf. Livy 36.27.

[16] Polybius 20.10.5–9.

[17] Gruen, "Greek Πίστις and Roman *Fides*," 63; cf. Morgan, *Roman Faith and Christian Faith*, 98.

[18] For example, Polybius 2.11.5–10; 3.100.3; 18.38.5.

[19] Polybius 18.38.3–9; Livy 33.13.6–12.

[20] Flaccus is also the one who comes to the defense of the Aetolians when Glabrio threatens to put the envoys in chains (Polybius 20.10.10; cf. Livy 36.26.7, 36.28.8); cf. Gruen, "Greek Πίστις and Roman *Fides*," 59.

Gruen explains that the likely reason for Phaeneas's shock and confusion at the whole situation was more likely related to the extreme nature of Glabrio's demands,[21] as Phaeneas himself interrupts Glabrio and says, "But what you demand, O General, is neither just nor Greek."[22] Gruen postulates the likely contributing factor of Glabrio's hot-tempered personality and underhanded motivations. Just as Glabrio had been enraged against the city of Chalcis but was allayed by an intervention from Flaminius,[23] he also seemed to have exploded against Phaeneas and his comments and needed to be mollified by Flaccus.[24] Indeed, Glabrio being a *novus homo*[25] with a history of successful negotiations was probably motivated to be strategic and potentially manipulative here as well. Even Polybius remarks that Glabrio was intending to scare his opponents with his words and actions.[26] Thus, Glabrio's behavior might have been more of an act that backfired when the Aetolians became even angrier and refused to meet to discuss Rome's demands.[27]

Because this seems to be the sole extant narrative of cultural misunderstanding regarding *pistis/fides*, Gruen's argument that Hellenic and Roman perceptions of *pistis/fides* were mutually intelligible makes sense and has been widely accepted by scholars today.[28] However, it still does not explain why Polybius would have offered a cultural explanation to this particular situation when Polybius himself had discussed the *pistis* to the Romans elsewhere (as mentioned above). Polybius would have been an ideal observer of such linguistic and cultural nuances between the Greeks and Romans, having been an Achaean himself who also spent significant time in Rome.[29] Indeed, his awareness of the cultural differences would probably have been developed from his youth, having been a hipparch (cavalry commander) of the Achaean Confederacy in 170 BCE[30] just like his father, Lycortas of Megalopolis, who had (unsuccessfully) been working toward equality with Rome for many years.[31]

---

[21] Gruen, "Greek Πίστις and Roman *Fides*," 67. Cf. Polybius 20.11.6–9.
[22] Polybius 20.11.6 (Paton, Walbank, and Habicht, LCL). Cf. Livy 36.28.4 in which Phaeneas is noted as saying, "What we did was to entrust ourselves to your good faith, not put ourselves in slavery."
[23] Plutarch, *Flaminius* 16.1–2.
[24] Polybius 20.10.7–10.
[25] That is, the first man of a family to reach the senate or the first man of a senatorial family to reach the consulship. Cf. *Bellum Africum* 57; Cicero, *De officiis* 1.138. See also, Henriette van der Blom, *Cicero's Role Models: The Political Strategy of a Newcomer* (Oxford: Oxford University Press, 2010); and T. P. Wiseman, *New Men in the Roman Senate, 139 BC–AD 14* (London: Oxford University Press, 1971).
[26] Polybius 20.10.7.
[27] Polybius 20.10.12–16; cf. Livy 36.28.9–36.29.1 in which the Aetolians actually reject the demands. Gruen, "Greek Πίστις and Roman *Fides*," 56, 67.
[28] Morgan, *Roman Faith and Christian Faith*, 98.
[29] After the Romans triumphed over the Macedonians at Pydna in 168 BCE, Polybius was among a thousand prominent Achaeans deported to Rome and subsequently detailed without trial (cf. Polybius 30.13.6–11; Livy 45.31.9–11; Pausanias 7.10.7–11; Zonaras 9.31). He was able to befriend powerful Romans such as Cornelius Scipio Aemilianus, whom Polybius mentored in preparing Scipio for his public career (cf. Plutarch, *Moralia* 199F).
[30] Polybius 28.6.9.
[31] Cf. Pausanias 9.9.4; Plutarch, *Philopoemen* 21. See also, R. M. Errington, *Philopoemen* (Oxford: Clarendon Press, 1969); Arthur M. Eckstein, "Polybius, Phylarchus, and Historiographical Criticism," *Classical Philology* 108, no. 4 (2013): 314–38.

Thus, it is unclear as to why Polybius would present the issue as a cultural misunderstanding. It is suggested that Polybius was fully aware of what he was doing and that his point was not about asserting that Greek and Latin speakers genuinely understood *pistis* and *fides* differently but that Phaeneas and Glabrio were *pretending* to misunderstand one another for political reasons.[32] Both leaders wanted to get the best possible deal: Phaeneas was motivated to receive clemency for the Aetolians, and Glabrio was motivated to acquire *deditio* and dictate his own terms so that he could add to his accomplishments and rise in political power.[33]

For the purposes of this research, Polybius is valuable in understanding how *pistis/fides* operated in the context of Roman military victories. Both Greeks and Romans experienced the *pistis* of the Romans from opposite ends, as the conquered and the conquerors, respectively. Not all Greeks may have seen themselves as "the conquered ones," and not all Romans may have seen themselves as "conquerors," but both sides would probably have acknowledged that there was an asymmetrical relationship in which the Romans were ultimately the ones in power. The *pistis* of the Romans for the purposes of Roman victory and rule was a significant strategy that helped develop the culture that led to the Roman Empire.

Pistis to the Roman Empire

In the first century CE, Rome continued to achieve victory through an emphasis on *pistis*. The writings of Josephus reveal that the Romans used their strong military to solidify their domination in the Roman Empire. Josephus was a Pharisee, and thus a religious and well-educated Jew, but in his writings, he indicates that his intended audience is not necessarily the Jewish community. When he explains that he is a Pharisee, he compares his training to that of the Greek Stoic school[34] suggesting that he is writing for a Hellenistic audience.[35] Josephus also indicates this in his use of *pistis*, commonly using the intellectual Greek meaning referring to "loyalty," rather than the religious Jewish meaning referring to the faith of the people or the faithfulness of God.[36] Though he comes from a different background to Polybius, Josephus is similar in that he was a historian who chose to write about Rome after he was captured as a prisoner of war.[37] Josephus not only became friendly with some powerful Romans, but he later sided with Rome against his own people, reaping the benefits of his betrayal, which included Roman citizenship and a house that was a former lodging of Vespasian.[38] Josephus was familiar with Polybius's work,[39] and was therefore aware of the idea of the *pistis* of the Romans, but he himself also experienced the concept

---

[32] Morgan, *Roman Faith and Christian Faith*, 98.
[33] Cf. Gruen, "Greek Πίστις and Roman *Fides*," 67.
[34] Josephus, *Life* 12.
[35] Cf. Dennis R. Lindsay, *Josephus and Faith: Πίστις and Πιστεύειν as Faith Terminology in the Writings of Flavius Josephus and in the New Testament* (Leiden: Brill, 1993), 185.
[36] Lindsay, *Josephus and Faith*, 185–7.
[37] Cf. Josephus, *Life* 351.
[38] Josephus, *Life* 416, 423.
[39] Josephus, *Ant.* 12.135–7, 358–9.

firsthand and references several times the fate of cities that did or did not choose to enter into the *pistis* of the Romans.

The language varies slightly between the two historians; while Polybius most often speaks about entering into the *pistis* of the Romans (εἰς τὴν Ῥωμαίων πίστιν), Josephus talks about *pistis* to/with the Romans (τὴν πρὸς Ῥωμαίους πίστιν). It could be argued that entering into the *pistis* of the Romans might suggest a nuance of subjugation in which the conquered people group places themselves under Rome, while *pistis* to/with the Romans could suggest a more positive narrative of partnership. Indeed, in comparison to Polybius, Josephus does seem to present a more positive narrative overall about the relationships between Rome and other nations. Regardless of any underlying nuances, however, the similarities between Josephus and Polybius demonstrate that there was a continued culture of *pistis* in the Roman military context for several centuries not only during the Roman Republic but also into the Roman Empire.

In *Jewish Antiquities,* which relays the history of the Jews to Greek readers, Josephus writes about an edict of Claudius in 41 CE regarding the strife between Jews and Greeks in the city of Alexandria. In response to a petition from Agrippa and Herod, Claudius grants the Jews the right to observe their customs:

> I very gladly consented, not merely in order to please those who petitioned me, but also because in my opinion the Jews deserve to obtain their request on account of their loyalty and friendship to the Romans. In particular, I did so because I hold it right that not even Greek cities should be deprived of these privileges, seeing that they were in fact guaranteed for them in the time of the divine Augustus. It is right, therefore, that the Jews throughout the whole world under our sway should also observe the customs of their fathers without let or hindrance.
>
> ἥδιστα συνεχώρησα οὐ μόνον τοῦτο τοῖς αἰτησαμένοις με χαριζόμενος, ἀλλὰ καὶ αὐτοὺς ὑπὲρ ὧν παρεκλήθην ἀξίους κρίνας διὰ τὴν πρὸς Ῥωμαίους πίστιν καὶ φιλίαν, μάλιστα δὲ δίκαιον κρίνων μηδεμίαν μηδὲ Ἑλληνίδα πόλιν τῶν δικαίων τούτων ἀποτυγχάνειν, ἐπειδὴ καὶ ἐπὶ τοῦ θείου Σεβαστοῦ αὐταῖς ἦν τετηρημένα. καλῶς οὖν ἔχειν καὶ Ἰουδαίους τοὺς ἐν παντὶ τῷ ὑφ' ἡμᾶς κόσμῳ τὰ πάτρια ἔθη ἀνεπικωλύτως φυλάσσειν.[40]

Claudius grants the Jews in Alexandria the right to religious tolerance because of the Jews' *pistis* to the Romans. This religious tolerance toward Jews throughout the Roman world may seem ironic because Claudius was also known for expelling the Jews from Rome.[41] However, the expulsion in Rome, from Claudius's perspective, was likely more about his concern over the political disturbances rather than a concern about religion.[42]

In the immediate context of Jews in Alexandria, Claudius grants religious tolerance because he feels that the Jews deserve it; they have historically demonstrated their loyalty (πίστις) and friendship (φιλία). The use of the word "friendship" might initially

---

[40] Josephus, *Ant.* 19.288–90 (Feldman, LCL).
[41] Cf. Acts 18:2; Suetonius, *Claudius* 25.4.
[42] Cf. Leonard Victor Rutgers, "Roman Policy towards the Jews: Expulsions from the City of Rome during the First Century CE," *Classical Antiquity* 13, no. 1 (April 1994): 66.

appear to undermine the sense that this is a serious *pistis* relationship between the Romans and the Jews. However, the word "friendship" was often used in a military context,[43] and therefore it is not an indication that this *pistis* was a lighthearted one. The context in Alexandria actually involved the threat of violence because the Greeks under the approval of Caligula had been violent against the Jews when they had refused to acknowledge the emperor as a god.[44] Josephus explains that Claudius grants the Jews their deserved benefit of religious tolerance because they had lived in the area from centuries before when they supported Alexander the Great against the Egyptians and remained loyal subjects when Augustus established the Roman Empire.[45]

This account shows Rome's high value for *pistis*, as something that could reap a reward. The steadfastness of keeping *pistis* would create a sense of obligation on the part of the Romans to the extent that Jews would not have to worship the emperor as a god because it contradicted their own religious views. *Pistis* surpassed worship of the emperor because *pistis* for the Romans was not really about religious belief but rather about devotion and loyalty. The Jews in this case had proven their loyalty to Rome, and so their worship of the emperor was not necessary.

For the Romans, *pistis* was important because it ultimately meant keeping the peace, as seen in *Jewish War*. Josephus recounts an event during the time of the emperor Nero in 66 CE when Cestius, the Roman governor of Syria, dispatches the tribune Neapolitanus to Jerusalem to determine why there had been some fighting in the city:

> Having traversed the city and satisfied himself as to the amenable temper of the inhabitants, Neapolitanus went up to the Temple. Here he called the multitude together, highly commended them for their loyalty to the Romans and earnestly exhorted them to keep the peace; then, after paying his devotions to the sanctuary of God from the permitted area, he returned to Cestius.

> ὁ δ' ὡς διοδεύσας πεῖραν ἱκανὴν ἔλαβεν τῆς πραότητος αὐτῶν, εἰς τὸ ἱερὸν ἀναβαίνει. ἔνθα συγκαλέσας τὸ πλῆθος, καὶ πολλὰ μὲν εἰς πίστιν αὐτοὺς τὴν πρὸς Ῥωμαίους ἐπαινέσας, πολλὰ δὲ εἰς τὸ τηρεῖν τὴν εἰρήνην προτρεψάμενος καὶ τοῦ θεοῦ προσκυνήσας ὅθεν ἐξῆν τὰ ἅγια, πρὸς Κέστιον ἐπανῄει.[46]

Neapolitanus had been sent to Jerusalem because the procurator Gessius Florus had accused the Jews of revolt, while the Jews insisted that they had remained loyal to Rome and that Florus was the one who had unfairly attacked them.[47] After verifying that everything seemed to be under control, Neapolitanus commends the Jews for their *pistis* to the Romans and exhorts them "to keep the peace" (εἰς τὸ τηρεῖν τὴν εἰρήνην).

"Keeping the peace" in the *pistis* to the Romans is ultimately about avoiding violence. When the initial *pistis* is extended, the threat of violence is imminent. Once *pistis* is

---

[43] For example, Josephus, *Ant.* 8.163, 8.261, 18.96; cf. Josephus, *War* 1.181, 1.391; Polybius 1.16.6, 2.32.2, 2.58.5, 3.77.5.
[44] Josephus, *Ant.* 19.284.
[45] Josephus, *Ant.* 19.281–2; cf. *War* 2.487; *Apion* 2.42.
[46] Josephus, *War* 2.341 (Thackeray, LCL).
[47] Josephus, *War* 2.333.

established, however, the goal is to have no more fighting and death. Further violence is to be avoided as much as possible. That is why keeping the *pistis* is so important to both the Jews and the Romans. If *pistis* was indeed broken, as Florus suggested, then the consequences would be severe. Rebellion toward the emperor might inspire further rebellion from other cities, which would be a threat to the entire Empire; Rome would be highly motivated to eliminate anyone who broke their *pistis* to the Romans. Thus, the Jews assure Neapolitanus that they have kept their *pistis,* and Neapolitanus demonstrates Rome's respect for the Jews by going to the temple to worship their god, staying in the outer court where Gentiles are allowed.

The Romans eventually did destroy the temple in Jerusalem. Ironically, Josephus was the commander of Galilee during this time. However, in the First Jewish Revolt against Rome (66–74 CE), he played an ambiguous role in which he was meant to be a Jewish leader but, after his capture, ended up serving the Romans. In *The Life*, Josephus tries to defend his actions in an address to the Jewish leader, Justus of Tiberias.[48] Josephus contrasts the two largest cities of Galilee, Sepphoris and Justus's native city of Tiberias,[49] which Josephus writes were models of those who had kept their *pistis* to Rome (Sepphoris) versus those who had not (Tiberias). Josephus compliments the pro-Roman Sepphoris, saying:

> Now, Sepphoris, situated in the heart of Galilee, surrounded by numerous villages, and in a position, without any difficulty, had she been so inclined, to make a bold stand against the Romans, nevertheless decided to remain loyal to her masters.[50]
>
> ἀλλὰ Σέπφωρις μὲν ἐν τῷ μεσαιτάτῳ τῆς Γαλιλαίας κειμένη καὶ περὶ αὐτὴν κώμας ἔχουσα πολλάς, καί τι καὶ θρασύνεσθαι δυναμένη πρὸς Ῥωμαίους, εἴπερ ἠθέλησεν, εὐχερῶς, διεγνωκυῖα τῇ πρὸς τοὺς δεσπότας ἐμμένειν πίστει.[51]

Josephus says that, practically speaking, it would have made sense for Sepphoris to rebel because the city had a lot of support nearby. However, the Jews there chose to remain loyal to Rome.

By contrast, Josephus says to Justus regarding the city of Tiberias:

> With no Jewish city in the vicinity, might easily, had it so desired, have kept faith with the Romans. You were a populous community and well supplied with arms. But, you maintain, it was I who was responsible for your revolt at that time.

---

[48] Josephus, *Life* 345–54.
[49] In the New Testament, Tiberias is mentioned in the context of significant events, but only appears in the Gospel of John (6:1, 23; 21:1).
[50] The word "master" (δεσπότης) does not necessarily have the same negative connotation that modern readers might associate with it today as with the English connotation to the word "despot." Cf. LSJ, s.v. "δεσπότης." As seen in this context, Josephus is speaking positively about the city and their *pistis* to Rome.
[51] Josephus, *Life* 346 (Thackeray, LCL).

μηδεμιᾶς δὲ πόλεως Ἰουδαίων παρακειμένης, εἰ ἤθελεν τὴν πρὸς Ῥωμαίους πίστιν φυλάττειν, ῥᾳδίως ἐδύνατο. καὶ γὰρ πολὺς ἦτε δῆμος καὶ ὅπλων ηὐπορεῖτε. ἀλλ᾽, ὡς σὺ φῄς, αἴτιος ὑμῖν ἐγὼ τότε.[52]

Justus and Josephus seemingly blame one another for the troubles that have happened with Tiberias,[53] which had recently been ousted by Sepphoris as the capital of Galilee. The central problem was a bitter animosity between Jews and Greeks in multiple cities, including Gadara, Hippos, and Scythopolis, against which Justus had led violent raids. These conflicts, however, could not take place without involving the Romans.[54] Thus, Josephus points to *pistis* being broken as the central issue. The people of Tiberias experienced the problems that they did because they had broken their *pistis* to the Romans.

Josephus was critical of both Greeks and Jews with regard to their *pistis*. When he describes what happened at Scythopolis, he points to the lack of *pistis* on the part of the Greeks in the city. Josephus, along with other Jewish leaders, had hoped that the Romans would come and help quell the revolution by Jewish rebels.[55] However, Cestius and the Roman army were defeated in 66 CE, and this led to even further chaos because the rebels hoped to defeat the Romans completely. Cities in Syria panicked and began to kill all Jewish residents, even women and children. However, Josephus says that the Greek natives of Scythopolis were the worst offenders as they had no sense of *pistis* toward their Jewish neighbors:

> They compelled their own Jewish residents to bear arms against their compatriots, which we are forbidden to do, and with their assistance engaged and defeated the invaders; and then, after the victory, with no thought of the allegiance due to fellow-citizens and confederates, put them all, to the number of many thousands, to the sword.
>
> τοὺς παρ᾽ αὐτοῖς Ἰουδαίους ἐβιάσαντο κατὰ τῶν ὁμοφύλων ὅπλα λαβεῖν, ὅπερ ἐστὶν ἡμῖν ἀθέμιτον, καὶ μετ᾽ ἐκείνων συμβαλόντες ἐκράτησαν τῶν ἐπελθόντων· ἐπειδὴ δ᾽ ἐνίκησαν, ἐκλαθόμενοι τῆς πρὸς τοὺς ἐνοίκους καὶ συμμάχους πίστεως πάντας αὐτοὺς διεχρήσαντο πολλὰς μυριάδας ὄντας.[56]

When rebels attacked Scythopolis, the Jews who already lived in the city helped the native Greeks to fight against the invading Jews, their own ethnic brethren. After the rebels were defeated, however, the Greeks turned on their own Jewish neighbors and killed all of the Jews who had just fought alongside them. They had no *pistis*—no sense of loyalty—and Josephus was appalled by the Greeks' lack of compassion and *pistis* toward the neighbors who had just supported them.

---

[52] Josephus, *Life* 349–50 (Thackeray, LCL).
[53] Cf. Josephus, *Life* 37, 41.
[54] Cf. Tessa Rajak, "Justus of Tiberias," *ClQ* 23, no. 2 (Nov 1973): 352.
[55] Josephus, *Life* 23.
[56] Josephus, *Life* 26–7 (Thackeray, LCL).

Josephus's high regard for *pistis* may be reflective of the culture at large, or may be influenced by what appears to be the Romans' strong value for *pistis*. As seen above, the Romans clearly regarded *pistis* between themselves and other cities as important. However, Josephus indicates that they also had a clear expectation for *pistis* among the Romans themselves. This was especially true in the context of the *pistis* between soldiers. *Pistis* was valued so highly that it was considered more important than a victory itself. Josephus offers his eyewitness perspective of the importance of *pistis* when Titus, who would later become emperor, besieged Jerusalem in 70 CE. During the siege, some Jews managed to trick some of the Roman soldiers to come close to the gates.[57] Without awaiting any orders, the soldiers had gone to the gates, expecting the Jews to open them because they had supposedly wanted peace, but instead, the feigning Jewish soldiers attacked the unsuspecting Romans. Titus had been suspicious of the Jews' behavior because he had invited them to terms through Josephus the day before. He had told the soldiers to remain where they were, but the men who were closest to the front had not yet heard. Without waiting for orders, they made the mistake of going ahead and falling straight into a trap.

The scheme was not completely successful as the Roman soldiers managed to get away. However, Titus was furious, and he reprimanded them, pointing to *pistis* among the Jews as the reason they were able to dupe some of the Romans:

> Their schemes are further favored by fortune because of their obedience and their mutual loyalty and confidence
>
> ἕπεται δ᾽ αὐτῶν ταῖς ἐνέδραις καὶ τύχη διὰ τὸ πειθήνιον καὶ τὴν πρὸς ἀλλήλους εὔνοιάν τε καὶ πίστιν[58]

Titus recognized that the Jews kept their *pistis* to one another; even though the Jews were the ones who were besieged, and thus on the more vulnerable side, their *pistis* had allowed them to achieve a small victory over their powerful enemy.

Regarding his own soldiers, however, Titus says that they are a disgrace because they have broken their *pistis*. He even goes so far as to say:

> These rash adventurers shall learn forthwith that, among Romans, even a victory without orders given is held dishonorable.
>
> γνώσεσθαί γε μὴν αὐτίκα τοὺς ἀπαυθαδισαμένους ὅτι καὶ τὸ νικᾶν παρὰ Ῥωμαίοις δίχα παραγγέλματος ἀδοξεῖται.[59]

Titus suggests the high value with which the Romans regard their *pistis*. He implies that other nations may not value *pistis* as highly; as long as the victory is won, *pistis* may not matter. Or perhaps, the victory could make up for the fact that *pistis* was

---

[57] Josephus, *War* 5.109–13.
[58] Josephus, *War* 5.122 (Thackeray, LCL).
[59] Josephus, *War* 5.125 (Thackeray, LCL).

broken. However, Titus declares that, for the Romans, *pistis* is even more important than the victory itself. Even if the Romans had succeeded in this case, he would still be upset because the rogue soldiers had broken their *pistis* to him.

Despite the failings of some of his soldiers, Titus eventually does succeed in the siege of Jerusalem, and the Romans destroy the city because the Jews supposedly fail to demonstrate their *pistis* to Rome. As a result, all of Jerusalem's valuables are taken, and the most valued place, the temple, is completely destroyed.[60] When he returns to Rome, Titus is given a triumph, a parade of honor, which Josephus describes in detail. Included in the procession ritual are statues of the victory goddess:

> After these, and last of all the spoils, was carried a copy of the Jewish Law. Then followed a large party carrying statues of Nike, all made of ivory and gold. Behind them drove Vespasian, followed by Titus.
>
> ὅ τε νόμος ὁ τῶν Ἰουδαίων ἐπὶ τούτοις ἐφέρετο τῶν λαφύρων τελευταῖος. ἐπὶ τούτοις παρῆεσαν πολλοὶ Νίκης ἀγάλματα κομίζοντες· ἐξ ἐλέφαντος δ᾽ ἦν πάντων καὶ χρυσοῦ ἡ κατασκευή. μεθ᾽ ἃ Οὐεσπασιανὸς ἤλαυνε πρῶτος καὶ Τίτος εἵπετο.[61]

The inclusion of Nike is appropriate to the celebration as she is often associated with the military (as seen in Section 2.2) and is a visual representation of the victory itself. Josephus specifically notes that she is made of valuable material, ivory and gold, and it is not one, but several statues[62] of the goddess that accompany the celebration. It is interesting that there are multiple statues of her being carried by several people. This could indicate that she is a visual representation of the belief of assured victory, or perhaps the Romans are showing the extent of their victory by including multiple statues of her. In either case, the message is that the Romans had the favor of the gods, and they demonstrated this by including statues of Nike and of many other gods as well.[63] After Titus's death, the procession was commemorated with the Arch of Titus, which remains in Rome to this day (Figure 5).[64]

Pistis/Fides, Nike/Victoria, and the Emperor

We have seen that the concept of *pistis/fides* was important to the Romans. The word *fides* itself was an ambivalent and open norm with no fixed definition, and thus it appeared in a variety of contexts, mostly with a positive nuance that could connote trust, confidence, trustworthiness, loyalty, and fidelity to one's word.[65] However, *fides*

---

[60] Josephus blames the Jews, however, for the destruction of the temple, cf. Josephus, *War* 6.166–7.
[61] Josephus, *War* 7.150–2 (Thackeray, LCL).
[62] The LCL translation uses "images," but ἀγάλματα might more helpfully be translated "statues." Cf. LSJ, s.v. "ἄγαλμα."
[63] Josephus, *War* 7.136–7.
[64] The Jewish spoils—the table of shew bread, incense cups, and trumpets—as borne in the procession are also depicted on one side of the Arch.
[65] Gérard Freyburger, *Fides: étude Sémantique Et Religieuse Depuis Les Origines Jusqu'à L'époque Augustéenne* (Paris: Belles Lettres, 1986), 16.

Figure 5 "Roman Forum: Arch of Titus." (c. 81 CE) depicting Titus crowned by Nike (top right) for his military victory. Photograph by Gary Lee Todd.

often held moral implications with an expectation of magnanimity, honesty, and impartiality, and a man of *fides* was expected to fulfill his duties and to do the right thing of his own accord without succumbing to external pressure.[66]

The Romans' high regard for *fides* is reflected in the way they honored the goddess Pistis/Fides, the personification of good faith. Roman historian Livy writes about Numa Pompilius (715–673 BCE), Rome's pious second king, establishing her cult:

> He also established an annual worship of Fides, to whose chapel he ordered that the flamens should proceed in a two-horse hooded carriage, and should wrap up their arms as far as the fingers before sacrificing, as a sign that faith must be kept, and that even in men's clasped hands her seat is sacred.

> Et Fidei sollemne instituit. Ad id sacrarium flamines bigis curru arcuato vehi iussit, manuque ad digitos usque involuta rem divinam facere, significantes fidem tutandam sedemque eius etiam in dexteris sacratam esse.[67]

Clasped hands became a ubiquitous symbol for good faith, reflecting the relational nature of trust between two parties having faith in one another. Clasped hands would appear as imagery on coins, often along with images of the goddess Fides.[68]

---

[66] John M. Barry, "*Fides* in Julius Caesar's *Bellum Civile*: A Study in Roman Political Ideology at the Close of the Republican Era" (PhD Diss, University of Maryland, College Park, 2005), 5, 22.
[67] Livy, *History of Rome* 1.21.4 (Foster, LCL). Cf. Plutarch, *Numa* 16.
[68] Seth William Stevenson, *A Dictionary of Roman Coins: Republican and Imperial* (London: George Bell, 1889), 385–7.

When Greek historian Dionysius of Halicarnassus writes about Numa establishing the Pistis/Fides cult, he adds that Numa had established the cult because other gods had been sufficiently worshipped:

> But that Pistis, than which there is nothing greater nor more sacred among men, was not yet worshipped either by states in their public capacity or by private persons. As the result of these reflections he, first of all men, erected a temple to the Public Faith and instituted sacrifices in her honor at the public expense in the same manner as to the rest of the gods. And in truth the result was bound to be that this attitude of good faith and constancy on the part of the State toward all men would in the course of time render the behavior of the individual citizens similar. In any case, so revered and inviolable a thing was good faith in their estimation, that the greatest oath a man could take was by his own faith, and this had greater weight than all the testimony taken together.
>
> Πίστιν δέ, ἧς οὔτε μεῖζον οὔτε ἱερώτερον πάθος ἐν ἀνθρώποις οὐδέν, οὔπω σεβασμῶν τυγχάνειν οὔτ' ἐν τοῖς κοινοῖς τῶν πόλεων πράγμασιν οὔτ' ἐν τοῖς ἰδίοις. ταῦτα δὴ διανοηθεὶς πρῶτος ἀνθρώπων ἱερὸν ἱδρύσατο Πίστεως δημοσίας καὶ θυσίας αὐτῇ κατεστήσατο, καθάπερ καὶ τοῖς ἄλλοις θεοῖς, δημοτελεῖς. ἔμελλε δὲ ἄρα σὺν χρόνῳ τὸ κοινὸν τῆς πόλεως ἦθος πιστὸν καὶ βέβαιον πρὸς ἀνθρώπους γενόμενον τοιούτους ἀπεργάσασθαι καὶ τοὺς τῶν ἰδιωτῶν τρόπους. οὕτω γοῦν σεβαστόν τι πρᾶγμα καὶ ἀμίαντον ἐνομίσθη τὸ πιστόν, ὥστε ὅρκον τε μέγιστον γενέσθαι τὴν ἰδίαν ἑκάστῳ πίστιν καὶ μαρτυρίας συμπάσης ἰσχυροτάτην.[69]

Both Livy and Dionysius not only reflect the importance with which Pistis/Fides was regarded in Greco-Roman history but they also indicate that *pistis/fides* was considered sacred. *Pistis/fides* was valued for oneself, between men, and also before the gods. As a result, the goddess Pistis/Fides became an icon of trust and loyalty in the context of relationships.

The cult of Pistis/Fides was important for the Romans especially because the divine-human *fides* was woven into every aspect of the Roman public life and even some parts of domestic life. We have already seen that *pistis/fides* to the Romans was important in the military context, and the goddess Pistis/Fides was said to sanction *pistis/fides* in war and preside over treaties, oaths, and contracts.[70] When a temple to the goddess was erected on Capitoline Hill in Rome around the third century BCE, the walls were said to have been covered with texts of international treaties as she was the patron of diplomatic relations.[71]

Fides to the emperor was particularly valued and promoted throughout the Empire. Roman legions were granted the title of *pia fidelis* (pious and faithful) when they showed exceptional loyalty to an emperor during his bid for power or when he

---

[69] Dionysius of Halicarnassus, *Roman Antiquities* 2.75 (Cary, LCL).
[70] Morgan, *Roman Faith and Christian Faith*, 127; Freyburger, *Fides*, 231–8, 282–98.
[71] Freyburger, *Fides*, 266.

Figure 6 A bronze dupondius of Marcus Aurelius showing Pistis/Fides with Nike in her right hand (170–1 CE), Rome. (RIC III Marcus Aurelius 999) ANS 1944.100.49173. Courtesy of the American Numismatic Society.

was putting down a revolt.⁷² The title was akin to a reward from an emperor for such loyalty, and demonstrates the significance with which the emperors valued *fides* in their soldiers. Emperors needed this loyalty so that they could trust their soldiers to help maintain power.

Many emperors understandably took advantage of the association of the benevolent Fides who was also connected with wealth and power, and imprinted her on their coins. The emperors Galba, Vespasian, and Domitian were some of the emperors who had coins of Fides and the words Fides Publica(e) imprinted on them to foster loyalty among the people.⁷³ The emperors also imprinted Nike/Victoria⁷⁴ along with Fides on their coins to demonstrate the *pistis/fides* that led to victory in the Roman Empire. The connection is seen on the coins of emperors such as Marcus Aurelius (Figure 6) and Septimius Severus, which were imprinted with the image of the goddess Fides holding a small Nike in her right hand.⁷⁵ The emperor took advantage of the military associations of Nike and coupled her with Fides to convey a message of good faith and loyalty between the soldiers and their ruler.⁷⁶ The coins seem to reinforce the notion that trust was necessary for victory, and that Fides and Nike, as overseers of society, could grant (and withdraw) their blessing.

---

[72] Morgan, *Roman Faith and Christian Faith*, 82.
[73] *RIC I*² Galba 135; *RIC II*², Part 1 Vespasian 301; *RIC II*², Part 1 Domitian 215.
[74] In Latin, Nike was known as Victoria, but for consistency and readability, I will refer to the victory goddess primarily as "Nike," and refer to Pistis/Fides primarily as Fides because she is operating within the mostly Roman context.
[75] *RIC III* Marcus Aurelius 999; *RIC IV* Septimius Severus 651. Nike could be seen on coins from as early as fifth century BCE (Rawles, "Early Epinician," 22, 23). See also, the Zeus with Nike in his right hand mentioned in Section 2.1, and the Athena with Nike in her right hand in Section 2.2.
[76] Cf. Morgan, *Roman Faith and Christian Faith*, 84.

Pistis to the *Divi Filius*

Pistis/fides to the Roman Empire was encouraged through the perception of the emperor as the *divi filius,* the divine son, a title that was often used to designate the emperor. The conception of the emperor as the *divi filius* initially began when the Roman senate officially recognized Julius Caesar as *Divus Iulius* (the divine Julius) almost two years after his assassination.[77] Octavian, as the adopted son of Caesar, then called himself *divi filius* or *divi Iuli filius* (son of the divine Julius) to garner support and perpetuate favor from the people. He had already been trying to legitimize his being Caesar's heir so that he might distinguish himself as worthy of sole leadership of Rome. By hosting funeral games in honor of Caesar in 44 BCE, Octavian strategically sought the support of the army veterans and the *plebs* (general Roman citizens) by evoking Caesar's memory.[78] A comet supposedly flew over these games, and Octavian declared it as a sign that he was meant to be the next Roman ruler.[79] He later displayed the "celestial sign" on coins that he issued,[80] and from as early as 40 BCE, Octavian issued coins from the Roman mint imprinted with the words *divi filius*.[81] The *divi filius* title was not only written on coins but was also disseminated on inscriptions and monuments as part of official titulature.[82]

The divine status of Caesar, and Octavian's claim that he was therefore *divi filius,* was simultaneously foreign to the political and religious Roman elite, and appealing because of the strong Roman tradition of the relationship between political leaders and the gods.[83] When the *divus* title was first granted to Julius Caesar, in some ways, it was not such a radical step because he had received honors that were akin to the status of a god even while he was alive.[84] He had a priest (*flamen*) for his cult,[85] was allowed to adorn his house with a pediment to look like a temple, and place his own image in formal processions of images of the gods. Soon after his death, he was also given altars,

---

[77] Cf. Beard, North, and Price, *Religions of Rome,* 208–10.
[78] Paul Zanker, *The Power of Images in the Age of Augustus,* Jerome Lectures, Sixteenth Series, tr. Alan Shapiro (Ann Arbor: University of Michigan Press, 1988), 34.
[79] Cf. Pliny the Elder, *Natural History* 2.93–4; Seneca the Younger, *Natural Questions* 7.17.2; Cassius Dio, *Roman History* 45.6.4–7.1; John T. Ramsey and A. Lewis Licht, *The Comet of 44 BC and Caesar's Funeral Games* (ACS 39; Atlanta: Scholars Press, 1997), 155. Ironically, the Romans usually viewed comets as a sign of misfortune (cf. Cicero, *De Divinatione* 1.11.18; 2.28.60). Previous Roman political discourse had incorporated celestial events, but Octavian made the comet into an icon for apotheosis. When the emperor Vespasian many years later saw a comet on his deathbed, he joked that he was turning into a god (Suetonius, *Life of Vespasian* 23.4).
[80] For example, a silver denarius of Augustus from *c.* 19–18 BCE shows the emperor on one side, and the comet of 44 BCE and the words *divus Iulius* (the divine Julius) on the reverse (*RIC* I² Augustus 37A).
[81] Lily Ross Taylor, *Divinity of the Roman Emperor,* American Philological Association Monograph Series 1 (Middletown, CT: American Philological Association, 1931), 130.
[82] Taylor, *Divinity of the Roman Emperor,* 106.
[83] From at least the second century BCE, Roman generals and governors received various forms of divine honors from eastern cities. However, it was not clear even to the Romans about what exactly happened in apotheosis and to what degree a deified human related with established gods like Zeus/Jupiter and Ares/Mars. Cf. Cicero, *On the Nature of the Gods* 3.49–50; Beard, North, and Price, *Religions of Rome,* 141–8.
[84] Beard, North, and Price, *Religions of Rome,* 140.
[85] Cf. Cicero, *Philippic* 2.110–11, a speech delivered in 44 BCE.

Figure 7 A gold quinarius aureus of Tiberius (22–3 CE), Lugdunum, imprinted with 'TIDIVIF' (Tiberius *divi filius*) and with Nike sitting on a globe and holding a victory wreath. (RIC I [2nd edn.] Tiberius 8) ANS 1956.184.18. Courtesy of the American Numismatic Society.

sacrifices, and a temple, all markers of divine status. He received a formal decree of deification in 42 BCE, making him *divus* Julius.[86]

The senate as a motley unwieldy body of a thousand members, some of whom were freedmen and of provincial stock, were initially unsure about Octavian.[87] After many years, however, Octavian strategically used the title of *divi filius* to advance his political position and overcome rivals in the senate. He was officially conferred the title of "Augustus" in 27 BCE, and became the first of many emperors who were known as *divi filius*. After his death, Augustus was promoted to divine status as well and was supposedly witnessed ascending to heaven.[88]

Not all emperors were granted apotheosis by the senate after their deaths, and thus, the title of *divi filius* could not be applied to all emperors,[89] but many of the succeeding emperors, including Tiberius, Nero, and Domitian, proliferated the title during their reigns. Like Augustus, these three emperors similarly stamped the *divi filius* title on coins that they issued, and they often included the image of the victory goddess Nike/Victoria (Figure 7).[90] The coins helped propagate their message as divine sons because Roman coins were in use, not only in Rome but also across Africa, Greece, and Gaul, and Roman soldiers throughout the Empire were paid with the imprinted coins.[91]

---

[86] It is controversial as to whether Caesar officially became a Roman god before his death as Roman writers and modern scholars offer different and often contradictory views, but he was nevertheless clearly granted a degree of divine status (Beard, North, and Price, *Religions of Rome*, 141).
[87] Taylor, *Divinity of the Roman Emperor*, 150.
[88] Suetonius, *Augustus* 100.4; Cassius Dio 56.46.2; *Inscriptiones Italiae* xiii.2, p. 510.
[89] Cf. Georg Wissowa, *Religion Und Kultus Der Römer*, 2nd edn (München: Beck, 1912), 596–7.
[90] See, for example, *RIC I²* Tiberius 8 (seen above); *RIC I²* Nero 10; *RIC II²*, Part 1 Domitian 63 which all have "*divi f*" inscribed on them. They also all have the image of the goddess Nike/Victoria.
[91] Michael Crawford, "coinage, Roman," in *OCD*.

The religious dominance of the emperors can be seen in the landscape of Roman religion, which changed radically under the Empire; almost half of the twenty or so new state temples built between the reigns of Augustus and Constantine were dedicated to deified emperors, and most of these temples were large and conspicuous.[92] The temples reflected the monumental prominence of the Roman emperors, which was promoted in the Greco-Roman culture, and the imperial cult was regarded as important because it was tied to political, social, and economic structures. For example, at the festivals that honored the emperor, the struggles of competitors to win, the fight for honorific positions, and the concern for social status presupposed and enhanced the importance of the imperial cult.[93] The cult of the emperor helped enforce order and consolidate the social and political hierarchies as well as ensure that the subjects of Rome would submit to the authority of the emperor and not participate in subversive activities.

The association of the emperors with the divine became an assumed part of the culture especially among the Greeks because they would refer to the emperor as "god" (θεός) even when he was alive. They did recognize the strict distinction between *divus* (one who posthumously received official divine status through recognition from the senate) and *deus* (an immortal who had never experienced a mortal existence) in Rome, but there was no readily available translation of *divus* into Greek.[94] Therefore, Greek speakers employed the word θεός, and all of the first century CE emperors were called θεός even though they were not all *divi* or *divi filius*, indicating that θεός was probably applied broadly to the emperor throughout the Empire by all social classes.[95] Even in the stricter culture of distinct terms in Rome, Domitian apparently demanded to be addressed as *dominus et deus noster* (our master and god) in his effort to reinforce the divinity and authority of the emperor.[96] Thus, the culture under the Roman Empire in the early centuries recognized and propagated the conception of the emperor as "god" or as "the son of god," and a failure to recognize the divine son could have been interpreted as subversive, not only in a political sense but potentially also in a religious context.

5.2 A Countercultural Battle over *Pistis*

In light of this cultural context, which achieves victory through a *pistis* to the Romans and proliferates a *pistis* in the emperor as the divine son, we now turn to the Johannine community that was situated within this culture and examine the letter that proclaims another *pistis* victory. Through this analysis, it becomes clear that the author of 1 John is deliberately countering the notions of *pistis* in the wider culture, and proclaiming a

---

[92] Beard, North, and Price, *Religions of Rome*, 253.
[93] Simon Price, *Rituals and Power: The Roman Imperial Cult in Asia Minor* (Cambridge: Cambridge University Press, 1984), 130–2.
[94] Price, *Rituals and Power*, 75; John Scheid, "deus, divus" in *OCD*.
[95] Michael Peppard, *The Son of God in the Roman World: Divine Sonship in Its Social and Political Context* (New York: Oxford University Press, 2011), 41–2; cf. Wissowa, *Religion Und Kultus Der Römer*, 596–7.
[96] Suetonius, *Domitian* 13.2; Pliny the Younger, *Panegyricus* 2.3, 52.2.

countercultural victory of *pistis* so that the Johannine believers can be assured in the truth of their *pistis* and remain vigilant against anything from the culture that might threaten to sway them from it.

Emphasizing *Pistis* in 1 John

Because the noun *pistis* appears only once (1 Jn 5:4) among the Johannine letters and the Gospel of John, one could presume that *pistis* is not a major concern in Johannine literature in comparison to every other book of the New Testament where the noun *pistis* appears more than once. However, verbal forms appear many times in John's Gospel and nine times in 1 John (3:23; 4:1, 16; 5:1, 5, 10 [3x], 13), and the adjectival form occurs in the letters as well (1 Jn 1:9; 3 Jn 5; cf. Jn 20:27). In conjunction with the conquering language throughout the letter, which expresses the author's concerns about what is "from the world" (1 Jn 2:16; 4:5) and "in the world" (2:15, 16; 4:3, 4; cf. 4:1), and the concluding warning about idols, we see that the fundamental battle in 1 John is the battle over *pistis*. The conquering language and *pistis* language that he has utilized several times in the five short chapters of the letter come together in the victory of *pistis* proclaimed in the final chapter (5:4):

> For everyone who is born of God conquers the world. And this is the victory that has conquered the world, our faith.
>
> ὅτι πᾶν τὸ γεγεννημένον ἐκ τοῦ θεοῦ νικᾷ τὸν κόσμον· καὶ αὕτη ἐστὶν ἡ νίκη ἡ νικήσασα τὸν κόσμον, ἡ πίστις ἡμῶν.

The writer poses the Johannine believers as Johannine conquerors because he wants them to fight against the *pistis* of the Greco-Roman world, and he assures that the *pistis* of the culture cannot compare to the strength and power of the Johannine *pistis*.

The challenge of defining *pistis* has been contentious in scholarship, partially because *pistis* in the Greco-Roman world had multiple and layered meanings including "belief," "trust," and "loyalty."[97] As seen above, I have followed most English translations[98] and left the translation of *pistis* as "faith" (5:4). The word "faith" is probably commonly used for this verse in English because it more readily reflects a spiritual nuance in comparison to the word "belief."[99] However, the writer of 1 John would likely not have objected to *pistis* as "belief" or even "trust" or "loyalty," as all of these would encompass what he is trying to emphasize: the distinction between what the Johannine community

---

[97] The issue of *pistis Christou* has been especially highly debated (cf. Matthew C. Easter, "The *Pistis Christou*: Main Arguments and Responses in Summary," *CurBR* 9, no. 1 [Sep 2010]: 33–47). Teresa Morgan's book *Roman Faith and Christian Faith* has been helpful in trying to bridge the gap between the *pistis* in New Testament texts and the *pistis* as understood by classicists looking at the Greco-Roman context. Cf. LSJ s.v. "πίστις."

[98] For example, NIV, ESV, NLT, NKJV, NASB, CEV, NRSV.

[99] The word "belief" in English seems to have a broader range. For example, someone might have certain government beliefs or beliefs about education, but with religious belief, the word "faith" might also be used. By contrast, if one referred to government faith or faith in education, the connotation would either suggest religious faith in those contexts or the degree of trustworthiness.

believes and what beliefs prevail in the culture of the Greco-Roman world. By looking at the *pistis*-related verses in 1 John, the contention between the two and its relation to the conquering language of the letter becomes clear.

The first allusion to *pistis* appears in Chapter 1, in which the writer uses the adjective πιστός to refer to the one who is faithful (1:9).

> If we confess our sins, he who is faithful and just will forgive us our sins and cleanse us from all unrighteousness.
>
> ἐὰν ὁμολογῶμεν τὰς ἁμαρτίας ἡμῶν, πιστός ἐστιν καὶ δίκαιος, ἵνα ἀφῇ ἡμῖν τὰς ἁμαρτίας καὶ καθαρίσῃ ἡμᾶς ἀπὸ πάσης ἀδικίας.

In this verse, the writer is referring to God as the faithful one,[100] and he appears to use this pattern of identifying God with the concepts that he wishes his disciples to embody as well.[101] Just as the writer establishes God in connection with light (1:5, 7), righteousness (2:1, 29), and love (4:8, 16), the association of *pistis*, and in this case, the first reference to the concept, is with God himself.

The next allusion to *pistis* appears two chapters later, in which the author emphasizes the importance of what the readers should believe (3:23):

> And this is his command, that we should believe in the name of his Son Jesus Christ and love one another, just as he gave a command to us.
>
> καὶ αὕτη ἐστὶν ἡ ἐντολὴ αὐτοῦ, ἵνα πιστεύσωμεν τῷ ὀνόματι τοῦ υἱοῦ αὐτοῦ Ἰησοῦ Χριστοῦ καὶ ἀγαπῶμεν ἀλλήλους, καθὼς ἔδωκεν ἐντολὴν ἡμῖν.

Chapter 3 in particular is saturated with verbs in the first-person plural, emphasizing the Johannine community as a whole, including their collective identity as children of God (e.g., 3:1, 2), their obligation to respond in love for one another (3:11, 14), and their willingness to even lay down their lives for one another (3:16). The subjunctives earlier in the chapter (3:1, 11) may emphasize the sense of urgency in the letter.[102] They lead to the final aorist subjunctive verb of the chapter (πιστεύσωμεν, 3:23), which is also the first time the verb πιστεύω is used in 1 John.

The importance of their *believing* is conveyed with the declaration that it is a command (ἐντολή) from God.[103] He underlines the significance of the command by

---

[100] Cf. Deut. 7:9; 32:4 (LXX) where God's character is also described as πιστός (Lieu, *I, II & III John*, 58).

[101] Cf. the many references to "remain" (μένω) in God/Jesus (2:6, 24, 27, 28; 3:6, 24; 4:13, 15, 16), which emphasize his point about the disciples reflecting the attributes of God.

[102] Variation among manuscripts in verb tense and its implications have been debated, but the overall emphasis on the importance of belief and love are evident (cf. Brown, *The Epistles of John*, 462; Lieu, *I, II & III John*, 159).

[103] "Command" (ἐντολή) occurs at 1 Jn 2:3, 4, 7 (3x), 8; 3:22, 24; 4:21; 5:2, 3 (2x); cf. 2 Jn 4, 5, 6 (2x). The plural appears eight times in the Johannine letters, and the singular appears ten times. In the immediate context, v. 23 is in the singular (as opposed to the plural in vv. 22, 24), which may convey the fundamental divine command to believe in Jesus (and to respond with love). The frequent use of "command" amplifies the sense of urgency and obligation. Cf. also Smalley, *1, 2, 3 John*, 207.

referring to it four times within three verses (3:22-4).[104] The Johannine believers, along with the writer himself, *must* believe, and he specifies what they are all believing *in*; the Johannine community should believe in the name of Jesus Christ as the Son of God. The dative construction (πιστεύσωμεν τῷ ὀνόματι) is unique as elsewhere the letter uses εἰς with the accusative τὸ ὄνομα. There is probably no fundamental difference in meaning, but the explicit reference to believing in the name of Jesus conveys the significance of his character, personhood, and authority.[105] The writer also recapitulates the necessity of loving one another, which he will reference again with regard to *pistis* in the next chapter (see more below).

In contrast to the collective first-person address about the necessity of believing in Jesus, the next *pistis*-related verse uses a second-person imperative to declare what *not* to believe (4:1):

> Beloved, do not believe every spirit, but test the spirits to see whether they are from God; for many false prophets have gone out into the world.
>
> Ἀγαπητοί, μὴ παντὶ πνεύματι πιστεύετε, ἀλλὰ δοκιμάζετε τὰ πνεύματα εἰ ἐκ τοῦ θεοῦ ἐστιν, ὅτι πολλοὶ ψευδοπροφῆται ἐξεληλύθασιν εἰς τὸν κόσμον.

The two verses about what the Johannine community should believe (3:23) and what they should not believe (4:1) being so close to one another and in direct opposition to one another underscores one of the primary reasons that the author is writing his letter: he wants them to retain their *pistis* in Jesus and guard against anything, particularly from the Greco-Roman culture, that threatens this *pistis*. He draws the distinction between what the Johannine community *should* believe and what they *should not* believe, because he recognizes the contention between them, and the author wants to ensure that the Johannine readers acknowledge the correct *pistis* and not be swayed by the false prophets, antichrists, the evil one, or any cultural influence that might cause them to believe otherwise (see also Section 3.1–3.3).

The author of 1 John returns to the first-person plural in Chapter 4, in which he gives his discourse on love (4:7–5:3). In the middle of this discourse, he makes another allusion to what they believe (4:16):

> So we have known and believed the love that God has for us. God is love, and those who remain in love remain in God, and God remains in them.
>
> καὶ ἡμεῖς ἐγνώκαμεν καὶ πεπιστεύκαμεν τὴν ἀγάπην ἣν ἔχει ὁ θεὸς ἐν ἡμῖν. Ὁ θεὸς ἀγάπη ἐστιν, καὶ ὁ μένων ἐν τῇ ἀγάπῃ ἐν τῷ θεῷ μένει καὶ ὁ θεὸς ἐν αὐτῷ μένει.

This time, the verb is in the perfect tense: "we have believed" (πεπιστεύκαμεν),[106] indicating a completed action in which the content of what is believed is the love that

---

[104] The sense of importance increases as the indirect imperative of v. 22 becomes a direct imperative in v. 23 (Bultmann, *The Johannine Epistles*, 58).
[105] Smalley, *1, 2, 3 John*, 208; Lieu, *I, II & III John*, 158. Cf. also believing εἰς τὸ ὄνομα at Jn 1:12; 2:23; 3:18, a construction which is not seen elsewhere in the NT.
[106] Cf. similar language in Jn 6:69.

God has for the Johannine community. While the previous emphasis was on believing in the name of Jesus, he remains appropriate to the focus of the exhortation and states that the Johannine community has already known and already believed in the love of God because they could not be Johannine Christians without it; love was the reason why God had sent Jesus to earth (4:10; cf. Jn 3:16). The verse is a reminder of what they have already believed in the past, which has distinguished them from those who do not know or believe in the love of God and are more consumed with fear instead (cf. 4:18, see also Section 4.1).

The final chapter underlines the Johannine writer's primary concern as he alludes to *pistis* six times. The beginning verse of the chapter sets the stage before his climax on the importance of *pistis* (5:4-5) with the first in a series of participles about those who believe (5:1):

> Everyone who believes that Jesus is the Christ has been born of God, and everyone who loves the parent loves the child.
>
> Πᾶς ὁ πιστεύων ὅτι Ἰησοῦς ἐστιν ὁ Χριστὸς, ἐκ τοῦ θεοῦ γεγέννηται, καὶ πᾶς ὁ ἀγαπῶν τὸν γεννήσαντα ἀγαπᾷ τὸν γεγεννημένον ἐξ αὐτοῦ.

This verse echoes the previous reference to believe in Jesus Christ as the Son of God (3:23, cf. 5:1, 5)[107] and draws a parallel to the one who loves the parent (God) and the child (other believers). The aim in the latter phrase is to establish the evidence that a person who believes in Jesus and loves God is also expected to love other children of God who also believe in Jesus as the Son of God.[108] Thus, believing in Jesus as the Christ has implications for a person's identity (being a child who is born of God), which in turn also has implications for how that person should respond (loving others, cf. 5:2).

Having alluded to the importance of what is believed in previous verses, and the contention between those who believe in Jesus as the Son of God and those who do not (3:23; 4:1), the writer makes a clear and distinct proclamation on the importance of *pistis* (5:4):

> For everyone who is born of God conquers the world. And this is the victory that has conquered the world, our faith.
>
> ὅτι πᾶν τὸ γεγεννημένον ἐκ τοῦ θεοῦ νικᾷ τὸν κόσμον· καὶ αὕτη ἐστὶν ἡ νίκη ἡ νικήσασα τὸν κόσμον, ἡ πίστις ἡμῶν.

Thus far, he has utilized conquering language and discussed what is believed, but in this verse, he equates the two by declaring that the victory itself is "our *pistis*" (ἡ πίστις ἡμῶν). The writer uses the first-person plural possessive to emphasize that the Johannine community, including the writer himself, collectively conquers the world with *pistis*. He makes sure to distinguish that he is referring to "*our pistis*," which conveys the subtext of "not *their pistis*," that is, the *pistis* of the Greco-Roman world.

---

[107] See more on the Son of God below.
[108] Cf. Marshall, *The Epistles of John*, 227.

While the verbs for "believe" and "conquer" have been seen previously throughout the letter, the noun *pistis* appearing for the first and only time, and identifying "our *pistis*" as *nikē*, also in noun form for the first and only time, acts like a neon sign, drawing attention to the victory proclamation.

Immediately after, the writer of 1 John poses a rhetorical question to reinforce the importance of the victorious *pistis* (5:5):

> Who is the one who conquers the world except the one who believes that Jesus is the Son of God?
>
> τίς ἐστιν δὲ ὁ νικῶν τὸν κόσμον εἰ μὴ ὁ πιστεύων ὅτι Ἰησοῦς ἐστιν ὁ υἱὸς τοῦ θεοῦ;

The question echoes the previous participle (5:1) that identified the characteristics of a Johannine believer as one who *believes* in Jesus as the Son of God, and in believing this, the Johannine believer is also identified as "the one who conquers the world" (ὁ νικῶν τὸν κόσμον).[109] The two participles placed in parallel to one another, and in conjunction with the victory proclamation in the previous verse, emphasizes the Johannine identity as believers who have *pistis* in Jesus as the Son of God that also signifies their identity as conquerors of the Greco-Roman world, which adopts a different *pistis*.

In the next few verses, the writer of 1 John highlights the importance of testimony for *pistis* (see more on testimony below), and the participles appear again to define the distinction that the author has been reiterating throughout the entire letter in the contention between the one who believes and the one who does not believe (5:10):

> The one who believes in the Son of God has the testimony in himself. The one who does not believe in God has made him a liar because he has not believed in the testimony which God has testified concerning his Son.
>
> ὁ πιστεύων εἰς τὸν υἱὸν τοῦ θεοῦ ἔχει τὴν μαρτυρίαν ἐν αὐτῷ,[110] ὁ μὴ πιστεύων τῷ θεῷ ψεύστην πεποίηκεν αὐτόν, ὅτι οὐ πεπίστευκεν εἰς τὴν μαρτυρίαν ἣν μεμαρτύρηκεν ὁ θεὸς περὶ τοῦ υἱοῦ αὐτοῦ.

Similarly to the previous chapter in which he emphasized the importance of not believing in every spirit (4:1), the writer of 1 John separates the Johannine believer from "the one who does not believe," for that person makes God a "liar" (ψεύστης), a word he has used to delineate conflict several times before, especially in 1:10 where he also references God being made a liar.[111] The declaration of God as a liar seems extreme, and although it may not be as incendiary to its audience as it might sound to

---

[109] The question here also balances the rhetorical question of 2:22: "Who is the liar but the one who denies that Jesus is the Christ?" Cf. Painter, *1, 2, and 3 John*, 229.

[110] The well-attested variant, "in him" can only mean "in himself," indicating the internalization of God's testimony (Lieu, *I, II & III John*, 218).

[111] See also, 1 Jn 1:10; 2:4, 22; 4:20; cf. Jn 8:44, 55. The word ψεύστης appears most frequently in 1 John among New Testament texts.

a person reading it in English today,[112] the writer of 1 John makes the point to show the implications of the one who believes versus the one who does not. There is the distinction not only in the content of their *pistis* (what is believed) but also that the "liar" does not have the same *pistis* because he has not believed in the testimony from God himself. The perfect tense of the verbs (πεποίηκεν, πεπίστευκεν, μεμαρτύρηκεν) underscore that God has already given his testimony in the past, and the writer seems to allude to those (such as the antichrists who left the community, 2:19) who have already chosen not to believe and have therefore designated God as a liar.

The final allusion to *pistis* is at the start of the epilogue in which the author gives the concluding reason for his writing (5:13):[113]

> I have written these things to you who believe in the name of the Son of God, so that you may know that you have eternal life.
>
> Ταῦτα ἔγραψα ὑμῖν ἵνα εἰδῆτε ὅτι ζωὴν ἔχετε αἰώνιον τοῖς πιστεύουσιν εἰς τὸ ὄνομα τοῦ υἱοῦ τοῦ θεοῦ.

This time, the author does not include himself in using the first-person plural to emphasize the collective group (cf. 3:23; 4:16), and he does not focus on the identity of each individual (e.g., 5:5, 10; cf. 5:1). Instead, the dative plural participle distinguishes the writer from his audience. The reason for his writing is his concern over what they believe. He wants to remind and assure his disciples about their *pistis* and the implications for their *pistis*. They will have eternal life because of what they believe.

From the verses above, and especially with their concentration in the final chapter, it is clear that the core concern of 1 John is the Johannine *pistis* and the contention against those in the Greco-Roman world who believe in a different *pistis*. The fundamental battle is a battle over *pistis,* and thus, the writer repeatedly emphasizes the importance of what *pistis* the audience believes and exhorts and assures his disciples of why they should retain this *pistis*.

Pistis in the Son of God

In the battle over *pistis* in 1 John, the writer emphasizes that the victorious *pistis* is specifically in Jesus as "the Son of God" (ὁ υἱὸς τοῦ θεοῦ, 5:5):

> Who is the one who conquers the world except the one who believes that Jesus is the Son of God?
>
> τίς δέ ἐστιν ὁ νικῶν τὸν κόσμον εἰ μὴ ὁ πιστεύων ὅτι Ἰησοῦς ἐστιν ὁ υἱὸς τοῦ θεοῦ;

Nikē, pistis, and "the Son of God" come together as the conqueror of the Greco-Roman world is also the one who has *pistis* in Jesus as the Son of God. As we have discussed, the

---

[112] Cf. Yarbrough, *1–3 John*, 84–5.
[113] Cf. the frequent references to the reason why he is writing: "We write" (γράφομεν, 1:4), "I am writing to you" (γράφω ὑμῖν, 2:1, 7, 8, 12, 13 (2x)) or "I wrote/I have written to you" (ἔγραψα ὑμῖν, 2:14 (3x), 21, 26).

word *nikē* would likely evoke the imagery and associations of the goddess Nike, who was a prominent part of the culture for both Greeks and Romans for many centuries.[114] However, we have seen that Nike was also affiliated with the emperor and that the title "the son of god" would evoke a reference to him. Before Jesus was the renowned Son of God, the first well-known figure to receive that title during the Roman Empire was the emperor.[115] Having demonstrated that the Greco-Roman culture advocates *pistis* in the emperor as the *divi filius*, we can see that the Johannine author is making a countercultural proclamation against this Greco-Roman *pistis*.

In the short letter of 1 John, the word "son" (υἱός) appears twenty-two times,[116] all in reference to Jesus, and of the twenty-two occurrences, the phrase "the Son of God" (ὁ υἱὸς τοῦ θεοῦ) appears seven times. Although the word "son" appears in every chapter of the letter, ten of the references are concentrated in the final chapter in which believing in Jesus as the Son of God is emphasized, and where the writer of 1 John declares the *pistis* victory. One could argue that the emphasis on "the son" is simply to refer to the incarnation of Jesus. If that were so, then a reader might expect the words "flesh" (σάρξ) or "body" (σῶμα) in the letter, as in the Gospel of John, where the emphasis on "son" and "the Son of God" is also apparent.[117] While "flesh" (σάρξ) appears thirteen times in John's Gospel, often regarding the flesh of Jesus,[118] the only two instances of "flesh" in 1 John are in reference to "the desire of the flesh" (ἡ ἐπιθυμία τῆς σαρκὸς) in the world (2:16, see also Section 3.3), and identifying spirits that confess that Jesus has come "in the flesh" (ἐν σαρκὶ, 4:2).[119] This brief reference is the only direct allusion to the incarnation in 1 John.[120]

The word "body" (σῶμα) similarly does not appear in the Johannine Letters,[121] although it appears a number of times in John's Gospel referring to the literal body of Jesus.[122] The reference to the incarnation of Jesus in 1 John 4:2 demonstrates that the author *does* consider it important, but it is not necessarily the focus of the contention over *pistis* in the letter. Instead, the writer of 1 John frequently emphasizes the importance of believing in Jesus as the "Son of God."

---

[114] See more in Sections 2.1 and 2.2.
[115] Peppard, *The Son of God*, 4.
[116] See "son" (υἱός) at 1 Jn 1:3, 7; 2:22, 23 (2x), 24; 3:8, 23; 4:9, 10, 14, 15; 5:5, 9, 10 (2x), 11, 12 (2x), 13; 20 (2x); cf. 2 Jn 3, 9. "The Son of God" (ὁ υἱὸς τοῦ θεοῦ) appears at 1 Jn 3:8; 4:15; 5:5, 10, 12, 13, 20.
[117] Of the fifty-five occurrences of υἱός in John's Gospel, υἱὸς θεοῦ appears nine times at Jn 1:34, 49; 3:18; 5:25; 10:36; 11:4, 27; 19:7; 20:31.
[118] Cf. Jn 1:14; 6:52, 53, 54, 55, 56.
[119] Cf. 2 Jn 7 where deceivers do not confess that Jesus has come "in the flesh." Flesh (σάρξ) appears in most books of the NT, (but not in 1 and 2 Thessalonians, 2 Timothy, Titus, and 3 John), and often in a negative context (e.g., Mt. 26:41; Rom. 13:14; Gal. 5:19; 1 Pet. 2:11; Rev. 17:16). Among the Gospels, σάρξ appears much more frequently in the Gospel of John than in the Synoptic Gospels, probably because of the christological emphasis on the incarnation in John's Gospel.
[120] A few verses later, the writer makes a related reference to the incarnation in God sending his son "into the world" (4:9, cf. Jn 3:16).
[121] "Body" (σῶμα) also appears in almost every NT book, but does not appear in 2 Thessalonians, 1 and 2 Timothy, Titus, Philemon, 2 Peter, and the Johannine letters. Many of the references to σῶμα in the NT refer to the human body in general, as opposed to the human body of Jesus.
[122] Cf. Jn 2:21, 19:31, 38 (2x), 40; 20:12. The word σῶμα seems to be used in John's Gospel mostly to refer to Jesus's body after the crucifixion.

The Johannine author frames "the Son of God" as the key source of conflict in the battle over *pistis*. He refers to the Son in the first two chapters (1:3, 7; 2:22, 23, 24), but the first time he mentions "the Son of God" is in Chapter 3, when he places the Son of God in direct opposition to the devil (3:8):

> The one who commits sin is of the devil; for the devil has been sinning from the beginning. The Son of God was revealed for this purpose, to destroy the works of the devil.
>
> ὁ ποιῶν τὴν ἁμαρτίαν ἐκ τοῦ διαβόλου ἐστιν, ὅτι ἀπ' ἀρχῆς ὁ διάβολος ἁμαρτάνει· εἰς τοῦτο ἐφανερώθη ὁ υἱὸς τοῦ θεοῦ, ἵνα λύσῃ τὰ ἔργα τοῦ διαβόλου.

As with much of the conquering language that we have seen in this letter, the author speaks from the place of triumph, and depicts the Son of God as the conqueror. The Son of God is the destroyer of the opposition, who is the devil. The language of the devil sinning "from the beginning" (ἀπ' ἀρχῆς) hearkens back to the prologue, which referred to what was "from the beginning" (1:1), the fathers who know him who is "from the beginning" (2:13, 14), and what the readers heard "from the beginning" (2:24).[123] All of the references relate to Jesus, but he is not named directly. Instead, he is a figure associated with "the beginning." It is also notable that the name "Jesus" and the word "Christ" do not appear in Chapter 3 until much later on in verse 23. In the immediate context of 3:8, the figure who was "from the beginning" is now given the title of "the Son of God," who is revealed on earth as the countering conqueror to the devil who has been sinning "from the beginning." The purpose of the Son of God is to triumph over the devil and destroy his works.

The next time the writer mentions the Son of God is in the middle of his discourse on love in Chapter 4 (4:14-15):

> And we have seen and do testify that the Father has sent his Son as the Savior of the world. God remains in those who confess that Jesus is the Son of God, and they remain in God.
>
> καὶ ἡμεῖς τεθεάμεθα καὶ μαρτυροῦμεν ὅτι ὁ πατὴρ ἀπέσταλκεν τὸν υἱὸν σωτῆρα τοῦ κόσμου. ὃς ἐὰν ὁμολογήσῃ ὅτι Ἰησοῦς ἐστιν ὁ υἱὸς τοῦ θεοῦ, ὁ θεὸς ἐν αὐτῷ μένει καὶ αὐτὸς ἐν τῷ θεῷ.

Here we see two titles that were used for the emperor: the Savior of the World (1 Jn 4:14; cf. Jn 4:42)[124] and the Son of God. Verse 15 is also the first time that Jesus is directly referred to as "the Son of God" (although he is referred to as "the Son" previously at 1:3, 7; 3:23; cf. 2:22).

The conquering message here is not in a direct conflict (as with the devil in 3:8). Instead, the emphasis is on the importance of remaining (μένω), which the author

---

[123] See also Section 3.3 for more on 2:13-14.
[124] Cf. Koester, "Savior of the World," 666–7 regarding "Savior of the World" (ὁ σωτὴρ τοῦ κόσμου) as a title used for Roman emperors.

mentions six times in 4:12-16. The tension is between those who confess that Jesus is the Son of God, and therefore remain in God (4:15), and those who do not remain in God (cf. 4:8, 18, 20). The reference to the Son of God is within the love discourse (4:7–5:3) to help identify true Johannine believers: one indication is the confession of Jesus as the Son of God (4:14-15), and the other is the demonstration of the love of God (4:7, 11, 12). These indications guide the readers in discerning who is from God and who is from the world (cf. 4:1-6).

It is striking that in the final chapter of 1 John, the author concentrates the language of sonship. The word "son" is mentioned ten times in Chapter 5, of which the remaining five occurrences of "the Son of God" appear. Having alluded to the contention between the Son of God and the devil (3:8) and the conflict between Johannine believers and those of the world in Chapter 4, the first declaration of sonship in the final chapter is in the context of victory (5:5):

> Who is the one who conquers the world except the one who believes that Jesus is the Son of God?
>
> τίς δὲ ἐστιν ὁ νικῶν τὸν κόσμον εἰ μὴ ὁ πιστεύων ὅτι Ἰησοῦς ἐστιν ὁ υἱὸς τοῦ θεοῦ;

"The one who conquers the world" and the "one who believes" are placed in parallel to demonstrate that the Johannine conqueror is the believer who specifically has *pistis* in the Son of God. The Greco-Roman culture also encouraged *pistis* in the *divi filius*,[125] as the imperial cult was implemented throughout the Roman Empire. However, the writer makes clear with his rhetorical question, which presumes an obvious response, that the Johannine conqueror is victorious over the world when they have *pistis* specifically in *Jesus* as the Son of God, and no one else.

The author uses the identity of "the one who believes" (ὁ πιστεύων) again with regard to the Son of God, but with a slight adjustment (5:10):

> The one who believes in the Son of God has the testimony in himself. The one who does not believe in God has made him a liar because he has not believed in the testimony which God has testified concerning his Son.
>
> ὁ πιστεύων εἰς τὸν υἱὸν τοῦ θεοῦ ἔχει τὴν μαρτυρίαν ἐν αὐτῷ, ὁ μὴ πιστεύων τῷ θεῷ ψεύστην πεποίηκεν αὐτόν, ὅτι οὐ πεπίστευκεν εἰς τὴν μαρτυρίαν ἣν μεμαρτύρηκεν ὁ θεὸς περὶ τοῦ υἱοῦ αὐτοῦ.

The Johannine believer is not just "the one who believes" (ὁ πιστεύων) *that* (ὅτι) Jesus is the Son of God, alluding to the content of their *pistis*; the believer is "the one who believes in the Son of God" (ὁ πιστεύων εἰς τὸν υἱὸν τοῦ θεοῦ). Believing in the Son of God, and specifically *Jesus* as the Son of God, is a core part of their identity as Johannine believers, which is attested by the testimony of the Spirit within them (5:6,

---

[125] Cf. the centurion's identification of Jesus as the Son of God relating with the emperor in the Gospel of Mark (Adela Yarbro Collins, "Mark and His Readers: The Son of God among Greeks and Romans," *HTR* 93, no. 2 [April 2000]: 85–100).

10; cf. 4:13). The statement offers reassurance to those who might waver in their *pistis* and reminds them of their distinction from "the one who does not believe in God" (ὁ μὴ πιστεύων τῷ θεῷ).

In the final three references to the Son of God, we see a similar emphasis on "life" (ζωή) and specifically "eternal life" (ζωὴ αἰώνιος). Just before his epilogue, the author underlines the conflict of *pistis* between the Johannine believers and the ones who do not believe in the Son of God, with the added dimension of "life" (5:12):

> The one who has the Son has life; the one who does not have the Son of God does not have life.
>
> ὁ ἔχων τὸν υἱὸν ἔχει τὴν ζωήν, ὁ μὴ ἔχων τὸν υἱὸν τοῦ θεοῦ τὴν ζωὴν οὐκ ἔχει.

The verb "to have" (ἔχω) being used four times in the verse emphasizes the sense of identity and the testimony of *pistis* within believers. "The one who believes in the Son of God" (ὁ πιστεύων εἰς τὸν υἱὸν τοῦ θεοῦ, 5:10, cf. 5:1, 5) and is "the one who conquers" (ὁ νικῶν, 5:5), is also "the one who has the Son [of God]" (ὁ ἔχων τὸν υἱὸν [τοῦ θεοῦ]). It may sound a bit awkward to *have* the Son, but it underscores the sense of the internalized *pistis* in the Johannine believer-conquerors and the testimony of the Spirit within them (5:6-10). It is also consistent with the Johannine message to "remain" (μένω).[126]

The added dimension is the distinction of having "life" (ζωή). The Johannine believer-conqueror who has the Son also *has* life (ἔχει τὴν ζωήν), while "the one who does not have the Son of God" does not *have* life. He then clarifies that this "life" is "eternal life," a connection he makes in the last two references to the Son of God (5:13, 20). The connection between *pistis* in the Son of God and eternal life will be examined further below, but the final point here is about the exhortation by the author concerning *pistis* in the true Son of God.

When the writer begins his epilogue, he declares the identity of the readers once again as those who have *pistis* in the Son of God (5:13):

> I have written these things to you who believe in the name of the Son of God, so that you may know that you have eternal life.
>
> Ταῦτα ἔγραψα ὑμῖν ἵνα εἰδῆτε ὅτι ζωὴν ἔχετε αἰώνιον τοῖς πιστεύουσιν εἰς τὸ ὄνομα τοῦ υἱοῦ τοῦ θεοῦ.

He is writing "to you who believe in the name of the Son of God" (τοῖς πιστεύουσιν εἰς τὸ ὄνομα τοῦ υἱοῦ τοῦ θεοῦ). It is an even longer title for the Johannine believers than "the one who believes in the Son of God" (ὁ πιστεύων εἰς τὸν υἱὸν τοῦ θεοῦ) seen in 5:10. This time, he specifies *pistis* in the "name" (ὄνομα) of the Son of God. He has alluded to Jesus's "name" before, referring to sins being forgiven on account

---

[126] The writer of 1 John emphasizes the importance to remain (μένω), especially to remain in God/Jesus (2:6, 24, 27, 28; 3:6, 24; 4:13, 15, 16), cf. other occurrences of μένω at 1 Jn 2:10, 14, 17, 19, 28; 3:9, 14, 15, 17, 24; 4:12; 2 Jn 2, 9 (2x).

of his name (2:12) and the command to believe in the name of his Son, Jesus Christ (3:23). However, the phrasing in 5:13 is the only time "name" is mentioned as part of the identity of the Johannine believer. The readers are "believers in the name of the Son of God."

In the penultimate verse, the Johannine author reveals the underlying countercultural reason for his frequent emphasis on the "Son" throughout his letter, and especially, "the Son of God" in the final chapter (5:20):

> And we know that the Son of God has come and has given us understanding so that we may know him who is true; and we are in him who is true, in his Son Jesus Christ. He is the true God and eternal life.

> οἴδαμεν δὲ ὅτι ὁ υἱὸς τοῦ θεοῦ ἥκει καὶ δέδωκεν ἡμῖν διάνοιαν ἵνα γινώσκομεν τὸν ἀληθινόν, καὶ ἐσμεν ἐν τῷ ἀληθινῷ ἐν τῷ υἱῷ αὐτοῦ Ἰησοῦ Χριστῷ. οὗτός ἐστιν ὁ ἀληθινὸς θεὸς καὶ ζωὴ αἰώνιος.

In contrast to the emperor, who is "the son of the god" uplifted in the Greco-Roman culture, the writer of 1 John has emphasized the victorious *pistis* in Jesus, the *true* Son of God. He uses the adjective "true" (ἀληθινὸς) three times in the verse to make his point.[127] He has alluded to the distinction between truth and lie before, for example, in reference to the truth not being in a hypocritical person (1:8, 2:4) or in reference to the spirit of truth (4:6, 5:6).[128] However, he emphasizes the true Son of God, in contrast to the idols around them (his final word in 5:21), which includes the *pistis* in the emperor as the divine ruler of the Greco-Roman world. The author gives the final declaration of his focus on the victorious *pistis* that supersedes the Greco-Roman world, which is *pistis* in Jesus, the true divine Son of God.

Skeptical readers may doubt that the writer of 1 John is referencing the emperor as he does not use the word "emperor" (αὐτοκράτορος) directly in his letter. However, the fact that the only titular use of "the Son of God" outside of the New Testament in the first century CE was for the Roman emperor suggests a countercultural narrative.[129] It would be hard to imagine that the writer of 1 John is not aware of the cultural association he would provoke by emphasizing "the Son of God." He does not need to use the word "emperor" directly because the title of "the Son of God" would already provoke allusions to the emperor. Moreover, he does not discuss the emperor directly because the writer of 1 John wants to emphasize the *true* Son of God. While the culture may subscribe to a *pistis* in the emperor as the divine son, the Johannine believers counter the culture and conquer the Greco-Roman world with their *pistis* in Jesus as the true Son of God.

---

[127] Cf. the only other reference to the adjective in the letter at 1 Jn 2:8.
[128] The word "truth" (ἀλήθεια) occurs at 1 Jn 1:6, 8; 2:4, 21 (2x); 3:18, 19; 4:6; 5:6, cf. 2 Jn 1 (2x), 2, 3, 4; 3 Jn 1, 3 (2x), 4, 8, 12.
[129] Peppard, *The Son of God*, 28.

Testifying to Johannine *Pistis*

The *pistis* victory of 1 John is a positive and triumphant message. However, the letter is not like the victory odes from the athletic games that celebrate a victory for the purposes of the glory of the Johannine community (see Section 2.1). The contentious undertone of the Johannine believers needing to conquer several opponents suggests that the war against the Greco-Roman world is not fully over. The author is writing his letter to assure the readers of their triumphant *pistis* in Jesus as the Son of God because the audience may not feel secure in their *pistis*.

Like many New Testament writers, the Johannine author reflects his awareness of the fragility of others' experience as the basis for *pistis*.[130] The news of Jesus's resurrection and glorification was dependent on the testimony of a relatively small group of people who were personally unknown to most converts, and this was problematic because the Greco-Roman culture of *pistis* typically relied on personal experience and the testimony of those closest to them.[131] People would form their *pistis* based on what they saw and heard with their own eyes and ears as a form of self-trust.[132] If something could not be experienced directly, then there would be increased doubt. Diodorus Siculus, for example, warns his readers about some earlier untrustworthy historians who believed in false reports.[133] Thus, when writing about the past, historians would often try to verify the information personally and get as close to the original source as possible.[134]

Believing in something that one could not test or prove was considered foolish, childish, and reflective of the uneducated masses.[135] Therefore, if one had to rely on the testimony of another, it was better if the testimony could be investigated for oneself.[136] For earlier events that could not be directly verified, multiple testimonies that were in agreement were considered more reliable and credible. Dionysius of Halicarnassus, for example, encourages having as "numerous and indisputable testimonies" (μαρτυριῶν ... πολλῶν καὶ δυσαντιλέκτων) as possible regarding earlier historical accounts in order to deem them more "credible" (πισταί).[137] If there was a consensus from multiple sources, then it would more likely be a truth worth believing.

The possibility of dubious false reports, the importance of direct experience, and the testimony of multiple witnesses who agree with one another to form a reliable *pistis*

---

[130] For example, Lk. 1:14; 1 Cor. 2:3–5; 2 Thess. 1:10, 1 Tim. 2:6–7; Tit. 1:13-14; Heb. 2:1-4; cf. Morgan, *Roman Faith and Christian Faith*, 245.

[131] Morgan, *Roman Faith and Christian Faith*, 65, 245.

[132] Cf. Dionysius of Halicarnassus, *Roman Antiquities* 5.8.1, which mentions that it comes naturally for men to judge one another based on what they experience personally (as opposed to hearsay about the person). The more cynical Dio Chrysostom in his *On Distrust* Oration 74, promotes distrusting almost everyone but never suggests that a person cannot trust himself. Trusting in one's senses hardly needed to be made explicit because it was simply assumed (Morgan, *Roman Faith and Christian Faith*, 42).

[133] Diodorus Siculus, *The Library of History* 1.5.1, 1.23.7–8, 1.26.1–3, 1.29.5–6.

[134] Cassius Dio claims to begin his history with when he can establish the clearest account of events (*Roman History* 1.3).

[135] Morgan, *Roman Faith and Christian Faith*, 67.

[136] Cf. Lucian, *Slander* 31.

[137] Dionysius of Halicarnassus, *Roman Antiquities* 7.70.2 (Cary, LCL).

are all reflected in the letter of 1 John. The author knows that in the battle over *pistis* in the Greco-Roman world, the readers must be certain that there is evidence for the Johannine *pistis* superseding any other in the culture. Like many other New Testament writers, the Johannine author uses testifying (μαρτυρέω) or testimony (μαρτυρία),[138] which are strong terms, often used for eyewitness testimony or irrefutable proof of experience of the resurrection.[139] Within the short letter of 1 John, he refers to testifying or testimony a total of twelve times,[140] ten of which are in the final chapter, where he also emphasizes *pistis* and declares the victory of *pistis*. He mentions testimony throughout the letter, and especially in the final chapter, because he wants the Johannine audience to be assured that their *pistis* is not an abstract ideology, or *pistis* in something that is trendy or the latest fad in the culture. It is a substantial and true *pistis* that is supported by evidence from both people and God himself.

The import of proving the Johannine *pistis* is apparent from the first three verses of the prologue in 1 John (1:1-3):

> What was from the beginning, what we have heard, what we have seen with our eyes, what we have looked at and touched with our hands, concerning the word of life—and the life was revealed, and we have seen and testify, and proclaim to you the eternal life that was with the Father and was revealed to us—and we proclaim to you what we have seen and heard so that you also may have fellowship with us; and truly our fellowship is with the Father and with his Son Jesus Christ.

> Ὃ ἦν ἀπ' ἀρχῆς, ὃ ἀκηκόαμεν, ὃ ἑωράκαμεν τοῖς ὀφθαλμοῖς ἡμῶν, ὃ ἐθεασάμεθα καὶ αἱ χεῖρες ἡμῶν ἐψηλάφησαν περὶ τοῦ λόγου τῆς ζωῆς—καὶ ἡ ζωὴ ἐφανερώθη, καὶ ἑωράκαμεν καὶ μαρτυροῦμεν καὶ ἀπαγγέλλομεν ὑμῖν τὴν ζωὴν τὴν αἰώνιον ἥτις ἦν πρὸς τὸν πατέρα καὶ ἐφανερώθη ἡμῖν—ὃ ἑωράκαμεν καὶ ἀκηκόαμεν, ἀπαγγέλλομεν καὶ ὑμῖν, ἵνα καὶ ὑμεῖς κοινωνίαν ἔχητε μεθ' ἡμῶν. καὶ ἡ κοινωνία δὲ ἡ ἡμετέρα μετὰ τοῦ πατρὸς καὶ μετὰ τοῦ υἱοῦ αὐτοῦ Ἰησοῦ Χριστοῦ.

The writer begins with an emphasis on the testimony of "what was from the beginning," (Ὃ ἦν ἀπ' ἀρχῆς), referring to Jesus.[141] He uses the first-person plural to indicate who is testifying; unlike later in the letter when he is referring to the Johannine community as a whole,[142] in the prologue, the "we" seems to be referring to himself and others who

---

[138] The word μαρτύριον also appears in many NT books (e.g., Mt. 8:4; Mk 1:4; Lk. 5:14; Acts 4:33; 1 Cor. 1:6; 2 Thess. 1:10; 2 Tim. 1:8; Heb. 3:5; Jas 5:3; Rev. 15:5) but does not appear in the John's Gospel or the Johannine Letters. Cf. LSJ s.v. "μαρτύριον."

[139] Morgan, *Roman Faith and Christian Faith*, 315; LSJ s.v. "μαρτυρέω" and "μαρτυρία."

[140] Verbal forms of μαρτυρέω occur at 1 Jn 1:2; 4:14; 5:6, 7, 9, 10; cf. 3 Jn 3, 6, 12 (2x) and the noun μαρτυρία occurs at 1 Jn 5:9 (3x); 10 (2x), 11; cf. 3 Jn 12. The emphasis on testimony is clear in the Gospel of John as well, which uses μαρτυρέω and μαρτυρία a combined 44 times. See especially Jn 1:34; 3:11; 19:35.

[141] Cf. Marshall, *The Epistles of John*, 100–1; Smalley, *The Epistles of John*, 6.

[142] For example, 1 Jn 2:1, 3, 5, 18; 3:1, 2, 11; 4:11, 12, 13; 5:2, 3, 14.

have been eyewitnesses or those close to eyewitnesses of the incarnate Jesus,[143] and they are proclaiming the testimony "to you" (ὑμῖν, 1:2), his audience.[144]

The author of 1 John references the senses of the eyes, ears, and hands, which inform their testimony. Their *pistis* is not based on some abstract ideology or dream,[145] and it does not rely simply on what was *heard* (1:1, 3).[146] The Johannine *pistis* is not a weak baseless *pistis*, but a *pistis* based on what people have seen with their own eyes. The eyewitnesses have "seen," as with testimony in court in which witnesses testify based on what they have seen and what they know (see also Sections 3.1 and 4.2 regarding references to what "we know"). The expression "we have seen and testify" (ἑωράκαμεν καὶ μαρτυροῦμεν, 1:2) acts like a virtual swearing in at a deposition in court,[147] to give evidence and foundational substance to the Johannine *pistis* that is emphasized in the letter.

The writer uses a similar formula, "we have seen and do testify" in his next reference to testimony, which is in the middle of his discourse on love (4:14):

And we have seen and do testify that the Father has sent his Son as the Savior of the world.

καὶ ἡμεῖς τεθεάμεθα καὶ μαρτυροῦμεν ὅτι ὁ πατὴρ ἀπέσταλκεν τὸν υἱὸν σωτῆρα τοῦ κόσμου.

The verb for "see" (θεάομαι) in 4:14 differs from the one in 1:2 (ὁράω).[148] In 4:14, the writer may be using θεάομαι to express the nuance of what the eyewitnesses have seen and experienced that is not the invisible God or the incarnate Jesus.[149] The "seeing" may also include written accounts that have been circulating, as written testimony was often considered more reliable.[150] It is notable that the "see" verbs are in the perfect tense (ἑωράκαμεν, 1:2; τεθεάμεθα, 4:14); the eyewitnesses who have literally seen Jesus

---

[143] The prologue of John's Gospel also refers to the importance of the eyewitness testimony of John the Baptist for the purpose of *pistis* (Jn 1:7-8).

[144] Cf. Smalley, *1, 2, 3 John*, 103; Yarbrough, *1-3 John*, 37. The reference to fellowship "with us" (μεθ' ἡμῶν, 1:3) also indicates that the initial "we" of eyewitnesses is separate from the readers.

[145] Cf. Cicero's frustration over people who place confidence in dreams (*De Divinatione* 2.122).

[146] Hearing in the ancient world was not considered as reliable as seeing (e.g., Seneca the Younger, *De Ira* 2.24; cf. Yarbrough, *1-3 John*, 36-7).

[147] Thompson, *1-3 John*, 34.

[148] Cf. elsewhere in the New Testament regarding testimony about what has been "seen" at Jn 3:11, 32; Acts 7:44.

[149] Cf. Smalley, *1, 2, 3 John*, 251; LSJ s.v. "θεάομαι" and "ὁράω." The verb "ὁράω" also appears at 1:1, 3; 3:1, 2, 6; 4:20 (2x); 5:16; cf. 3 Jn 11, 14. The less common NT verb θεάομαι appears elsewhere in 1:1; 4:12. That both verbs appear in 1:1 may indicate the distinction of what has been seen directly with their eyes (ὁράω) and what other experiences they have had that support what they have seen directly (θεάομαι). This is especially true of 4:12 in which the verb θεάομαι is used in the reference to no one having *seen* God. Although God is invisible, the Johannine community can feel the love of God within them. The frequency of the two verbs of "seeing" in the letter indicates the importance of evidence for their *pistis*.

[150] Cf. John Marincola, *Authority and Tradition, in Ancient Historiography* (Cambridge: Cambridge University Press, 2003), 103. Livy says that he will be sure to give a "clearer and more definite account" of history because writing is "the sole trustworthy guardian of the memory of past events" (*History of Rome* 6.1.2).

and his death and resurrection have seen him in the past, and are now testifying in the present (reflected in the tense, μαρτυροῦμεν) to give evidence for what they have seen in the past. They are probably testifying by evangelizing to the general public but also to the audience of this letter. The succeeding verse refers to those who confess (ὁμολογέω)[151] that Jesus is the Son of God, further supporting the sense of testifying to others about what they know.

In the final chapter, references to testifying and testimony appear ten times, indicating the importance of what the writer is trying to convey to his audience: testimony gives evidence for their *pistis*. Immediately following the proclamation of the victorious *pistis* (5:4-5), the writer offers three distinct witnesses for the Johannine *pistis* (5:6-8):[152]

> This is the one who came by water and blood, Jesus Christ, not with the water only but with the water and the blood. And the Spirit is the one that testifies, for the Spirit is the truth. For there are three who testify: the Spirit and the water and the blood, and these three are in agreement.
>
> Οὗτός ἐστιν ὁ ἐλθὼν δι' ὕδατος καὶ αἵματος, Ἰησοῦς Χριστὸς οὐκ ἐν τῷ ὕδατι μόνον ἀλλ' ἐν τῷ ὕδατι καὶ ἐν τῷ αἵματι καὶ τὸ πνεῦμά ἐστιν τὸ μαρτυροῦν ὅτι τὸ πνεῦμά ἐστιν ἡ ἀλήθεια. ὅτι τρεῖς εἰσιν οἱ μαρτυροῦντες, τὸ πνεῦμα καὶ τὸ ὕδωρ καὶ τὸ αἷμα καὶ οἱ τρεῖς εἰς τὸ ἕν εἰσιν.

In verse 6, the Spirit is mentioned first as "the one that testifies" (τὸ μαρτυροῦν), and this is probably referring to the indwelling Spirit, as the writer has mentioned the Spirit being given to the Johannine believers (4:13). The indwelling Spirit testifies to the truth about Jesus, who came by water (referring to the baptism of Jesus) and blood (referring to Jesus's crucifixion).[153] As we have seen above, the culture relies foremost on trusting oneself, and the indwelling Spirit offers the testimony of personal experience in the truth (ἀλήθεια, 5:6).

The Johannine writer then clarifies that there are, in fact, three testimonies. Although spirit, water, and blood are all neuter nouns in Greek, the author personifies them with the collective masculine plural (μαρτυροῦντες) to emphasize the fact that there are three different witnesses who testify, and that their testimonies agree with one another.[154] The water and blood refer to past events, but the testimonies of these events, along with personal testimony from the indwelling Spirit, all cohere about Jesus. By framing the testimonies in this manner, the author of 1 John draws upon the culture of trusting in oneself and the agreement of multiple witnesses to reinforce the truth about the Johannine *pistis*.[155]

---

[151] See ὁμολογέω at 1:9; 2:23; 4:2, 3, 15 cf. 2 Jn 7. The distinction between ὁμολογέω and μαρτυρέω is that the ὁμολογέω literally means "agree with," but it can also mean "confess" or "be allowed;" cf. LSJ s.v. "ὁμολογέω." In 2:23, the one who "confesses" Jesus Christ as the Son of God is placed in contrast to the one who "denies" (ἀρνέομαι, cf. 2:22) him, suggesting the distinction between verbally agreeing with the Johannine *pistis* and rejecting it outright.
[152] Cf. Brown, *Epistles of John* 775-87 for issues of interpolation and variance of the so-called Johannine Comma in 5:7-8.
[153] Cf. Marshall, *The Epistles of John*, 231-4.
[154] Cf. Yarbrough, *1-3 John*, 282-4; Marshall, *The Epistles of John*, 237.
[155] Cf. other New Testament references to multiple witnesses: Mt. 18:16; Jn 8:17; 2 Cor. 13:1; 1 Tim. 5:19; Heb. 10:28.

Table 4 The Testimony

1 John 5:9	1 John 5:10
If we receive the testimony of men, the testimony of God is greater; for this is the testimony of God that he has testified concerning his Son.	The one who believes in the Son of God has the testimony in himself. The one who does not believe in God has made him a liar because he has not believed in the testimony which God has testified concerning his Son.
εἰ τὴν μαρτυρίαν τῶν ἀνθρώπων λαμβάνομεν, ἡ μαρτυρία τοῦ θεοῦ μείζων ἐστίν· ὅτι αὕτη ἐστὶν ἡ μαρτυρία τοῦ θεοῦ ὅτι μεμαρτύρηκεν περὶ τοῦ υἱοῦ αὐτοῦ.	ὁ πιστεύων εἰς τὸν υἱὸν τοῦ θεοῦ ἔχει τὴν μαρτυρίαν ἐν αὐτῷ, ὁ μὴ πιστεύων τῷ θεῷ ψεύστην πεποίηκεν αὐτόν, ὅτι οὐ πεπίστευκεν εἰς τὴν μαρτυρίαν ἣν μεμαρτύρηκεν ὁ θεὸς περὶ τοῦ υἱοῦ αὐτοῦ.

The reliability of a testimony is dependent on the one giving the testimony,[156] and so this may explain why the writer of 1 John adds to his initial emphasis on eyewitness testimony from people in the prologue to that of God himself testifying to his Son (5:9-10, see Table 4). The writer underscores his point here with the most saturated references of "testimony" and "testifying" appearing a combined seven times in the two verses. The writer initially distinguishes human testimony from the testimony of God (5:9).

The "testimony of men" (ἡ μαρτυρία τῶν ἀνθρώπων, 5:9) might be received by others as authoritative, but if people are willing to hear the testimonies of men, then surely they should receive the "testimony of God" (ἡ μαρτυρία τοῦ θεοῦ), which surpasses human testimony. He uses the perfect tense of the verb, "he has testified" (μεμαρτύρηκεν, 5:9, 10) to indicate that God himself has already testified in the past about his Son Jesus. The author of 1 John and the other eyewitnesses have testified (1:2); they are mere humans and offer the testimony of men, and people will usually accept and believe the testimony of men. However, the author repeats in verse 10 that God has testified as well, and the implication is that they should certainly believe God's testimony because his testimony is even greater (5:9).

Some people do not believe in God's testimony that he is shown through Jesus, his son, and if they do not believe, then they have identified God as a liar (cf. 1:10 and discussion on "liar" above). It seems that there are people who have not acknowledged God's testimony as greater and that there are also people who are testifying to a different *pistis*. They do not believe in the testimony that God has given about his Son (5:10). The Johannine leader is probably referring to the antichrists and false prophets that he has alluded to earlier.[157] Those who left the Johannine community (2:19) may have done so because of testimonies from those who denied that Jesus is the Christ (2:22-3).

---

[156] Cf. Sallust, *The War with Jugurtha* 17.7 in which the responsibility for reliable information comes from the sources themselves; cf. Marincola, *Authority and Tradition*, 105.

[157] See 1 Jn 2:18, 22; 4:3; cf. 2 Jn 7. See also section 3.2 on antichrists and false prophets.

They seem to have been swayed in their *pistis,* and the emphasis on God's testimony in the final chapter suggests that the author is concerned that others in the Johannine community might question their *pistis* as well.

Verse 10 emphasizes the connection between testimony and *pistis,* between those who have internalized the testimony of *pistis* in Jesus as the Son of God, and those who have chosen to reject this testimony. The readers of the letter have trusted in their Johannine teacher and believed his testimony thus far, possibly because they feel that they have a personal relationship with the man who addresses them as his "children."[158] However, there are many who have likely not seen Jesus firsthand and may struggle in their *pistis,* especially when confronted with another seemingly convincing testimony in an alternative *pistis.* They may also be tempted by what they see with their own eyes in their daily personal experiences of the world (2:16). Thus, the writer of 1 John warns his readers not to be tempted by the world (2:15) and cautions them about false testimonies from those who would deceive them (2:28; 3:7; cf. 4:1) in a similar manner to Diodorus Siculus, who cautioned his readers about historians reporting false testimonies.[159] Toward the end of 1 John, the author repeats the phrase (μεμαρτύρηκεν [ὁ θεὸς] περὶ τοῦ υἱοῦ αὐτοῦ, 5:9, 10) to emphasize the authoritative testimony of God, and he suggests the foolishness of those who would regard God as a "liar" when they would normally accept the testimony of men. He exhorts his readers to retain their *pistis* that is based in God's testimony about his Son.

In the final reference to testimony, the writer of 1 John offers the implications of *pistis* in God's testimony (5:11):

> And this is the testimony: that God gave us eternal life, and this life is in his Son.
>
> καὶ αὕτη ἐστὶν ἡ μαρτυρία ὅτι ζωὴν αἰώνιον ἔδωκεν ὁ θεὸς ἡμῖν, καὶ αὕτη ἡ ζωὴ ἐν τῷ υἱῷ αὐτοῦ ἐστιν.

In this simple statement, the author reveals his concern about why it is important to receive the testimony of both God and the eyewitnesses. Here, he is not trying to convey the content of the testimony (what God asserts) but the *result* of *pistis* in the testimony, which is eternal life. The consequences of *not* having *pistis* are great, and so the author wants to assure his audience that the testimony is more than reliable, and he wants to ensure that the readers retain their *pistis* and not assume any validity in the beliefs of the culture that would deem the Johannine *pistis* invalid. He specifies yet again that this life is "in his Son" (ἐν τῷ υἱῷ αὐτοῦ) who is connected to eternal life, as we shall explore in the final section below.

Victorious *Pistis* and Eternal Life

The reason why the *pistis* victory is so important to the Johannine author is because of the consequence of eternal life. In the Greco-Roman culture, the afterlife and the idea

---

[158] Cf. 1 Jn 2:1, 12, 14, 18, 28; 3:7, 18; 4:4; 5:21.
[159] Diodorus Siculus, *The Library of History* 1.5.1, 1.23.7–8, 1.26.1–3, 1.29.5–6.

of an eternal soul was something that was little understood but often sought. As we have seen, the athletes wanted a lasting glory in their victory odes (Section 2.1), and the emperors sought apotheosis and desired to be called "god" or "son of god" even while on earth (Section 5.1). The uncertainty around death fostered myths about the underworld,[160] and as we have seen in Section 4.1, different philosophical responses to life after death. The Romans under the Empire tried to cope with death through private deification, in which sacrifices were made to the dead, effectually rendering them as divine.[161]

The writer of 1 John offers a final countercultural message to the Greco-Roman culture, which longs for eternity and the afterlife, and yet seems to be dissatisfied in its responses. Finally, we see why the victorious *pistis* is so important to the author. It is not just about conquering the Greco-Roman world and having some personal pride in knowing more than the world. There is eternity at stake. The author repeatedly emphasizes eternal life as the countercultural consequence to the victorious *pistis* of 1 John.

From the prologue to the epilogue, the Johannine author connects the *pistis* in Jesus with eternal life. The word "life" (ζωή) appears thirteen times in the letter, of which six refer specifically to eternal life (ζωὴ αἰώνιος).[162] However, just as the language of *pistis*, testimony, and the Son of God are all concentrated in Chapter 5, the majority of references to "life" are also concentrated in the final chapter, suggesting yet another connection to *pistis*. Indeed, the Johannine author alludes to the connections between "life" and *pistis* in Jesus, starting from the prologue in which "life" appears three times in the first two verses (1:1-2):

> What was from the beginning, what we have heard, what we have seen with our eyes, what we have looked at and touched with our hands, concerning the word of life—and the life was revealed, and we have seen and testify, and proclaim to you the eternal life that was with the Father and was revealed to us.
>
> Ὃ ἦν ἀπ᾽ ἀρχῆς, ὃ ἀκηκόαμεν, ὃ ἑωράκαμεν τοῖς ὀφθαλμοῖς ἡμῶν, ὃ ἐθεασάμεθα καὶ αἱ χεῖρες ἡμῶν ἐψηλάφησαν περὶ τοῦ λόγου τῆς ζωῆς—καὶ ἡ ζωὴ ἐφανερώθη, καὶ ἑωράκαμεν καὶ μαρτυροῦμεν καὶ ἀπαγγέλλομεν ὑμῖν τὴν ζωὴν τὴν αἰώνιον ἥτις ἦν πρὸς τὸν πατέρα καὶ ἐφανερώθη ἡμῖν.

---

[160] Cf. Jan N. Bremmer, *The Rise and Fall of the Afterlife: The 1995 Read-Tuckwell Lectures at the University of Bristol*, Read-Tuckwell Lectures, University of Bristol 1995 (London: Routledge, 2002), 6.

[161] Veit Rosenberger, "Coping with Death: Private Deification in the Roman Empire," in *Burial Rituals, Ideas of Afterlife, and the Individual in the Hellenistic World and the Roman Empire*, ed. Katharina Waldner, Richard Gordon, and Wolfgang Spickermann (Stuttgart, Germany: Franz Steiner Verlag, 2016), 121.

[162] See ζωὴ αἰώνιος at 1 Jn 1:2; 2:25; 3:15; 5:11, 13, 20. Additional references to ζωή are at 1:1, 2; 3:14; 5:11, 12 (2x), 16. Cf. in John's Gospel: the first occurrence of ζωή is at 1:4, and the first reference to ζωὴ αἰώνιος is at 3:15. The theme of eternal life is clearly present in the Gospel as well; ζωὴ αἰώνιος in John's Gospel at 3:16, 36; 4:14, 36; 5:24, 39; 6:27, 40, 47, 54, 68; 10:28; 12:25, 50; 17:2, 3.

In verse 1, the author refers to Jesus with three different monikers: "the word of life" (ὁ λόγος τῆς ζωῆς), "the life" (ἡ ζωὴ), and "the eternal life" (ἡ ζωὴ ἡ αἰώνιος).[163] All three include the word "life" with the definite article, indicating more formally that these are titles for Jesus,[164] and the third title, eternal life, is the theme that the author of 1 John reinforces throughout his letter.

The life (ζωὴ) of 1 John is not to be confused with another word that could be translated "life" (βίος)[165] that appears in 1 Jn 2:16 and 3:17 (see also Section 3.3). The word βίος elsewhere in the NT appears as referring to everyday life (e.g., 2 Tim. 2:4) or to a person's livelihood (e.g., Mk 12:44; Lk. 21:4). However, the author uses βίος in reference to the life of the world. While ζωὴ reflects eternal life in Jesus Christ, the true Son of God, βίος is the life that is attached to the Greco-Roman world. The word ζωὴ is representative of the eternal life that the members of the Johannine community are living now and will continue to live after their physical deaths because they have *pistis* in Jesus as the Son of God.

The reference to "eternal life" appears only once in Chapter 2, but the context uses similar language to the prologue (2:24-5):

Let what you heard from the beginning remain in you. If what you heard from the beginning remains in you, you also will remain in the Son and in the Father. And this is the promise which he has promised us, eternal life.

ὑμεῖς ὃ ἠκούσατε ἀπ' ἀρχῆς ἐν ὑμῖν μενέτω. ἐὰν ἐν ὑμῖν μείνῃ ὃ ἀπ' ἀρχῆς ἠκούσατε, καὶ ὑμεῖς ἐν τῷ υἱῷ καὶ ἐν τῷ πατρὶ μενεῖτε. καὶ αὕτη ἐστὶν ἡ ἐπαγγελία ἣν αὐτὸς ἐπηγγείλατο ἡμῖν, τὴν ζωὴν τὴν αἰώνιον.

The sense of contention surrounds these two verses, as the verses before warn of antichrists and those who deny Jesus (2:18-23), and the verse immediately after warns of those who would deceive the readers. Verse 24 echoes the first verse of the letter, referring to what was heard "from the beginning" (ἀπ' ἀρχῆς). In contrast to the first-person plural verbs in the prologue, however, the verbs here place the focus on the readers ("you heard" [ἠκούσατε, 2x], "you will remain" [μενεῖτε]). Moreover, the restatement is placed in a conditional form: "if what you heard from the beginning remains in you" (ἐὰν ἐν ὑμῖν μείνῃ ὃ ἀπ' ἀρχῆς ἠκούσατε, 2:24), suggesting that the Johannine *pistis* needs to be appropriated by the person first.[166] We see the emphasis on "remaining" (μένω) repeated three times in the verse, which underlines the importance of not faltering in the Johannine *pistis*. As a result of their remaining in the true Son of God, they receive eternal life.

---

[163] In addition to the "the word of life" (ὁ λόγος τῆς ζωῆς, 1 Jn 1:1) having allusions to Jesus who is "the Word" (ὁ λόγος) in the Gospel of John (1:1, 14), "the life" (ἡ ζωὴ, 1 Jn 1:2) follows almost immediately after "the word of life," indicating that "the life" refers to "the word of life." Moreover, the repetition of ἐφανερώθη in 1:2 indicates that "the life" and "the eternal life" have the same referent.

[164] Cf. Yarbrough, *1–3 John*, 39. Cf. "life" also being identified with Jesus at the beginning of the Gospel of John (1:4).

[165] Cf. LSJ s.v. "βίος."

[166] Cf. Smalley, *1, 2, 3 John*, 119.

Eternal life is not just a possibility based on good behavior (reflecting a fear of divine judgment) or based on the whims of a Greco-Roman deity. The Johannine author offers a countercultural assurance that this eternal life is promised by God. The noun and verb for "promise" (ἐπαγγελία, ἐπαγγέλλομαι) make their sole appearance in the letter in reference to what God promised the Johannine believers: eternal life. Instead of referring directly to the incarnation of Jesus, the writer chooses to identify Jesus as "eternal life." The framing of the eternal life being a promise that God had already promised before, with the use of the aorist verb (ἐπηγγείλατο) that suggests an allusion to the prophesied Jesus, simultaneously suggests a reference to the past in which the promise was made and the future of the *effect* of eternal life.[167] However, as the conditional language suggests (2:24), the effect of an alternative *pistis*, that is, a *pistis* from the Greco-Roman world, produces a radically different result.

The Johannine author expresses the consequences of an alternative *pistis* with extreme language in Chapter 3 (3:13-15):

Do not be astonished, brothers, if the world hates you. We know that we have passed from death to life because we love one another. The one who does not love remains in death. Everyone who hates a brother is a murderer, and you know that every murderer does not have eternal life remaining in them.

μὴ θαυμάζετε, ἀδελφοί, εἰ μισεῖ ὑμᾶς ὁ κόσμος. ἡμεῖς οἴδαμεν ὅτι μεταβεβήκαμεν ἐκ τοῦ θανάτου εἰς τὴν ζωήν, ὅτι ἀγαπῶμεν τοὺς ἀδελφούς· ὁ μὴ ἀγαπῶν μένει ἐν τῷ θανάτῳ. πᾶς ὁ μισῶν τὸν ἀδελφὸν αὐτοῦ ἀνθρωποκτόνος ἐστίν. καὶ οἴδατε ὅτι πᾶς ἀνθρωποκτόνος οὐκ ἔχει ζωὴν αἰώνιον ἐν αὐτῷ μένουσαν.

The writer of 1 John places a division once again between the Johannine community and the world that can hate them (3:13). The implication is that they should *expect* the world to hate them (see also Section 3.3) as they have a *pistis* that does not align with the world's. In contrast to the hate from the world, the Johannine believers are expected to love one another (3:14). The author uses the extremities of life (ζωή) and death (θάνατος) to illustrate the differences in before and after *pistis* in Jesus as the Son of God. Every Johannine believer was remaining in the realm of death, just like every person in the Greco-Roman world. However, when the readers of 1 John accepted the Johannine *pistis*, they also received the promised eternal life. The author is indicating the severity of the change by saying that the readers have passed from death to life already and that love is the marker of their having done so (3:14). However, the lack of love is an indication that a person has not accepted the true Johannine *pistis*, and that person is remaining in death.

The Johannine author then takes one step further in the extreme by saying that the one who hates is a murderer (ἀνθρωποκτόνος, 3:15). The writer uses the language of "remaining" (μένω) once again to indicate that every murderer does not have eternal life remaining in them. Eternal life does not "remain" in murderers who demonstrate hate for their brothers. The severity of the language reveals the severe consequences of

---

[167] Cf. Yarbrough, *1–3 John*, 161.

the contention in 1 John. It is a battle in which there is the potential for violence and even death. The one in the world who hates also remains in death. But as discussed in Section 3.1, the Johannine author is drawing an even more extreme in referencing the one who hates a brother.

The references to "brother" have been to members within the Johannine community (e.g., 2:9-10; 3:10; 5:16), and it is especially apparent in the vocative that is used by the author in 3:13.[168] The references to Cain murdering his brother earlier in the chapter (3:12), and the emphasis that the Johannine community must not be like Cain underlines the sense of the finality of death. The inclination to respond like the world and hate others is an indication that a person still remains in the world of death. The author in verse 15 counters the culture by saying that the Johannine community must not be like the world and hate and do evil deeds, reflecting the *pistis* of the world and the *pistis* of the evil one who has authority over the world (3:12, 5:19). The people of that world do not have eternal life in them, but the Johannine believers do.

As we have discussed in the sections above, the final chapter emphasizes the Johannine victory through the most frequent references to *pistis* language, testimony, and the Son of God. The writer of 1 John similarly reinforces the countercultural message of eternal life in the last chapter to demonstrate the effect of their *pistis* in Jesus as the Son of God (5:11-12):

> And this is the testimony: that God gave us eternal life, and this life is in his Son. The one who has the Son has life; the one who does not have the Son of God does not have life.
>
> καὶ αὕτη ἐστὶν ἡ μαρτυρία ὅτι ζωὴν αἰώνιον ἔδωκεν ὁ θεὸς ἡμῖν, καὶ αὕτη ἡ ζωὴ ἐν τῷ υἱῷ αὐτοῦ ἐστιν. ὁ ἔχων τὸν υἱὸν ἔχει τὴν ζωήν, ὁ μὴ ἔχων τὸν υἱὸν τοῦ θεοῦ τὴν ζωὴν οὐκ ἔχει.

Pistis in the testimony about the Son of God is important because what is at stake is eternal life. He mentions life (ζωὴ) four times, with eternal life being referenced first, and the succeeding references simply being "life." The emphasis on "life" contrasts the previous allusions to "death" in Chapter 3, and serves as a counterpoint to the death he mentions in succeeding verses (5:16-17). As he concludes his reference to testimony in verse 12, he alludes to "life" four times to emphasize God's testimony, which is that God has granted eternal life to the Johannine believers in the past, and this eternal life is not available to those who do not have *pistis* in Jesus as the Son of God.

One might imagine that the Johannine believers should know this information. Seeing all of the eternal life verses in succession can make the Johannine author seem overly and unnecessarily repetitive. However, each time, the Johannine author emphasizes the effect of eternal life in a slightly different and nuanced way. In the case of 5:12, the author emphasizes the aspect of possession that is reminiscent of the indwelling Spirit (cf. 4:13) and the internalized testimony (5:10). The one who does not *have* the Son of God (ὁ μὴ ἔχων τὸν υἱὸν τοῦ θεοῦ), meaning the one who has not

---

[168] Cf. brotherhood language in Smalley, *1, 2, 3 John*, 189.

internalized *pistis* in the Son of God, does not possess eternal life. By contrast, the one who does *have* the Son (ὁ ἔχων τὸν υἱόν), meaning that he does have *pistis* in the Son of God, also possesses eternal life. In the Greco-Roman culture, someone may have *pistis* in the emperor as *divi filius*, but that would not result in the believer possessing eternal life. The political would be intertwined with the religious aspects of such *pistis*, and senators, for example, would be foolish to deify dead family members in an effort to afford some sense of eternity to them because it would be interpreted as a challenge to the emperor.[169]

When the Johannine writer finally begins his epilogue, he gives the reason for his writing, which is the assurance of eternal life for the Johannine believers (5:13):[170]

> I have written these things to you who believe in the name of the Son of God, so that you may know that you have eternal life.

> Ταῦτα ἔγραψα ὑμῖν ἵνα εἰδῆτε ὅτι ζωὴν ἔχετε αἰώνιον τοῖς πιστεύουσιν εἰς τὸ ὄνομα τοῦ υἱοῦ τοῦ θεοῦ.

As discussed in previous sections, the Johannine author has spent the earlier part of the chapter demonstrating that the Johannine *pistis* is not a weak or trendy *pistis* that is passing through the culture based on the testimonies of a couple men. It is a victorious *pistis* that is based on the testimony of God himself. As the Johannine believers come into conflict with the opponents who tempt the community to doubt their *pistis*, the author wants to assure the believers that the effect of their *pistis* is not a small one. It has eternal consequences. Eternal life through apotheosis in the culture was coveted by the emperors, who hoped to be deified after their death and sought to be as close to a divine figure in life as well. For them, deification was the prize, and in a way, the Johannine author is reminding his audience of the "prize" of eternal life that they receive through their *pistis* in Jesus as the Son of God. He is assuring them that the Johannine *pistis* is worth the battle against the Greco-Roman world.

In the final verses of the epilogue, the writer does not conclude with the standard greetings found in other New Testament letters. Instead, he offers several caveats including one about sin and how it can affect a person's life (5:16-17):

> If anyone sees his brother committing a sin that does not lead to death, he will ask, and he will give him life to the ones who commit sin not leading to death. There is sin leading to death; I do not say that he should pray about that. All unrighteousness is sin, but there is sin that does not lead to death.

> Ἐάν τις ἴδῃ τὸν ἀδελφὸν αὐτοῦ ἁμαρτάνοντα ἁμαρτίαν μὴ πρὸς θάνατον, αἰτήσει καὶ δώσει αὐτῷ ζωήν, τοῖς ἁμαρτάνουσιν μὴ πρὸς θάνατον. ἔστιν ἁμαρτία πρὸς θάνατον· οὐ περὶ ἐκείνης λέγω ἵνα ἐρωτήσῃ. πᾶσα ἀδικία ἁμαρτία ἐστίν, καὶ ἔστιν ἁμαρτία οὐ πρὸς θάνατον.

---

[169] Rosenberger, "Coping with Death," 120.
[170] A similar emphasis appears in the Gospel of John, which is said to be written for the purposes of the audience having *pistis* in the Son of God and receiving the effect of [eternal] life (Jn 20:31).

These verses provoke many questions including the question of what sin leads to death and what sin does not lead to death. Because the focus of the chapter, and indeed of the entire letter, has been the contention over *pistis,* this caveat in the epilogue likely indicates a concern over *pistis* as well.

The writer thus far has framed the battle over *pistis* in light of a worldly *pistis* from the culture that remains in death, in contrast to the Johannine *pistis,* which results in eternal life (cf. 3:12-16). We see similar language in 5:16-17 with references to life and death. Because every other verse that refers to life (ζωή) has been a reference to eternal life through *pistis* in Jesus, it seems that this reference to life in 5:16 would also be referring to eternal life. The one who is giving the life must therefore be a reference to God, who grants eternal life (5:11).

The writer brings up the issue of sin (ἁμαρτία), something he has addressed in every chapter of his letter.[171] He knows that his spiritual children may be tempted to sin, especially by the temptations of the Greco-Roman world (2:15-17), but he assures them that if they do sin, the Johannine members are not at a total loss and do have the support of Jesus himself (2:1). Regarding the distinctions between the sin that leads to death and the sin that does not lead to death, the previous references to death are helpful. The only other verse that has addressed death is 3:14, in which we saw that the author identifies those without the Johannine *pistis* to be in death. Therefore, the sin that leads to death suggests the extreme nature of a sin that is leading directly away from the Johannine *pistis* and toward the worldly one.

Despite the extreme language, the writer is actually presenting a positive message. When he says that the Johannine believers need not pray about the sin leading to death, he is not suggesting that they should abandon extreme sinners to their evil devices. That would be in contrast to the love discourse that permeates the letter (esp. 4:7-21). Rather, the author is saying that the Johannine members do not have to dwell on such matters. Instead, he focuses on the sin not leading to death, something he repeats three times in the two verses. When someone is struggling with sin, a fellow Johannine member can pray for that person, and have reassurance that they can still receive eternal life as a result of the Johannine *pistis.* Thus, sin is a concern, but it does not mean that a person is completely lost to the *pistis* of the world.

In the penultimate verse of the letter, the writer of 1 John emphasizes eternal life one last time (5:20):

And we know that the Son of God has come and has given us understanding so that we may know him who is true; and we are in him who is true, in his Son Jesus Christ. He is the true God and eternal life.

οἴδαμεν δὲ ὅτι ὁ υἱὸς τοῦ θεοῦ ἥκει καὶ δέδωκεν ἡμῖν διάνοιαν ἵνα γινώσκομεν τὸν ἀληθινόν, καὶ ἐσμενὲν τῷ ἀληθινῷ ἐν τῷ υἱῷ αὐτοῦ Ἰησοῦ Χριστῷ. οὗτός ἐστιν ὁ ἀληθινὸς θεὸς καὶ ζωὴ αἰώνιος.

---

[171] Cf. ἁμαρτία in 1 Jn 1:7, 8, 9 (2x); 2:2, 12; 3:4 (2x), 5 (2x) 8, 9; 4:10.

In contrast to the world that is under the power of the evil one mentioned in the previous two verses (5:18-19), the author summarizes his central countercultural message about the victorious *pistis* over the *pistis* of the Greco-Roman world. The victorious *pistis* that conquers the world is *pistis* in the true Son of God, who is Jesus Christ, and the Johannine believers receive eternal life through this *pistis*.

The closing verse, then, suggests an implicit "therefore" (5:21):

> [Therefore] little children, keep yourselves from idols.
>
> Τεκνία, φυλάξατε ἑαυτὰ ἀπὸ τῶν εἰδώλων.

The writer finishes with a final warning against the culture. The warning is appropriate, as the entire letter has been a countercultural narrative about the battle over *pistis*. Although the Johannine readers may face temptation (2:15-17), idolatry (5:21), and opponents[172] who try to promote a different *pistis* in the Greco-Roman world, they can be reassured that the Johannine *pistis* is in the true Son of God (esp. 5:20), which is attested by both God and man (1:1-4; 5:6-11). The Johannine believers are by nature Johannine conquerors because they contend against the polytheistic and imperial *pistis* of the culture and receive what the culture cannot achieve: eternal life through *pistis* in the true Son of God.

---

[172] Cf. the evil one (2:13, 14; 3:12; 5:18, 19), antichrists (2:18, 22; 4:3; cf. 2 Jn 7), false prophets (4:1), and the world itself (2:15-17; 3:1, 13; 5:4, 5, 19).

6

Conclusion and Final Reflections

This study has attempted to contribute to the scholarship of 1 John through its exegetical and cultural reading of the letter. The analysis of the "conquering" language with consideration to the cultural context aids modern readers, especially in demonstrating that the previously assumed intra-Johannine, sectarian contention of 1 John is more likely a contention with the culture of the Greco-Roman world in which the Johannine members lived and worked. While the broader culture touted a *pistis* to the emperor and to many gods, the writer of 1 John urges his spiritual children to fight against this cultural norm and to hold onto their *pistis* in Jesus as the true Son of God. In the battle over *pistis,* the countercultural message of 1 John would have been an encouraging letter to receive. The Johannine mentor is demonstrating to his spiritual children that he understands the challenges and temptations that they face in retaining their *pistis* in Jesus as the true Son of God, when the culture of the Greco-Roman world operates in a *pistis* in many gods and honors the emperor as *divi filius*. Thus, the triumphant declaration that the Johannine *pistis* is a *nikē*, which conquers the world (5:4), drives the believers of Jesus to persist in their *pistis* battle.

As we have seen, the conquering language toward a Johannine *nikē* utilizes militaristic undertones already familiar in the Greco-Roman culture, which associates the goddess Nike with military battles to underline the Johannine believers conquering their opponents. As discussed in Chapter 3, each of these opponents including the evil one, the antichrists, and the false prophets is affiliated with "the world," and it is ultimately the conquering of the world itself that marks the Johannine victory. Moreover, the repeated emphasis on "the world" as the ultimate opponent underscores the countercultural tone of Johannine resistance to the Greco-Roman world. Chapter 4 of this study has shown that the author of 1 John has already alluded to the culture with his reference to the negative fear of the divine in the polytheistic world, which contrasts the Johannine love of God (4:18), and that his countercultural message continues to the very end, with a concluding warning against the many idols of the Greco-Roman world.

Finally, we have seen that the battle with the Greco-Roman world in the First Letter of John is ultimately a conflict of *pistis*. Roman soldiers achieved military victories with a *pistis* to the emperor, who was also known as the *divi filius,* the son of god, and the repeated emphasis on Jesus as the true Son of God in 1 John demonstrates the writer's countercultural exhortation: for the Johannine believers to resist what is touted in the culture and to hold fast to their *pistis* in Jesus. While the culture promotes a *pistis* to the emperor, the Johannine author proclaims that the testimonies of both man and God prove that Jesus is the true divine Son. Though the Johannine believers need to be vigilant in resisting the antichrists, false prophets, and idols in the world that represent a different *pistis*, they can also be reassured that the minority community that holds a *pistis* in Jesus as the true Son of God conquers this world of opponents around them.

The countercultural victory of 1 John is especially striking when one considers the progression of the *pistis* battle in latter centuries of the Roman Empire. By the fourth century CE, the goddess Nike/Victoria became a visual representation of that battle as she was taken *in* and *out* of the Curia (Senate House) in Rome. After the unexpected conversion of the emperor Constantine to Christianity,[1] his son Constantius II removed the altar of Nike/Victoria, and established a law in 356 to make it a capital crime to sacrifice or take part in the worship of images.[2] By this time, the cult of Nike/Victoria had been practiced in Rome for some six and a half centuries, and the Altar of Victory had been the place where senators had sacrificed at her altar before each meeting and sworn oaths of loyalty to the emperor ever since Augustus first placed her there in 29 BCE.[3] Subsequent Christian emperors were more tolerant and allowed the cults of Rome to remain,[4] and the Altar of Victory was placed back in the Curia, probably during the brief reign of Julian in late 361 to mid-363.[5]

For most of the fourth century, and certainly under the time of Constantius II, the pressures on the Roman elite still strongly favored traditional practices,[6] but when the emperor Gratian stopped financial support of the cults in 382, and removed the altar of Nike/Victoria from the Curia for a second time, there seems to have been a noticeable shift in the culture.[7] Symmachus as prefect of the city of Rome wrote a lengthy memorandum to the emperor arguing for the restoration of the altar as it had come to represent the deep history of Roman imperial tradition and the religious customs that Symmachus believed had served the state well in fostering loyalty to the emperor.[8] For him, the goddess Nike/Victoria was synonymous with Rome. Thus, Symmachus's

---

[1] Beard, North, and Price, *Religions of Rome*, 366.
[2] *Codex Theodosianus* 16.10.6.
[3] John Matthews, *Western Aristocracies and Imperial Court, A.D. 364–425* (Oxford: Clarendon Press, 1975), 204.
[4] Beard, North, and Price, *Religions of Rome*, 374.
[5] Glen L. Thompson, "Constantius II and the First Removal of the Altar of Victory," in *A Tall Order: Writing the Social History of the Ancient World: Essays in Honor of William V. Harris*, ed. Jean-Jacques Aubert and Zsuzsanna Várhelyi (München, Germany: K. G. Saur, 2005), 103.
[6] Beard, North, and Price, *Religions of Rome*, 380.
[7] Cf. Symmachus, *Relations* 3.15. It seems only the altar was removed and the statue of Nike/Victoria herself may have been retained; cf. Claudian *De VI cons. Hon.* (of 404), 597–602; cf. Alan Cameron, *Claudian: Poetry and Propaganda at the Court of Honorius* (Oxford: Clarendon, 1970), 239; Matthews, *Western Aristocracies*, 204. The reason for the statue staying was probably because Nike/Victoria had become a symbol of rule and support of the senate, and it was the sacrifices that had been a problem for Constantius (Thompson, "Constantius II and the First Removal of the Altar of Victory," 92–3).
[8] Cf. Gerhard van den Heever, "The Usefulness of Violent Ends: Apocalyptic Imaginaries in the Reconstruction of Society," in *Reconceiving Religious Conflict: New Views from the Formative Centuries of Christianity*, ed. Wendy Mayer and Chris L. de Wet, Routledge Studies in the Early Christian World (Abingdon: Routledge, 2018), 282–335.

arguments were less directed against the issue of Christianity and more in favor of the toleration of the cults.⁹

Ambrose, the bishop of Milan, countered Symmachus with two letters that forcefully argued that it was the Christian duty of the emperor to fight for the church.¹⁰ The bishop seems to have presented a countercultural argument against the traditional culture at the highest level, regarding the once universally respected state religion, which Symmachus believed had made the Roman Empire prosperous, as the outdated enthusiasm of a local minority.¹¹ Ambrose was successful in his efforts, and after 382, with the brief exception of the reign of Eugenius from 392 to 394, "there was now only one true *religio.*"¹² What the writer of 1 John had presented centuries before as the countercultural victory of *pistis* against the Greco-Roman world had become the predominant norm.

---

[9] Beard, North, and Price, *Religions of Rome*, 386.
[10] Ambrose, *Epp.* 17–18. A more skeptical view of Ambrose suggests that his dispute over the altar was a low-risk opportunity to "flex his muscles" in the imperial court (Robert Chenault, "Beyond Pagans and Christians: Politics and Intra-Christian Conflict in the Controversy over the Altar of Victory," in *Pagans and Christians in Late Antique Rome*, ed. Michele Renee Salzman, Marianne Sághy, and Rita Lizzi Testa [Cambridge: Cambridge University Press, 2015], 48).
[11] Cf. Ambrose, *Ep.* 18.2; Matthews, *Western Aristocracies*, 207.
[12] Beard, North, and Price, *Religions of Rome*, 386.

Bibliography

Aberbach, Moses, and Leivy Smolar. "Aaron, Jeroboam, and the Golden Calves." *JBL* 86, no. 2 (June 1967): 129–40.
Akin, Daniel. *1, 2, 3 John*. NAC 38. Nashville, TN: Broadman & Holman Publishers, 2001.
Anderson, Paul. "Antichristic Crises: Proselytization Back into Jewish Religious Certainty—The Threat of Schismatic Abandonment." In *Text and Community: Essays in Commemoration of Bruce M. Metzger, Vol. 1*, edited by J. Harold Ellens, 217–40. Sheffield: Sheffield Phoenix Press, 2007.
Anderson, Paul. "Beyond the Shade of the Oak Tree: Recent Growth in Johannine Studies." *ExpTim* 119, no. 8 (2008): 365–73.
Anderson, Paul. "The Community that Raymond Brown Left Behind: Reflections on the Johannine Dialectical Situation." *Faculty Publications—College of Christian Studies* (2013): 275.
Ashton, John. *Understanding the Fourth Gospel*. Oxford: Oxford University Press, 2007.
Aune, David E., and Frederick E. Brenk, eds. *Greco-Roman Culture and the New Testament*. Leiden: Brill, 2012.
Barclay, John M. *Pauline Churches and Diaspora Jews*. Tübingen: Mohr Siebeck, 2011.
Barringer, Judy. "The Legacy of the Phidian Zeus at Olympia." In *Statue of Zeus at Olympia: New Approaches*, edited by Janette McWilliam, Sonia Puttock, Tom Stevenson, and Rashna Taraporewalla, 61–78. Newcastle upon Tyne: Cambridge Scholars Publishing, 2011.
Barry, John M. "*Fides* in Julius Caesar's *Bellum Civile*: A Study in Roman Political Ideology at the Close of the Republican Era." PhD Diss. University of Maryland, College Park, 2005.
Bauckham, Richard. *Gospel of Glory: Major Themes in Johannine Theology*. Grand Rapids: Baker Academic, 2015.
Beard, Mary, John North, and S. R. F. Price. *Religions of Rome, Vol. 1*. Cambridge: Cambridge University Press, 1998.
Beasley-Murray, George Raymond. *John*. WBC. Waco, TX: Word Books, 1987.
Blom, Henriette van der. *Cicero's Role Models: The Political Strategy of a Newcomer*. Oxford: Oxford University Press, 2010.
Bock, Darrell L. *Acts*. BECNT. Grand Rapids: Baker Academic, 2007.
Bowden, Hugh. *Mystery Cults in the Ancient World*. London: Thames & Hudson, 2010.
Bremmer, Jan N. *The Rise and Fall of the Afterlife: The 1995 Read-Tuckwell Lectures at the University of Bristol*. Read-Tuckwell Lectures, University of Bristol 1995. London: Routledge, 2002.
Brenk, Frederick E. *In Mist Apparelled: Religious Themes in Plutarch's Moralia and Lives*. Mnemosyne, Bibliotheca Classica Batava. Supplementum 48. Lugduni Batavorum: Brill, 1977.
Brown, Raymond. *The Epistles of John*. AB. London: Geoffrey Chapman, 1982.
Brown, Raymond. *The Gospel of John I–XII*. AB. Garden City, NY: Doubleday, 1966.
Bruce, F. F. *1 & 2 Thessalonians*. WBC 45. Waco, TX: Word Books, 1982.

Bruce, F. F. *The Epistles of John: Introduction, Exposition and Notes*. London: Pickering & Inglis, 1978.
Bujard, Sophie. "La Mosaïque aux Divinités d'Orbe-Boscéaz (Suisse): une lecture a choix multiples." In *La Mosaïque Gréco-romaine, 9*, Collection De L'École Française de Rome, 352, edited by Hélène Morlier, 227–34. Rome: École Française de Rome, 2005.
Bultmann, Rudolf. *The Johannine Epistles: A Commentary on the Johannine Epistles*. Hermeneia, edited by Robert W. Funk. Translated by R. Philip O'Hara, Lane C. McGaughy, and Robert Frank. Philadelphia, PA: Fortress, 1973.
Cameron, Alan. *Claudian: Poetry and Propaganda at the Court of Honorius*. Oxford: Clarendon Press, 1970.
Carter, Warren. *John and Empire: Initial Explorations*. London: T&T Clark, 2008.
Cassidy, Richard J. *John's Gospel in the New Perspective: Christology and the Realities of Roman Power*. Maryknoll, NY: Orbis Books, 1992.
Chaniotis, Angelos. "Empathy, Emotional Display, Theatricality, and Illusion in Hellenistic Historiography." In *Unveiling Emotions II: Emotions in Greece and Rome: Texts, Images, Material Culture*, edited by Angelos Chaniotis and Pierre Ducrey, 53–84. Stuttgart, Germany: Franz Steiner Verlag, 2013.
Chenault, Robert. "Beyond Pagans and Christians: Politics and Intra-Christian Conflict in the Controversy over the Altar of Victory." In *Pagans and Christians in Late Antique Rome*, edited by Michele Renee Salzman, Marianne Sághy, and Rita Lizzi Testa, 46–63. Cambridge: Cambridge University Press, 2015.
Clark-Soles, Jamie. *Death and Afterlife in the New Testament*. New York: T&T Clark, 2006.
Crook, Zeba. "Honor, Shame, and Social Status Revisited." *JBL* 128, no. 3 (Fall 2009): 591–611.
Culpepper, R. Alan. *The Gospel and Letters of John*. Nashville, TN: Abingdon Press, 1998.
DeConick, April. *The Gnostic Age: How a Countercultural Spirituality Revolutionized Religion from Antiquity to Today*. New York: Columbia University Press, 2016.
Dunn, James D. G. *Romans 1–8*. WBC 38A. Dallas, TX: Word Books, 1988.
Durham, John I. *Exodus*. WBC 3. Waco, TX: Word Books, 1987.
Easter, Matthew C. "The *Pistis Christou* Debate: Main Arguments and Responses in Summary." *CurBR* 9, no. 1 (Sep 2010): 33–47.
Eckstein, Arthur M. "Polybius, Phylarchus, and Historiographical Criticism." *Classical Philology* 108, no. 4 (2013): 314–38.
Edwards, M. J. "Martyrdom and the 'First Epistle' of John." *NovT* 31, Fasc. 2 (Apr 1989): 164–71.
Errington, R. M. *Philopoemen*. Oxford: Clarendon Press, 1969.
Farrar, Thomas J., and Guy Williams. "Diabolical Data: A Critical Inventory of New Testament Satanology." *JSNT* 39, no. 1 (2016): 40–71.
Fee, Gordon D. "Εἰδωλόθυτα Once Again: An Interpretation of 1 Corinthians 8–10." *Bib* 61, no. 2 (1980): 172–97.
Frey, Jörg. "Dualism and the World in the Gospel and Letters of John." In *The Oxford Handbook of Johannine Studies*, edited by Judith M. Lieu and Martinus C. de Boer, 274–91. Oxford: Oxford University Press, 2018.
Freyburger, Gérard. *Fides: étude Sémantique Et Religieuse Depuis Les Origines Jusqu'à L'époque Augustéenne*. Paris: Belles Lettres, 1986.
Griffith, Terry. *Keep Yourselves from Idols: A New Look at 1 John*. JSNTSup 233. London: Sheffield Academic Press, 2002.
Griffiths, J. Gwyn. *The Divine Verdict: A Study of Divine Judgement in the Ancient Religions*. Studies in the History of Religions 52. Leiden: Brill, 1990.

Grosheide, F. W. *Commentary on the First Epistle to the Corinthians*. NICNT. Grand Rapids: Eerdmans, 1972.
Gruen, Erich. "Greek Πίστις and Roman Fides." *Athenaeum* NS 60 (1982): 50–68.
Hamilton, Victor P. *The Book of Genesis: Chapters 18–50*. NICOT. Grand Rapids: Eerdmans, 1995.
Hays, Richard B. *Echoes of Scripture in the Letters of Paul*. New Haven, CT: Yale University Press, 1989.
Hays, Richard B. *First Corinthians*. Louisville, KY: John Knox Press, 1997.
Heever, Gerhard van den. "Finding Data in Unexpected Places (or: From Text Linguistics to Socio-rhetoric): Towards a Socio-rhetorical Reading of John's Gospel." *Neot* 33, no. 2 (1999): 343–64.
Heever, Gerhard van den. "The Usefulness of Violent Ends: Apocalyptic Imaginaries in the Reconstruction of Society." In *Reconceiving Religious Conflict: New Views from the Formative Centuries of Christianity*, edited by Wendy Mayer and Chris L. de Wet, 282–335. Routledge Studies in the Early Christian World. Abingdon: Routledge, 2018.
Heilig, Christoph. *Hidden Criticism?: The Methodology and Plausibility of the Search for a Counter-Imperial Subtext in Paul*. Tübingen: Mohr Siebeck, 2015.
Hills, Julian. "'Little Children, Keep Yourselves from Idols': 1 John 5:21 Reconsidered." *CBQ* 51, no. 2 (1989): 285–310.
Hooker, Morna Dorothy. *Endings: Invitations to Discipleship*. London: SCM Press, 2003.
Hornblower, Simon, Antony Spawforth, and Esther Eidinow, eds. *The Oxford Classical Dictionary*, 4th edn. Oxford: Oxford University Press, 2012.
Horsley, Richard A., ed. *Paul and Empire: Religion and Power in Roman Imperial Society*. Harrisburg, PA: Trinity Press International, 1997.
Hunter, Virginia J. *Thucydides: The Artful Reporter*. Toronto: Hakkert, 1973.
Käsemann, Ernst. *The Testament of Jesus*. Philadelphia, PA: Fortress, 1968.
Keener, Craig S. *The Gospel of John: A Commentary*. Peabody, MA: Hendrickson Publishers, 2010.
Koester, Craig. "The Antichrist Theme in the Johannine Epistles and Its Role in Christian Tradition." In *Communities in Dispute: Current Scholarship on the Johannine Epistles*, edited by R. Alan Culpepper and Paul N. Anderson, 187–96. Early Christianity and Its Literature 13. Atlanta: SBL Press, 2014.
Koester, Craig R. "'The Savior of the World' (John 4:42)." *JBL* 109, no. 4 (1990): 665–80.
Kooten, George van. "*Bildung*, Religion, and Politics in the Gospel of John: The Erastic, Philhellenic, Anti-Maccabean, and Anti-Roman Tendencies of the Gospel of 'the Beloved Pupil.'" In *Scriptural Interpretation at the Interface between Education and Religion*, edited by Florian Wilk, 123–77. Themes in Biblical Narrative 22. Leiden: Brill, 2019.
Kooten, George van. "Bleeding Blood, Not Ichor—Christ the 'Gottmensch.'" In *Über Gott: Festschrift für Reinhard Feldmeier zum 70. Geburtstag*, edited by Jan Dochhorn, Rainer Hirsch-Luipold, and Ilinca Tanaseanu-Doebler, 631–72. Tübingen: Mohr Siebeck, 2022.
Kooten, George van. "Christ and Hermes: A Religio-Historical Comparison of the Johannine Christ-Logos with the God Hermes in Greek Mythology and Philosophy." In *Im Gespräch mit C.F. Georg Heinrici: Beiträge zwischen Theologie und Religionswissenschaft*, edited by Marco Frenschkowski and Lena Seehausen, 273–324. Tübingen: Mohr Siebeck, 2021.

Kraft, Robert. "*Eis nikos* = Permanently/Successfully: 1 Cor 15.54, Matt 12.20." In *Septuagintal Lexicography*, edited by Robert Kraft, 153–6. Missoula, MT: Scholars Press, 1975.

Kruse, Colin. *The Letters of John*. PNTC. Grand Rapids: Eerdmans, 2000.

Kyle, Donald G. *Sport and Spectacle in the Ancient World*. 2nd edn. Chichester, West Sussex: John Wiley and Sons, 2015.

Liddell, Henry George, Robert Scott, Henry Stuart Jones, and Roderick McKenzie. *A Greek-English Lexicon*. 9th edn. Oxford: Clarendon Press, 1996.

Lieu, Judith. *I, II, & III John: A Commentary*. Louisville, KY: Westminster John Knox, 2008.

Lindsay, Dennis R. *Josephus and Faith: Πίστις and Πιστεύειν as Faith Terminology in the Writings of Flavius Josephus and in the New Testament*. Leiden: Brill, 1993.

Lloyd-Jones, Hugh. *The Justice of Zeus*. Sather Classical Lectures 41. Berkeley: University of California Press, 1971.

Loader, William. *The Johannine Epistles*. EC. London: Epworth, 1992.

Marincola, John. *Authority and Tradition in Ancient Historiography*. Cambridge: Cambridge University Press, 2003.

Marshall, I. Howard. *The Epistles of John*. NICNT. Grand Rapids: Eerdmans, 1978.

Martyn, J. Louis. *History and Theology in the Fourth Gospel*. 3rd edn. Louisville, KY: Westminster John Knox Press, 2003.

Martyn, J. Louis. "The Salvation-History Perspective in the Fourth Gospel." PhD Diss. Yale University, 1957.

Matthews, John. *Western Aristocracies and Imperial Court, A.D. 364–425*. Oxford: Clarendon Press, 1975.

McCormick, Michael. *Eternal Victory: Triumphal Rulership in Late Antiquity, Byzantium, and the Early Medieval West*. Past and Present Publications. Cambridge: Cambridge University Press, 1986.

Miller, Stephen G., ed. *Arete: Greek Sports from Ancient Sources*. 3rd edn. Berkeley: University of California Press, 2004.

Moloney, Francis. *The Gospel of John*. SP 4. Collegeville, MN: Liturgical Press, 1998.

Moo, Douglas J. *The Epistle to the Romans*. NICNT. Grand Rapids: Eerdmans, 1996.

Morgan, Teresa. *Roman Faith and Christian Faith: Pistis and Fides in the Early Roman Empire and Early Churches*. Oxford: Oxford University Press, 2015.

Morris, Leon. *The First Epistle of Paul to the Corinthians: An Introduction and Commentary*. TNTC. London: Tyndale Press, 1969.

Morris, Leon. *The First and Second Epistles to the Thessalonians: The English Text with Introduction, Exposition and Notes*. NICNT. Grand Rapids: Eerdmans, 1970.

Mulder, Stefan. "Early Christian Christology Contextualised: The Graeco-Roman Context of 'Christian' Docetism." MA Thesis. University of Groningen, 2016.

Nauck, Wolfgang. *Die Tradition und der Charakter des ersten Johannesbriefes: zugleich ein Beitrag zur Taufe im Urchristentum und in der alten Kirche*. Tübingen: Mohr, 1957.

Neyrey, Jerome H. *Paul, in Other Words: A Cultural Reading of His Letters*. Louisville, KY: Westminster/John Knox Press, 1990.

Nuffelen, Peter van. *Rethinking the Gods: Philosophical Readings of Religion in the Post-Hellenistic Period*. Cambridge: Cambridge University Press, 2011.

Painter, John. *1, 2, and 3 John*. SP 18. Collegeville, MN: Liturgical Press, 2002.

Patera, Maria. "Reflections on the Discourse of Fear in Greek Sources." In *Unveiling Emotions II: Emotions in Greece and Rome: Texts, Images, Material Culture*, edited by Angelos Chaniotis and Pierre Ducrey, 109–34. Stuttgart, Germany: Franz Steiner Verlag, 2013.

Patrich, Joseph. "Herod's Hippodrome-Stadium at Caesarea and the Games Conducted Therein." In *What Athens Has to Do With Jerusalem: Essays on Classical, Jewish, and Early Christian Art and Archaeology in Honor of Gideon Foerster*, edited by Leonard V. Rutgers, 29–68. Leuven: Peeters, 2002.

Peppard, Michael. *The Son of God in the Roman World: Divine Sonship in Its Social and Political Context*. New York: Oxford University Press, 2011.

Peristiany, John G., ed. *Honour and Shame: The Values of Mediterranean Society*. The Nature of Human Society. London: Weidenfeld and Nicolson, 1966.

Platt, Verity J. *Facing the Gods: Epiphany and Representation in Graeco-Roman Art, Literature and Religion*. Cambridge: Cambridge University Press, 2011.

Porter, Stanley E., and Andrew W. Pitts, eds. *Christian Origins and Greco-Roman Culture*. Leiden: Brill, 2013.

Price, Martin. "The Statue of Zeus at Olympia." In *The Seven Wonders of the Ancient World*, edited by Peter A. Clayton and Martin J. Price, 59–77. New York: Dorset, 1989.

Price, Simon. *Rituals and Power: The Roman Imperial Cult in Asia Minor*. Cambridge: Cambridge University Press, 1984.

Quatremère De Quincy, Antoine-Chrysostome. *Le Jupiter Olympien, Ou, L'art De La Sculpture Antique Considéré Sous Un Nouveau Point De Vue: Ouvrage Qui Comprend Un Essai Sur Le Goût De La Sculpture Polychrome, L'analyse Explicative De La Toreutique, Et L'histoire De La Statuaire En or Et Ivoire Chez Les Grecs Et Les Romains: Avec La Restitution Des Principaux Monuments De Cet Art Et La Démonstration Pratique Ou Le Renouvellement De Ses Procédés Mécaniques*. Paris: Firmin Didot, 1814.

Rajak, Tessa. "Justus of Tiberias." *ClQ* 23, no. 2 (Nov 1973): 345–68.

Ramsey, John T., and A. Lewis Licht. *The Comet of 44 B.C. and Caesar's Funeral Games*. ACS 39. Atlanta: Scholars Press, 1997.

Rawles, Richard. "Early epinician: Ibycus and Simonides." In *Reading the Victory Ode*, edited by Peter Agócs, Chris Carey, and Richard Rawles, 3–27. Cambridge: Cambridge University Press, 2012.

Rensberger, David. *1 John, 2 John, 3 John*. Nashville, TN: Abingdon Press, 1997.

Rensberger, David. "Completed Love: 1 John 4:11–18 and the Mission of the New Testament Church." In *Communities in Dispute: Current Scholarship on the Johannine Epistles*, edited by R. Alan Culpepper and Paul N. Anderson, 237–71. Early Christianity and its Literature 13. Atlanta: SBL Press, 2014.

Rensberger, David. *Overcoming the World: Politics and Community in the Gospel of John*. London: SPCK, 1989.

Richer, Nicholas. "Personified Abstractions in Laconia: Suggestions on the Origins of Phobos." In *Personification in the Greek World: From Antiquity to Byzantium*, edited by Emma Stafford and Judith Herrin, 111–22. Aldershot: Ashgate, 2005.

Rist, John M. *Stoic Philosophy*. Cambridge: Cambridge University Press, 1969.

Rives, James B. *Religion in the Roman Empire*. Blackwell Ancient Religions. Malden, MA: Blackwell Publishing, 2007.

Rogers, Guy MacLean. *The Mysteries of Artemis of Ephesos Cult, Polis, and Change in the Graeco-Roman World*. New Haven, CT: Yale University Press, 2012.

Rosenberger, Veit. "Coping with Death: Private Deification in the Roman Empire." In *Burial Rituals, Ideas of Afterlife, and the Individual in the Hellenistic World and the Roman Empire*, edited by Katharina Waldner, Richard Gordon, and Wolfgang Spickermann, 109–23. Stuttgart, Germany: Franz Steiner Verlag, 2016.

Rutgers, Leonard Victor. "Roman Policy towards the Jews: Expulsions from the City of Rome during the First Century C.E." *Classical Antiquity* 13, no. 1 (Apr 1994): 56–74.

Scanlon, Thomas Francis. *Eros & Greek Athletics*. Oxford: Oxford University Press, 2002.

Schmidt, Evamaria. *The Great Altar of Pergamon*. Translated by Lana Jaeck. London: Owen, 1965.

Schnackenburg, Rudolf. *The Johannine Epistles: Introduction and Commentary*. Translated by Reginald and Ilse Fuller. Tunbridge Wells: Burns & Oates, 1992.

Schnelle, Udo. *Antidocetic Christology in the Gospel of John*. Minneapolis: Fortress, 1992.

Schnelle, Udo. *Die Johannesbriefe*. Leipzig: Evangelische Verlagsanstalt, 2010.

Scully, Stephen. "Reading the Shield of Achilles: Terror, Anger, Delight." *Harvard Studies in Classical Philology* 101 (2003): 29–47.

Shapiro, Harvey A. *Personifications in Greek Art: The Representation of Abstract Concepts, 600–400 B.C.* Zurich: Akanthus, 1993.

Simon, Erika. *The Gods of the Greeks*. Translated by Jakob Zeyl. Edited by Alan Shapiro. Madison: University of Wisconsin Press, 2021.

Sinn, Ulrich. *Olympia: Cult, Sport, and Ancient Festival*. Translated by Thomas Thornton. Princeton, NJ: M. Wiener, 2000.

Smalley, Stephen S. *1, 2, 3 John*. WBC. Waco, TX: Word Books, 1984.

Spivey, Nigel Jonathan. *The Ancient Olympics*. 2nd edn. Oxford: Oxford University Press, 2012.

Stafford, Emma. "Masculine Values, Feminine Forms: On the Gender of Personified Abstractions." In *Thinking Men: Masculinity and Its Self-Representation in the Classical Tradition*, edited by Lin Foxhall and John Salmon, 43–56. London: Routledge, 1998.

Stevenson, Seth William. *A Dictionary of Roman Coins: Republican and Imperial*. London: George Bell, 1889.

Stevenson, Tom. "The Fate of the Statue of Zeus at Olympia." In *Statue of Zeus at Olympia*, edited by Janette McWilliam, Sonia Puttock, Tom Stevenson, and Rashna Taraporewalla, 155–72. Newcastle upon Tyne: Cambridge Scholars Publishing, 2011.

Stewart, Andrew F. *Art in the Hellenistic World: An Introduction*. Cambridge: Cambridge University Press, 2014.

Strecker, Georg. *The Johannine Letters: A Commentary on 1, 2, and 3 John*. Hermeneia. Translated by Linda M. Maloney. Edited by Harold W. Attridge. Minneapolis: Fortress, 1996.

Suggit, J. N. "1 JOHN 5:21: ΤΕΚΝΙΑ, ΦΥΛΑΞΑΤΕ ΕΑΥΤΑ ΑΠΟ ΤΩΝ ΕΙΔΩΛΩΝ." *JTS* 36 no. 2 (Oct 1985): 386–90.

Taraporewalla, Rashna. "Size Matters: The Statue of Zeus at Olympia and Competitive Emulation." In *Statue of Zeus at Olympia*, edited by Janette McWilliam, Sonia Puttock, Tom Stevenson, and Rashna Taraporewalla, 33–50. Newcastle upon Tyne: Cambridge Scholars Publishing, 2011.

Taylor, Lily Ross. *The Divinity of the Roman Emperor*. American Philological Association Monograph Series 1. Middletown, CT: American Philological Association, 1931.

Thatcher, Tom. *Greater than Caesar: Christology and Empire in the Fourth Gospel*. Minneapolis: Fortress, 2009.

Thompson, Glen L. "Constantius II and the First Removal of the Altar of Victory." In *A Tall Order: Writing the Social History of the Ancient World: Essays in Honor of William V. Harris*, edited by Jean-Jacques Aubert and Zsuzsanna Várhelyi, 85–106. Leipzig, Germany: K. G. Saur, 2005.

Thompson, Marianne Meye. *1–3 John*. IVP New Testament Commentary Series. Downers Grove, IL: InterVarsity Press, 1992.
Wahlde, Urban C. von. *Gnosticism, Docetism, and the Judaisms of the First Century: The Search for the Wider Context of the Johannine Literature and Why It Matters*. London: Bloomsbury, 2015.
Weinstock, Stefan. "Pax and the 'Ara Pacis.'" *Journal of Roman Studies*, no. 50, Parts 1 and 2 (1960): 44–58.
Weinstock, Stefan. "Victor and Invictus." *HTR* 50, no. 1 (1957): 211–47.
Wengst, Klaus. *Der erste, zweite und dritte Brief des Johannes*. Gütersloh: Mohn, 1978.
Westcott, Brooke Foss. *The Epistles of St. John: The Greek Text with Notes*. 2nd edn. Edited by F. F. Bruce. Abingdon: Marcham Manor Press, 1966.
Whitmarsh, Tim. *Battling the Gods: Atheism in the Ancient World*. London: Faber and Faber, 2016.
Wiseman, T. P. *New Men in the Roman Senate, 139 BC–AD 14*. London: Oxford University Press, 1971.
Wissowa, Georg. *Religion Und Kultus Der Römer*. 2nd edn. München: Beck, 1912.
Witherington, Ben. *The Acts of the Apostles: A Socio-rhetorical Commentary*. Grand Rapids: Eerdmans, 1998.
Worden, T. "The Literary Influence of the Ugaritic Fertility Myth on the Old Testament." *VT* 3, Fasc. 3 (Jul 1953): 273–97.
Wright, N. T. *Paul: Fresh Perspectives*. London: SPCK, 2005.
Wright, N. T. "Paul's Gospel and Caesar's Empire." In *Paul and Politics: Ekklesia, Israel, Imperium, Interpretation: Essays in Honor of Krister Stendahl*, edited by Richard A. Horsley, 160–83. Harrisburg, PA: Trinity Press International, 2000.
Wright, N. T., and J. P. Davies. "John, Jesus, and 'The Ruler of This World': Demonic Politics in the Fourth Gospel?" In *Conception, Reception, and the Spirit: Essays in Honor of Andrew T. Lincoln*, edited by J. Gordon McConville and Lloyd K. Pietersen, 71–89. Eugene, OR: Cascade Books, 2015.
Yarbro Collins, Adela. "Mark and His Readers: The Son of God among Greeks and Romans." *HTR* 93, no. 2 (Apr 2000): 85–100.
Yarbrough, Robert W. *1–3 John*. BECNT. Grand Rapids: Baker Academic, 2009.
Young, David C. *A Brief History of the Olympic Games*. Malden, MA: Blackwell, 2004.
Zanker, Paul. *The Power of Images in the Age of Augustus*. Jerome Lectures. Sixteenth Series. Translated by Alan Shapiro. Ann Arbor: University of Michigan Press, 1988.
Zimmerman, Ruben. "Eschatology and Time in the Gospel of John." In *The Oxford Handbook of Johannine Studies*, edited by Judith M. Lieu and Martinus C. de Boer, 292–310. Oxford: Oxford University Press, 2018.

Loeb Classical Library

Aeschylus. *Oresteia: Agamemnon. Libation-Bearers. Eumenides*. Edited and translated by Alan H. Sommerstein. LCL 146. Cambridge, MA: Harvard University Press, 2009.
Aristotle. *On the Soul. Parva Naturalia. On Breath*. Translated by W. S. Hett. LCL 288. Cambridge, MA: Harvard University Press, 1957.
Bacchylides, Corinna. *Greek Lyric, Volume IV: Bacchylides, Corinna, and Others*. Edited and translated by David A. Campbell. LCL 461. Cambridge, MA: Harvard University Press, 1992.

Cicero. *On the Nature of the Gods. Academics*. Translated by H. Rackham. LCL 268. Cambridge, MA: Harvard University Press, 1933.

Dio Cassius. *Roman History, Volume VI: Books 51–55*. Translated by Earnest Cary, Herbert B. Foster. LCL 83. Cambridge, MA: Harvard University Press, 1917.

Dio Cassius. *Roman History, Volume VII: Books 56–60*. Translated by Earnest Cary, Herbert B. Foster. LCL 175. Cambridge, MA: Harvard University Press, 1924.

Dio Chrysostom. *Discourses 12–30*. Translated by J. W. Cohoon. LCL 339. Cambridge, MA: Harvard University Press, 1939.

Dionysius of Halicarnassus. *Roman Antiquities, Volume I: Books 1–2*. Translated by Earnest Cary. LCL 319. Cambridge, MA: Harvard University Press, 1937.

Dionysius of Halicarnassus. *Roman Antiquities, Volume IV: Books 6.49–7*. Translated by Earnest Cary. LCL 364. Cambridge, MA: Harvard University Press, 1943.

Epictetus. *Discourses, Books 1–2*. Translated by W. A. Oldfather. LCL 131. Cambridge, MA: Harvard University Press, 1925.

Epictetus. *Discourses, Books 3–4. Fragments. The Encheiridion*. Translated by W. A. Oldfather. LCL 218. Cambridge, MA: Harvard University Press, 1928.

Herodotus. *The Persian Wars, Volume I: Books 1–2*. Translated by A. D. Godley. LCL 117. Cambridge, MA: Harvard University Press, 1920.

Herodotus. *The Persian Wars, Volume IV: Books 8–9*. Translated by A. D. Godley. LCL 120. Cambridge, MA: Harvard University Press, 1925.

Homer. *Odyssey, Volume I: Books 1–12*. Translated by A. T. Murray. Revised by George E. Dimock. LCL 104. Cambridge, MA: Harvard University Press, 1919.

Josephus. *Jewish Antiquities, Volume I: Books 1–3*. Translated by H. St. J. Thackeray. LCL 242. Cambridge, MA: Harvard University Press, 1930.

Josephus. *Jewish Antiquities, Volume IV: Books 9–11*. Translated by Ralph Marcus. LCL 326. Cambridge, MA: Harvard University Press, 1937.

Josephus. *Jewish Antiquities, Volume VIII: Books 18–19*. Translated by Louis H. Feldman. LCL 433. Cambridge, MA: Harvard University Press, 1965.

Josephus. *The Jewish War, Volume I: Books 1–2*. Translated by H. St. J. Thackeray. LCL 203. Cambridge, MA: Harvard University Press, 1927.

Josephus. *The Jewish War, Volume III: Books 5–7*. Translated by H. St. J. Thackeray. LCL 210. Cambridge, MA: Harvard University Press, 1928.

Josephus. *The Life. Against Apion*. Translated by H. St. J. Thackeray. LCL 186. Cambridge, MA: Harvard University Press, 1926.

Livy. *History of Rome, Volume I: Books 1–2*. Translated by B. O. Foster. LCL 114. Cambridge, MA: Harvard University Press, 1919.

Pausanias. *Description of Greece, Volume I: Books 1–2 (Attica and Corinth)*. Translated by W. H. S. Jones. LCL 93. Cambridge, MA: Harvard University Press, 1918.

Pausanias. *Description of Greece, Volume II: Books 3–5 (Laconia, Messenia, Elis 1)*. Translated by W. H. S. Jones, H. A. Ormerod. LCL 188. Cambridge, MA: Harvard University Press, 1926.

Philo. *On the Decalogue. On the Special Laws, Books 1–3*. Translated by F. H. Colson. LCL 320. Cambridge, MA: Harvard University Press, 1937.

Pindar. *Nemean Odes. Isthmian Odes. Fragments*. Edited and translated by William H. Race. LCL 485. Cambridge, MA: Harvard University Press, 1997.

Plato. *Laws, Volume II: Books 7–12*. Translated by R. G. Bury. LCL 192. Cambridge, MA: Harvard University Press, 1926.

Plutarch. *Lives, Volume I: Theseus and Romulus. Lycurgus and Numa. Solon and Publicola.* Translated by Bernadotte Perrin. LCL 46. Cambridge, MA: Harvard University Press, 1914.
Plutarch. *Lives, Volume IV: Alcibiades and Coriolanus. Lysander and Sulla.* Translated by Bernadotte Perrin. LCL 80. Cambridge, MA: Harvard University Press, 1916.
Plutarch. *Lives, Volume VI: Dion and Brutus. Timoleon and Aemilius Paulus.* Translated by Bernadotte Perrin. LCL 98. Cambridge, MA: Harvard University Press, 1918.
Plutarch. *Moralia, Volume II: How to Profit by One's Enemies. On Having Many Friends. Chance. Virtue and Vice. Letter of Condolence to Apollonius. Advice about Keeping Well. Advice to Bride and Groom. The Dinner of the Seven Wise Men. Superstition.* Translated by Frank Cole Babbitt. LCL 222. Cambridge, MA: Harvard University Press, 1928.
Plutarch. *Moralia, Volume XI: On the Malice of Herodotus. Causes of Natural Phenomena.* Translated by Lionel Pearson, F. H. Sandbach. LCL 426. Cambridge, MA: Harvard University Press, 1965.
Plutarch. *Moralia, Volume XIV: That Epicurus Actually Makes a Pleasant Life Impossible. Reply to Colotes in Defence of the Other Philosophers. Is "Live Unknown" a Wise Precept? On Music.* Translated by Benedict Einarson, Phillip H. De Lacy. LCL 428. Cambridge, MA: Harvard University Press, 1967.
Polybius. *The Histories, Volume I: Books 1–2.* Translated by W. R. Paton. Revised by F. W. Walbank, Christian Habicht. LCL 128. Cambridge, MA: Harvard University Press, 2010.
Polybius. *The Histories, Volume V: Books 16–27.* Translated by W. R. Paton. Revised by F. W. Walbank, Christian Habicht. LCL 160. Cambridge, MA: Harvard University Press, 2012.
Quintilian. *The Orator's Education, Volume V: Books 11–12.* Edited and translated by Donald A. Russell. LCL 494. Cambridge, MA: Harvard University Press, 2002.
Seneca. *Moral Essays, Volume II: De Consolatione ad Marciam. De Vita Beata. De Otio. De Tranquillitate Animi. De Brevitate Vitae. De Consolatione ad Polybium. De Consolatione ad Helviam.* Translated by John W. Basore. LCL 254. Cambridge, MA: Harvard University Press, 1932.
Strabo. *Geography, Volume IV: Books 8–9.* Translated by Horace Leonard Jones. LCL 196. Cambridge, MA: Harvard University Press, 1927.

Website Citations

Abraham, Ellie. "Nike Trainers Mocked Over Incorrect Use of Greek Lettering." *The Independent.* June 9, 2021. https://www.independent.co.uk/life-style/fashion/nike-trainers-greek-letter-mythology-b1862636.html (accessed June 10, 2021).
"culture, n." OED Online. December 2022. Oxford University Press. https://www.oed.com/view/Entry/45746?rskey=qKAVpn&result=1&isAdvanced=false (accessed February 06, 2023).
Jones, Sarah. "Here's How We'd Really Know that Trump Is the Antichrist." *New York Magazine.* August 21, 2019. https://nymag.com/intelligencer/2019/08/heres-how-wed-really-know-that-trump-is-the-antichrist.html (accessed May 25, 2021).
Jones, Serene. "Union Mourns Professor Lou Martyn." *Union News.* June 10, 2015. https://utsnyc.edu/union-mourns-professor-lou-martyn (accessed May 28, 2021).

"Nike of Delos." University of Cambridge Museum of Classical Archaeology Databases. https://museum.classics.cam.ac.uk/collections/casts/nike-delos (accessed May 27, 2021).

"Nike of Paionios." University of Cambridge Museum of Classical Archaeology Databases. https://museum.classics.cam.ac.uk/collections/casts/nike-paionios (accessed May 24, 2021).

"Olympic Medals." Olympics. https://olympics.com/en/olympic-games/olympic-medals (accessed June 16, 2021).

Harris, Paul. "One in Four Americans Think Obama May Be the Antichrist." *The Guardian.* April 2, 2013. https://www.theguardian.com/world/2013/apr/02/americans-obama-anti-christ-conspiracy-theories (accessed May 25, 2021).

"Statue of Jupiter." The State Hermitage Museum. https://bit.ly/3fiH79x (accessed May 25, 2021).

"Varvakeion Athena Parthenos." University of Cambridge Museum of Classical Archaeology Databases. https://museum.classics.cam.ac.uk/collections/casts/varvakeion-athena-parthenos (accessed May 27, 2021).

"Women's Air Force 1 Shadow: Goddess of Victory." Nike. https://www.nike.com/my/launch/t/womens-air-force-1-goddess-of-victory (accessed June 16, 2021).

Index of References

Old Testament

Genesis
3:6	51
4	28, 33
4:4-5	36
20:11	63
22:12	63
31:19	81, 83

Exodus
9:30	63
18:21	63
20:3	82
20:3-4	85
20:4	81
20:4-5	85
20:14	85
20:15	85
32	85

Leviticus
19:4	81, 83
25	36

Numbers
25:2	82
33:52	81

Deuteronomy
5:8	81
5:8-9	85
5:18	85
5:19	85
6:24	63
7:9	108
10:12	64
10:17	32
15	36
23:9 (LXX 23:10)	86
32:4	108

Joshua
4:24	32
6:18	86
24:14	63

Judges
7:3	63

1 Samuel
21:4 (LXX 21:5)	86

2 Samuel
22:31	32
22:32	32
22:33	32
23:3	63
23:5	32

1 Kings
11:2	82
12	30

2 Kings
14:23	84
23:24	81

1 Chronicles
16:25	63
16:26	81
21	27

2 Chronicles
34:7	81

Nehemiah
1:5	32

Job
1-2	27
22:13	32

33:29	32
34:31	32

Psalms
18:23 (LXX 17:24)	86
55:2	63
55:5	63
55:12	63
55:16	63
106 (LXX 105):14	50
119 (LXX 118):113	64
119 (LXX 118):119	64
119 (LXX 118):120	64
135 (LXX 134):15	81
148:12	30

Proverbs
1:7	63
7:5	86
9:10	64
20:29	30

Ecclesiastes
8:12	63

Isaiah
25:8	7
30:22	81
37:19	83
42:3	7
42:3-4	7
50:10	63

Jeremiah
16:19	81

Lamentations
5:14	30

Ezekiel
9:6	30
33:8	86

Daniel
9:4	32

Hosea
8:4	81
13:14	7

Joel
2:28	30, 41

Zechariah
3	27
8:4-5	30

New Testament

Matthew
2:13	30
2:20	30
3:16	44
4:1	56
4:1-11	32, 38, 40, 56
4:5	56
4:8	56
4:10	56
4:11	56
5:28	51
5:37	27
5:39	27
6:13	27
7:15	45
8:4	119
10:15	73
10:22	35
11:22	73
11:24	73
12:20	7
12:26	56
12:29	32
12:36	73
13:19	27
13:38	27
13:39	27, 56
16:7	50
16:23	56
18:16	121
19:20	28
19:22	28
21:1-11	60
23:35	35
24:9	35
24:11	45
24:24	45
24:27	72
24:37	72
24:39	72
25:41	56

26:36-46	57	8:14	51
26:41	113	8:43	51
26:56	54	10:17	57
27:27-31	58	10:18	56, 57
27:29	16	11:18	32, 56
		11:21	32
Mark		11:22	32
1:4	119	12:15	86
1:7	32	13:16	56
1:12-13	32, 38, 40, 56	13:24	16
1:13	56	15:12	51
3:23	56	15:30	51
3:26	56	16:3	73
4:15	56	19:28-40	60
4:19	50	21:4	51, 125
5:39	30	22:3	56
5:40	30	22:15	50
7:22	51	22:31	56
8:33	56	22:39-46	57
10:8	50	22:53	41
11:1-11	60	22:54	54
12:44	51, 125	24:39	50
13:22	45		
14:32-42	57	John	
14:50-2	54	1:1	125
14:51	28	1:4	124, 125
15:16-20	58	1:12	109
15:17	16	1:14	50, 113, 125
16:5	28	1:34	60, 113, 119
		1:49	60, 113
Luke		2:4	41
1:14	118	2:11	46
1:47	62	2:21	50, 113
1:49	62	2:23	109
1:49-50	62	3:1	56
1:50	62	3:11	119, 120
1:59	30	3:15	124
1:66	30	3:16	110, 113, 124
3:6	50	3:18	60, 109, 113
4:1-13	32, 38, 40, 56	3:32	120
4:2	56	3:36	124
4:3	56	4:14	124
4:6	56	4:23	41
4:13	56	4:36	124
5:14	119	4:42	60, 114
6:26	45	4:49	29
6:45	27	5:7	57
7:14	28	5:24	124
8:12	56	5:25	60, 113

5:39	46, 124	12:27	57
5:41	46	12:31	55–7, 60
5:44	46	12:41	46
5:45	46	12:42	56
6:1	97	12:43	46
6:23	97	12:47	86
6:27	124	12:50	124
6:40	124	13:1-19	57
6:47	124	13:2	56
6:52	113	13:21	57
6:53	50, 113	13:21-30	58
6:54	113, 124	13:27	56
6:55	113	13:29	46
6:56	113	13:33	29
6:63	50	13:34	31
6:68	124	13:34-5	29
6:69	109	13:36-8	58
6:70	56	13:37	37
7:18	46	13:38	37
7:20	56	14-17	57
7:26	56, 74	14:1	57, 58
7:48	56	14:3	59
8:17	121	14:18-19	59
8:44	36, 39, 50, 56, 111	14:27	54, 57, 58
8:48	56	14:28	59
8:49	56	14:30	55, 56, 58, 60
8:50	46	14:30-1	58
8:52	56	14:31	58
8:54	46	15:12	33
8:55	39, 111	15:13	37
9:24	46	15:18-19	35
10:11	37	15:20	54
10:15	37	16:2	41, 46, 54
10:17	37	16:7	59
10:20	56	16:11	55, 56, 59, 60
10:21	56	16:21	29
10:24	74	16:25	74
10:28	124	16:29	74
10:36	113	16:30	55
11:4	46, 60, 113	16:32	54, 59
11:13	46	16:33	5, 16, 50, 54–6, 59, 60
11:27	60, 113		
11:31	46	17:2	50, 124
11:33	57	17:3	124
11:40	46	17:5	46
11:48	59	17:11	50
11:56	46	17:12	86
12:12-19	57, 60	17:14	35
12:25	86, 124	17:15	27, 37

17:18	50	19:37	85
17:22	46	20:9	28
17:24	46	23:17	28
18	54	23:18	28
18:3	58	23:22	28
18:10-12	58		
18:12	58	Romans	
18:20	74	1:3	50
18:36	16, 60	1:23	85, 87
19:1-3	58	1:24	50
19:2	16	1:30	51
19:5	16	2:21-2	85
19:7	55, 60, 113	2:22	76, 85
19:11	60	3:4	39
19:12b	59	3:27	51
19:12-16	56	6:12	50
19:15	60	7:5	50
19:23-5	58	7:8	50
19:31	50, 113	8:6	50
19:35	119	8:9	44
19:38	50, 113	12:9	27
19:40	50, 113	13:14	51, 113
20:12	50, 113	16:17-20	84
20:15	46		
20:27	107	1 Corinthians	
20:31	60, 113, 128	1:6	119
21:1	97	2:3-5	118
21:5	29, 30	2:6	56
		2:8	56
Acts		2:11	44
2:17	28, 30, 41	3:16	44
2:26	50	5:5	50
4:33	119	5:13	27
5:10	28	7:40	44
7:40	85	8:1	76
7:41	76, 85	8:4	76, 85
7:44	120	8:5ff	87
7:58	28	8:7	76, 85
10:2	62	8:10	76, 85
10:22	62	9:24	16
10:35	62	9:24-6	15
13:6	45	9:25	15, 16
13:16	62	10:14	87
13:26	62	10:19	76, 85
15:20	76, 85	12:2	76, 85
17:23	77	14:20	30
17:29	87	15:23	72
18:2	95	15:31	51
19:24-41	17	15:54-5	7

15:57	7	4:5	84
16:13-14	84	4:12	16

2 Corinthians   1 Thessalonians

1:12	51	1:9	76, 85, 87
4:11	50	2:17	50
6:16	76	2:19	51, 72
7:1	62	3:13	72
7:15	62	4:5	50
7:15-16	63	5:22	84
10:8	73		
10:10	32	2 Thessalonians	
13:1	121	1:10	118, 119
13:5	84	3:3	27, 86
13:10	84	3:6-15	84

Galatians   1 Timothy

2:2	16	1:10	39
5:7	16	2:2	51
5:16	51	2:6-7	118
5:19	50, 113	3:16	50
6:8	50	4:10	16
6:17	84	5:1-2	30
		5:17	30
Ephesians		5:19	121
2:3	51	5:20	84
2:14	50	6:9	50
4:22	50	6:12	16
5:21	62		
5:22-6:9	30	2 Timothy	
6:5	62	1:8	119
6:10-20	84	2:4	51, 125
6:16	27	2:5	16
		2:22	50
Philippians		3:2	51
1:20	73	3:6	50
1:23	50	4:3	50
2:12-13	62	4:7	16
2:16	16	4:8	16
3:3	50		
3:12-14	16	Titus	
3:14	16	1:5	30
		1:12	39
Colossians		1:13-14	118
1:29	16	2:1-6	30
3:5	50	2:12	50
3:18-4:1	30	3	84
3:22	62	3:3	50

Philemon		3:17	84
16	50		
21	84	1 John	
		1:1	31–3, 51, 53, 114, 120, 124, 125
Hebrews			
1:2	41	1:1-2	51, 124
2:1-4	118	1:1-3	119
2:13	30	1:1-4	130
2:14	30	1:2	119, 120, 122, 124, 125
3:5	119		
5:7	50	1:3	53, 113, 114, 120
6:18	32	1:4	112
10:28	121	1:5	30, 53, 108
11:4	35	1:6	39, 117
12:1	16	1:7	30, 85, 108, 113, 114, 129
13:9	84		
13:22	84	1:7-8	120
		1:7-9	29
James		1:8	39, 43, 85, 117, 129
1:12	16	1:9	85, 107, 108, 121, 129
1:14-15	50	1:10	32, 39, 85, 111, 122
1:27	86	2:1	29, 30, 44, 73, 85, 86, 108, 112, 119, 123, 129
4:16	51		
5	84		
5:3	50, 119	2:1-2	29
5:14	30	2:2	1, 45, 48, 85, 129
		2:3	108, 119
		2:4	39, 108, 111, 117
1 Peter		2:5	50, 61, 72, 119
1:14	50	2:6	33, 37, 108, 116
1:17	62	2:7	29, 31, 33, 53, 108, 112
1:20	41	2:8	29, 39, 52, 108, 112, 117
2:11	51, 113		
4:2	52	2:8-11	30
4:3	50	2:9-10	127
4:16	73	2:10	29, 33, 61, 116
5:1	30	2:11	30, 51, 52
5:1-5	30	2:12	28–30, 38, 44, 73, 85, 86, 112, 117, 123, 129
5:5	30		
5:8	84	2:12-14	28, 29, 35, 50
		2:13	1, 16, 25, 27–31, 33, 40, 41, 48, 81, 89, 112, 114, 130
2 Peter			
1:4	50		
2:1	45	2:13b	26
2:9	73	2:13-14	26, 28, 32, 37, 38, 52, 86, 114
2:10	51		
2:14	51	2:14	1, 16, 25, 27–33, 37, 39–41, 48, 49, 81, 86, 89, 112, 114, 116, 123, 130
2:18	51		
3:3	50		
3:7	73		

2:15	1, 45, 48, 49, 52, 86, 107, 123	3:8-10	36, 40
		3:9	32, 37, 85, 86, 116, 129
2:15-17	27, 39, 41, 48–50, 61, 74, 129, 130	3:10	28, 33, 34, 37, 38, 40, 56, 86, 127
2:15-18	26	3:10-12	34
2:16	1, 36, 45, 48, 50, 51, 107, 113, 123, 125	3:11	31, 33, 37, 53, 74, 108, 119
2:17	1, 45, 48, 52, 116	3:11-12	32, 33
2:18	1, 25, 27, 29, 30, 40, 41, 45, 53, 73, 86, 119, 122, 123, 130	3:11-15	35, 40, 61
		3:12	1, 16, 25–8, 33–40, 52, 55, 86, 127, 130
2:18-23	125	3:12-16	129
2:19	42, 45, 47, 112, 116, 122	3:13	1, 27, 29, 35–7, 39, 45, 48, 49, 52, 53, 86, 126, 127, 130
2:20	30		
2:20-3	42	3:13-15	126
2:21	29, 39, 112, 117	3:14	26, 51, 52, 74, 108, 116, 124, 126, 129
2:22	1, 25, 27, 39, 40, 43, 76, 111, 113, 114, 121, 122, 130	3:14-15	35
		3:14-18	34
		3:15	26, 36, 51, 52, 55, 116, 124, 126, 127
2:22-3	46, 122		
2:23	43, 113, 114, 121	3:16	37, 108
2:24	32, 33, 37, 53, 108, 113, 114, 116, 125, 126	3:17	1, 36, 37, 45, 48, 51, 74, 116, 125
2:24-5	125		
2:25	51, 124	3:18	29, 30, 39, 86, 117, 123
2:26	29, 39, 43, 112	3:19	39, 117
2:26-8	43	3:21	29, 72
2:27	30, 32, 33, 39, 43, 108, 116	3:22	108, 109
		3:22–4	109
2:28	29, 30, 37, 44, 72–4, 86, 108, 116, 123	3:23	30, 74, 107–10, 112–14, 117
2:29	86, 108	3:24	26, 32, 37, 44, 108, 116
2:29-3:12	34	4:1	1, 25–7, 29, 44, 45, 48, 86, 107, 109–11, 123, 130
3-4	61		
3:1	1, 27, 45, 48, 86, 108, 119, 120, 130		
		4:1-2	44
3:2	29, 73, 86, 108, 119, 120	4:1-3	16
		4:1-4	53
3:3	33	4:1-5	1, 4
3:4	85, 129	4:1-6	115
3:4-9	30	4:2	26, 44, 45, 47, 50, 51, 113, 121
3:5	85, 129		
3:6	37, 85, 108, 116, 120	4:2b	46
3:7	29, 30, 33, 34, 39, 43, 86, 123	4:2-3	40, 76
		4:3	1, 25–7, 40, 44, 45, 47, 48, 53, 107, 121, 122, 130
3:7-10	34		
3:8	28, 30, 31, 33, 34, 38, 56, 85, 113–15, 129		
		4:3-5	49

4:4	1, 16, 28–31, 48, 50, 86, 107, 123	5:8		26, 44
4:5	1, 47, 48, 52, 53, 107	5:9		87, 113, 119, 122, 123
4:6	26, 39, 44, 47, 53, 117	5:9-10		122
4:7	29, 74, 86, 115	5:10		39, 87, 107, 111–13, 115, 116, 119, 122, 123, 127
4:7-21	61, 129			
4:7-5:3	109, 115	5:11		74, 87, 113, 119, 123, 124, 129
4:8	62, 65, 108, 115			
4:9	1, 48, 113	5:11-12		127
4:10	30, 85, 110, 113, 129	5:11-13		51
4:11	29, 74, 115, 119	5:12		87, 113, 116, 124, 127
4:12	72, 74, 115, 116, 119, 120	5:13		29, 30, 74, 87, 107, 112, 113, 116, 117, 124, 128
4:12-16	115			
4:13	26, 32, 37, 44, 108, 116, 119, 121, 127	5:13-21		75, 85
		5:14		53, 72, 119
4:14	1, 48, 60, 113, 114, 119, 120	5:14-15		75
		5:14-21		75
4:14-15	114, 115	5:15		53
4:15	32, 37, 38, 74, 76, 108, 113, 115, 116, 121	5:16		26, 51, 85, 120, 124, 127, 129
4:16	37, 62, 65, 74, 107–9, 112, 116	5:16-17		127–9
		5:16-18		30, 87
4:16b-17	65	5:17		26, 85
4:17	1, 48, 50, 72–4	5:18		1, 16, 25, 27, 37, 38, 40, 75, 85, 86, 130
4:18	5, 61, 64, 65, 72, 74, 77, 110, 115, 131	5:18-19		30, 86, 130
4:20	39, 52, 111, 115, 120	5:18-20		37, 75, 86
4:21	108	5:19		1, 4, 16, 25, 27, 38, 39, 48, 49, 52, 127, 130
5:1	76, 86, 87, 107, 110–12, 116	5:20		38, 39, 51, 74–7, 81, 87, 88, 113, 116, 117, 124, 129, 130
5:2	86, 108, 110, 119			
5:3	108, 119			
5:4	1, 4, 5, 7, 16, 26–8, 37, 48, 53, 54, 74, 86, 89, 107, 110, 130, 131	5:21		1, 5, 26, 29, 30, 40, 61, 74, 75, 77, 81, 84, 86, 88, 117, 123, 130
5:4-5	1, 5, 16, 25, 26, 31, 38, 49, 53, 54, 88, 110, 121	2 John		
5:4-13	75	1		30, 86, 117
5:5	1, 16, 27, 28, 38, 48, 53, 76, 87, 89, 107, 110–13, 115, 116, 130	1-4		39
		2		116, 117
		3		113, 117
5:6	26, 39, 44, 76, 87, 115, 117, 119, 121	4		86, 108, 117
		5		108
5:6-8	46, 121	6		53, 108
5:6-10	116	7		1, 27, 40, 43, 46, 48, 51, 113, 121, 122, 130
5:6-11	130			
5:7	119	9		113, 116
5:7-8	121	10-11		84

11	16, 27	
13	75, 86	

3 John

1	30, 39, 117
2	29
3	39, 117, 119
4	39, 53, 86, 117
5	29, 107
6	119
8	39, 117
11	16, 29, 84, 120
12	39, 117, 119
14	120
15	75

Jude

6	73
7-8	50
11	35
16	50
17-23	84
18	50

Revelation

2:10	16
2:14	76
2:20	76
9:20	76, 85
12:9	57
13	40
13:15	87
15:5	119
16:13	45
17:16	50, 113
19:18	50
19:20	45
20:10	45

Deuterocanonical Works and Septuagint

Wisdom of Solomon

4:12	50
5:8	51
17:7	51

2 Maccabees

1:24	32
9:8	51
15:6	51

4 Maccabees

8:19	51
18:11	35

Old Testament Pseudepigrapha

Ascension of Isaiah

4.1-18	40

Sibylline Oracles

3.63-74	40

Testament of Reuben

4:8	86

Other Ancient Sources

Aeschylus, *Agamemnon*

839	77
921	65
946–7	65

Aeschylus, *Choephoroe*

1048–50	66

Aeschylus, *Eumenides*

48–56	66
175–8	66
339–40	66
582–4	66
794–807	66

Aeschylus, *Prometheus Vinctus*

516	67

Ambrose, *Epistulae*

17–18	133
18.2	133

Apollodorus, *The Library*

3.12	50

Athenaeus, *The Learned Banqueters*

6.243e	17

Aristophanes, *Birds*

573	17

Aristotle, *Nicomachean Ethics*

1149b15–16	50

Index of References

Aristotle, *On Prophecy in Sleep*
464b9   79

Aristotle, *Politics*
1.3   30

Bacchylides
3.5   10
11.1   10
12.5   10

Bellum Africum
57   93

Cassius Dio, *Roman History*
1.3   118
21.3   30
37.25.2   79
41.61.4   22
45.6.4–7.1   104
51.17.5   79
51.22.1–2   24
56.24.3–5   22
56.46.2   105
59.26.5   25
63.16.2   79
67.19.2   79

Cicero, *De Divinatione*
1.11.18   104
2.28.60   104
2.122   120

Cicero, *De Natura Deorum*
1.86   71
1.117–18   71
3.49–50   104

Cicero, *De Officiis*
1.138   93

Cicero, *Orationes Philippicae*
2.110–11   104

Claudian, *De VI cons. Hon.*
597–602   132

Codex Theodosianus
16.10.6   132

Demosthenes, *On the Crown*
18.186   42

Dio Chysostom, *Discourses*
12.25   13
12.51–2   13
74   118

Diodorus Siculus, *The Library of History*
1.5.1   118, 123
1.23.7–8   118, 123
1.26.1–3   118, 123
1.29.5–6   118, 123

Diogenes Laertius, *Lives of Eminent Philosophers*
10.1   71

Dionysius of Halicarnassus, *On Literary Composition*
16.46   66
16.64   66

Dionysius of Halicarnassus, *Roman Antiquities*
1.38.2–3   80
1.59.5   81
1.68.2   81
1.77.2   81
2.75   102
5.8.1   118
6.13.4   81
7.68.4   81
7.70.2   118
10.2.3   81

Epictetus, *Discourses*
1.6.24   13
2.18   50

Epictetus, *Encheiridion*
16   69

Herodotus, *The Persian Wars*
1.51   80
1.87   68
1.91   68
4.72   28

8.67	49
8.77	24
8.106	68
9.42	42
9.105	8

Hesiod, *The Shield*

144	67
195	66, 67
463	66

Hesiod, *Theogony*

217	67
230	67
383–403	16, 19
904	67
933-5	66

Hesiod, *Works and Days*

11–26	8

Homer, *Homeric Hymns*

8.4	17

Homer, *Iliad*

1.304	42
4.440	66
5.451	78
5.739	67
11.37	66
15.119	66
19.87	67
19.90–4	67
19.126–31	67

Homer, *Odyssey*

4.796	78
11.171–3	17
11.476	78

Ignatius, *To the Smyrnaeans*

5.2	46

Ignatius, *To the Trallians*

10	46

Irenaeus, *Adversus haereses*

1.26.1	46

Josephus, *Antiquities*

1.250	49
8.163	96
8.261	96
9.99	84
9.205	84
9.243	84
9.273	84
10.50	84
10.65	84
10.69	84
12.135–7	94
12.358–9	94
15.341	9
16.137	9
18.96	96
19.281–2	96
19.284	96
19.288–90	95

Josephus, *Apion*

2.42	96

Josephus, *Life*

12	94
23	98
26–7	98
37	98
41	98
345–54	97
346	97
349–50	98
351	94
416	94
423	94

Josephus, *War*

1.25.1	30
1.181	96
1.391	96
1.425	9
2.333	96
2.341	96
2.487	96
5.109–13	99
5.122	99
5.125	99
5.513	84
6.166–7	100

7.136–7	100	Philostratus of Athens, *Heroicus*	
7.150–2	100	25.7.6	66

Livy
1.21.4	101
6.1.2	120
10.33.9	11
10.47.3	11
29.14.13	11
33.13.6–12	92
36.22.5–24.12	91
36.26.7	92
36.27	91, 92
36.28.4	93
36.28.8	92
36.28.9–29.1	93
45.31.9–11	93

Lucian, *Anacharsis, or Athletics*
9	11, 15

Lucian, *Slander*
31	118

Lucretius, *De Rerum Natura*
6.68–79	69

Pausanias
1.1.3	14
1.8.4	72
1.24.7	18
1.25.2	19
1.28.6	66
5.10.4	14
5.11.1–2	12
5.13.8–14.2	11
5.19.4	67
5.26.1	14
7.10.7–11	93
8.25	66
8.42	66
10.20.9	91

Philo, *On the Account of the World's Creation*
103–5	30

Philo, *On the Special Laws*
1.28	84

Pindar, *Fragments*
131.3	78

Pindar, *Isthmian Odes*
2.26	9
5.8–11	9

Pindar, *Nemean Odes*
4.6	9
5.42	9
5.52	8

Plato, *Laws*
959b	78

Plato, *Phaedo*
66c	79

Plato, *Sophist*
266b	79

Pliny (the Elder), *Naturalis historia*
2.93–4	104
35.58	8

Pliny (the Younger), *Panegyricus*
2.3	106
52.2	106

Plutarch, *Agis and Cleomenes*
8.3	66

Plutarch, *Alexander*
31.9	66

Plutarch, *Brutus*
39.3–6	21
50.5	68

Plutarch, *Caesar*
9.1	68
47.1	22

Plutarch, *Crassus*
21.1	68

Plutarch, *Dion*
26.7	68
51.4	68

Plutarch, *Flaminius*
16.1–2	93

Plutarch, *Letter of Consolation to Apollonius*
35.120C	78

Plutarch, *Lucullus*
29.5	68

Plutarch, *Moralia*
97C–100	68
165C	70
199F	93
237	28
237D	30
316C–26C	68
674D–5B	8
757B	50
873B	17, 24
1104B	70
1104B–C	71

Plutarch, *Numa*
16	101

Plutarch, *Otho*
13.3	68

Plutarch, *Philopoemen*
21	93

Plutarch, *Publicola*
14	49

Plutarch, *Pyrrhus*
13.1	68

Plutarch, *Sulla*
11.1	23
19.5	17, 23

Plutarch, *Theseus*
27.2	66

Polybius
1.16.6	96
1.63.9	68
2.11.1–8	89
2.11.3–7	90
2.11.5	90, 92
2.11.5–7	90
2.11.5–10	92
2.11.7	90
2.11.10	90
2.11.12	90
2.32.2	96
2.58.5	96
3.77.5	96
3.100.3	90, 92
9.9.4	93
9.32.4	8
15.6.8	68
18.38.3–9	92
18.38.5	92
18.38.5–6	91
18.38.9	91, 92
20.9	91
20.9.10–12	92
20.10.5–9	92
20.10.7	93
20.10.7–10	93
20.10.10	92
20.10.12–16	93
20.11.6	93
20.11.6–9	93
28.6.9	93
30.10.1	68
30.13.6–11	93
39.8.2	68

Polycarp, *Letter to the Philippians*
7.1	40

Quintilian
12.10.9	13

Quintus Smyrnaeus
8	66
243	66

Sallust, *The War with Jugurtha*
17.7	122

Seneca the Younger, *De Ira*			6.13	50
2.24	120			
			Xenophanes, *Fragments*	
Seneca the Younger, *De Tranquillitate Animi*			2.5	8
15.4	69		Zonaras	
			9.31	93
Seneca the Younger, *Quaestiones Naturales*			**Material Culture**	
7.17.2	104		Dessau, *ILS*	
			8744	24
Sextus Empiricus, *Against the Physicists*			IE IV	
1.188	67		1069.2	17
			1077.2	17
Strabo, *Geography*				
8.3.30	13		*IG* XIV	
			747	8
Suetonius, *Augustus*				
100.4	105		*RIC* I²	
			Augustus 37A	104
Suetonius, *Claudius*			Galba 135	103
25.4	95		Nero 10	105
			Tiberius 8	105
Suetonius, *Domitian*				
4.4	8		*RIC* II², Part 1	
13.2	106		Domitian 61	19
			Domitian 63	105
Suetonius, *Nero*			Domitian 215	103
22–5	11		Vespasian 301	103
Suetonius, *Vespasian*			*RIC* III	
23.4	104		Marcus Aurelius 999	103
Symmachus, *Relations*			*RIC* IV	
3.15	132		Septimius Severus 651	103
Thucydides			*Syll.*³	
2.89	8		1122	67
6.11.6	68, 69			

www.ingramcontent.com/pod-product-compliance
Lightning Source LLC
Chambersburg PA
CBHW071934240426
43668CB00038B/1756